Dark Ages II
When the Digital Data Die

ISBN 0-13-066107-4

Dark Ages II
When the Digital Data Die

Bryan Bergeron

Prentice Hall PTR
Upper Saddle River, New Jersey 07458
www.phptr.com

Library of Congress Cataloging-in-Publication Data

Bergeron, Bryan P.
    Dark Ages II: when the digital data die/Bryan Bergeron.
      p. cm.
    Includes bibliographical references and index.
    ISBN 0-13-066107-4
    1. Information superhighway. 2. Information technology. 3. Digital communications. 4.
Information society. 5. Computers and civilization. I. Title: Dark Ages two. II. Title.

    ZA3225 .B47 2002
    303.48'33—dc21
                                                                2001046158

Editorial/production supervision: *Jane Bonnell*
Cover design director: *Jerry Votta*
Cover design: *Nina Scuderi*
Interior design: *Gail Cocker-Bogusz*
Manufacturing buyer: *Maura Zaldivar*
Acquisitions editor: *Mark L. Taub*
Editorial assistant: *Sarah Hand*
Development editor: *Jennifer L. Blackwell*
Marketing manager: *Bryan Gambrel*

Prentice Hall books are widely used by corporations and government agencies for training, marketing, and resale.
The publisher offers discounts on this book when ordered in bulk quantities. For more information, contact Corporate Sales Department, Phone: 800-382-3419; FAX: 201-236-7141; E-mail: corpsales@prenhall.com
Or write: Prentice Hall PTR, Corporate Sales Dept., One Lake Street, Upper Saddle River, NJ 07458.

Company and product names mentioned herein are the trademarks or registered trademarks of their respective owners.

Printed in the United States of America
10 9 8 7 6 5 4 3 2 1

ISBN 0-13-066107-4

Pearson Education LTD.
Pearson Education Australia PTY, Limited
Pearson Education Singapore, Pte. Ltd.
Pearson Education North Asia Ltd.
Pearson Education Canada, Ltd.
Pearson Educación de Mexico, S.A. de C.V.
Pearson Education—Japan
Pearson Education Malaysia, Pte. Ltd.

To Miriam Goodman

Contents

PART TWO
Technology

Foreword

My father was one of those people who liked to store all the images and sounds that documented his life. So upon his untimely death at the age of 58 in 1970, I inherited his archives which I treasure to this day. I have my father's 1938 doctoral dissertation at the University of Vienna containing his unique insights into the contributions of Brahms to our musical vocabulary. There are albums of neatly arranged newspaper clippings of his acclaimed musical concerts as a teenager in the hills of Austria. There are the urgent letters to and from the American music patrons who sponsored his flight from Hitler just before "Krystalnacht" made such escape impossible. These items are among dozens of aging boxes containing a myriad of old remembrances, including photographs, musical recordings on vinyl and magnetic tape, personal letters, and even old bills.

I also inherited his penchant for preserving the records of one's life, so along with my father's boxes, I have several hundred boxes of my own. My father's productivity assisted by the technology of his manual typewriter and carbon paper cannot compare with my own prolificacy, aided and abetted by computers and high speed printers which can reproduce my thoughts in all kinds of permutations.

Tucked away in my own boxes are also various forms of digital media: punch cards, paper tape reels, and digital magnetic tapes and disks of various sizes and formats. I often think about just how accessible this information remains. Ironically, the ease of approaching this information is inversely proportional to the level of advancement of the technology used to create it. Most straightforward are the paper documents, which although showing the signs of age, are imminently readable. Only slightly more challenging are the vinyl records and analog sound tape recordings. Although some basic equipment is required, these are not difficult items of equipment to find or use. The punch cards are somewhat more difficult, but it's still possible to find punch card readers, and the formats are uncomplicated.

By far, the most difficult information to retrieve is that contained on the digital disks and tapes. Consider the challenges involved. For each one, I have to figure out exactly which disk or tape drive was used. I then have to recreate the exact hardware configuration from many years ago. Try finding an IBM 1620 circa 1960 or Data General Nova I circa 1973 with exactly the right disk drive and controller, and you'll quickly discover the difficulties involved. Then once you've assembled the requisite old equipment, there are layers of software to deal with: the appropriate operating system, disk information drivers, and application programs. Then just who are you going to call when you run into the inevitable scores of problems inherent in each layer of hardware and software? It's hard enough getting contemporary systems to work, let alone systems for which the help desks were disbanded decades ago. Even the Computer Museum, which used to be located in Boston, has been disbanded, and even when it was in business, most of the old computers on display had stopped functioning many years earlier.

Assuming that you prevail through all of these obstacles, the actual magnetic data on the disks has probably decayed. So even if we assume that the old hardware and software that you assembled are working perfectly, and that you have aging human experts to assist you with perfect recall of long since obsolete equipment, these old computers would still generate mostly error messages.

So is the information gone? The answer is: not entirely. Even though the magnetic spots may no longer be readable by the original equipment, the faded magnetic regions could be enhanced by suitably sensitive equipment using methods that are analogous to the image enhancement often used on images of the pages of old books. So the information is still there, albeit extremely difficult to get at. With enough devotion and historical research one might actually retrieve it. If we had reason to believe that one of these disks contained secrets of enormous value, we would probably succeed in recovering the information. But the mere motivation of nostalgia is unlikely to be sufficient for this formidable task. I will say that I did largely anticipate this problem, so I do have paper printouts of most of these old files. Invariably, that will be how I solve this problem. The bottom line is that accessing information stored in digital form decades (and sometimes even just years) later is extremely difficult if not impossible.

However, keeping all our information on paper is not the answer. Hard copy archives present a different problem. Although I can readily read even a century-old paper manuscript if I'm holding it in my hand, finding a desired document from among thousands of only modestly organized file folders can be a frustrating and time consuming task. It can take an entire afternoon to locate the right folder, not to mention the risk of straining one's back from moving dozens of heavy file boxes from one stack to another. Using the more compact form of hard copy known as microfilm or microfiche may alleviate some of the problems, but the difficulties of locating the right document remain.

So I have had a dream of taking all of these archives, scanning them into a massive personal data base, and then being able to utilize powerful contemporary search and retrieve methods on the hundreds of thousands of scanned and OCR'd (Optical Character Recognized) records. I even have a name for this project: DAISI (Document And Image Storage Invention), and I have been accumulating the ideas for this little venture for many years.

DAISI will involve the rather formidable task of scanning and OCR'ing hundreds of thousands of documents, and patiently cataloguing them into a data base. But the real challenge to my dream of DAISI is the one that Bryan Bergeron articulates so eloquently in this volume, namely how can I possibly select appropriate hardware and software layers that will give me the confidence that my archives will be viable and accessible decades from now?

Of course my own archival desires are a microcosm of the exponentially expanding knowledge base that the human civilization is accumulating. It is this shared species-wide knowledge base that distinguishes us from other animals. Other animals communicate, but they don't accumulate an evolving and growing base of knowledge to pass down to the next generation. Given that we are writing our precious heritage in what Bergeron calls "disappearing ink," our civilization's legacy would appear to be at great risk. The danger appears to be growing exponentially along with the exploding size of our knowledge bases. The problem is further exacerbated by the accelerating speed with which we turn over to new standards in the many layers of hardware and software needed to store information.

Is there an answer to this dilemma? Bergeron's insightful volume articulates the full dimension of the problem as well as a road map to ameliorating its destructive effects. I will summarize my own response to this predicament below, but first we need to consider yet another source of knowledge.

There is another valuable repository of information stored in our own brains. Our memories and skills, although they may appear to be fleeting, do represent information, stored in vast patterns of neurotransmitter concentrations, interneuronal connections, and other salient neural details. I have estimated the size of this very personal data base at thousands of trillions of bytes (per human brain), and we are further along than many people realize in being able to access this data and understand its encoding. We have already "reverse engineered" (i.e., scanned and understood the methods of) several dozen of the hundreds of regions of the brain, including the way in which information is coded and transmitted from one region to another.

I believe it is a conservative scenario to say that within thirty years we will have completed the high resolution scan of the human brain (just as we have completed today the scan of the human genome) and will have detailed mathematical models of the hundreds of information processing organs we call the human brain. Ultimately we will be able to access and understand the thousands of trillions of bytes of information we have tucked away in each of our brains.

This will introduce the possibility of reinstantiating the vast patterns of information stored in our electrochemical neural mechanisms into other substrates (i.e., computational mechanisms) that will be much more capable in terms of speed, capacity, and in the ability to quickly share knowledge. Today, our brains are limited to a mere hundred trillion connections. Later in this century, our minds won't have to stay so small.

Copying our minds to other mediums raises some key philosophical issues, such as "is that really me," or rather someone else who just happens to have mastered all my thoughts and knowledge? Without addressing all of these issues in this foreword, I will mention that the idea of capturing the information and information processes in our brains has raised the specter that we (or at least entities that act very much like we do) could "live forever." But is that really the implication?

For eons, the longevity of our mental software has been inexorably linked to the survival of our biological hardware. Being able to capture and reinstantiate all the details of our information processes would indeed separate these two aspects of our mortality. But the profound implication of Bergeron's *Dark Ages II* is that software does not necessarily live forever. Indeed there are formidable challenges to it living very long at all.

So whether information represents one man's sentimental archive, or the accumulating knowledge base of the human-machine civilization, or the mind files stored in our brains, what can we say is the ultimate resolution regarding the longevity of software? The answer is simply this: information lasts only so long as someone cares about it. The conclusion that I've come to with regard to my DAISI project, after several decades of careful consideration, is that there is no set of hardware and software standards existing today, nor any likely to come along, that will provide me with any reasonable level of confidence that the stored information will still be accessible (without unreasonable levels of effort) decades from now. The only way that my archive (or any one else's) can remain viable is if it is continually upgraded and ported to the latest hardware and software standards. If an archive remains ignored, it will ultimately become as inaccessible as my old 8 inch disk platters.

In this pioneering work, Bergeron describes the full dimensions of this fundamental issue, and also provides a compelling set of recommendations to preserve key sources of information beyond the often short-sighted goals underlying the design of most contemporary information processing systems. The bottom line will remain that information will continue to require continual maintenance and support to remain "alive." Whether data or wisdom, information will only survive if we want it to.

We are continually recreating our civilization's trove of knowledge. It does not simply survive by itself. We are constantly rediscovering, reinterpreting, and reformatting the legacy of culture and technology that our forbears have bestowed to us. We will eventually be able to actually access the vast patterns of information in our brains, which will provide the opportunity to back up our memories and skills. But all of this information will be fleeting if no one cares about it. Translating our currently hardwired thoughts into software will not necessarily provide us with immortality. It will simply put the means to determine how long we want our lives and thoughts to last into our own figurative hands.

Ray Kurzweil

Preface

The Declaration of Independence, the Magna Carta, a letter from a deceased relative, the photo of a long-lost childhood friend, a marriage contract, and a dog-eared Pulitzer Prize-winning novel—all mere marks and symbols on paper—variably represent national treasures, personal mementos, and heirlooms that may span generations or centuries. These objects not only have social, economic, and sentimental value but they also provide a glimpse at the aspirations of an embryonic nation, insight into the social fabric of everyday life, and a window into the minds of the authors.

Letters, photos, books, and other written and printed documents endure because of the durability of the media on which they are recorded, the care with which they are stored and viewed, and, in part, because they can be interpreted without an intermediary. A letter can be held, the texture and color of the paper can be appreciated, and, assuming the writing is legible and in a language known to the reader, understood in an instant or pondered over for hours. The reader can then fold the letter and carefully place it in the envelope that was used to mail it decades ago and tuck it away for future reading. To a social scientist, the penmanship or type font, like the paper quality and texture, provide part of the overall impression of the author's mood and aesthetic, as well as the author's access to a typewriter, printer, or other technology.

Today, pen and paper have been largely supplanted by digital computers, LCD displays, and laser printers. Email is increasingly the preferred mode for interpersonal communications, especially in business, and digital signatures hold the same weight as those made with a pen. Although the quantity of paper used in printing email and other electronic documents has steadily climbed since the introduction of desktop publishing in the 1980s, the majority of electronic documents that are printed find their way to the shredder or recycling bin.

The common practice is to create and store data—whether legal documents, books, computer programs, databases, ordinary text documents, music, photographs, animations, or videos—in a digital form that is not directly observable. That is, the stream of 0's and 1's encoded as magnetic fluctuations in the iron oxide coating on a tape or disc, pits in a plastic CD-ROM or DVD, or the states of the matrix of transistors in a memory stick must be used in conjunction with a complex electro-mechanical intermediary or translator to be experienced. Unlike the case with a hundred-year-old photographic negative, it takes more than holding a warped and dusty CD-ROM up to the light to appreciate the images, programs, or music it once held.

Dark Ages II: When the Digital Data Die is a critical exploration of the vast social, technologic, and economic impact of the Dark Ages that will result if the implicit management of the exponentially increasing pool of data continues along the current trajectory. The book looks at the ephemeral quality of data on the Web, in eBooks, and in email as well as the fleeting durability and lack of enduring standardization of CDs, tapes, memory sticks, and other electronic media. This book explores how, paradoxically, as a technologic society in which knowledge is the medium of business and professional life, we are documenting the majority of our actions and creating intellectual property in what amounts to disappearing ink.

Dark Ages II: When the Digital Data Die is an accessible book, with just enough technical depth to allow an intelligent reader to appreciate the challenges that lie ahead. It provides an overview of the most relevant technologies in enough depth for the reader to understand the social and economic implications that the wide-scale loss of data would have on today's information-dependent, socio-technologic infrastructure.

For easier study, this book is divided into five parts: History, Technology, Economics, Society, and Solutions. Each part provides a freestanding reference for readers with specific needs. For example, the reader interested primarily in the societal factors that favor a second Dark Ages can focus on the Society section. A glossary of terms and abbreviations at the end of the book provides a handy reference for the occasional technical term.

Part I, History, reviews the way in which humanity's store of accumulated knowledge—in the form of oral, painted, inscribed, and written data—has either passed from one generation to the next or was not passed on because of disease, war, religious beliefs, intentional destruction, or benign neglect. A discussion highlights how the current, exponential growth in the socio-technical infrastructure will not continue unabated indefinitely, given that no society in the history of the planet has been able to escape the inevitable waxing and waning of its technological base.

Part II, Technology, explores the concepts of data, information, and knowledge as the lifeblood of our technologic society, explains the loss of data that occurs daily, in personal, corporate, and government settings, and illustrates our society's dependence on data integrity and a robust information technology infrastructure. The exploration continues with the rapid evolution of the personal computer, software applications, media types, and data formats, with a view to a future world in which many of us will work as knowledge brokers who live by our intellectual property holdings that we manage in personal data warehouses.

Part III, Economics, examines the economics of our information infrastructure. It looks at the cost of incessant media format and operating system upgrades that result in the loss of software applications and data. It considers the economic penalties of data loss because of improper collection methods, the ill-conceived changes in corporate strategies, the vicissitudes of the global economy, and the significance of acquisitions and mergers. Consideration is given to the economic ramifications of the recent popularity of centralized and network-based data storage, as well as the business practices, such as data mining, that can extract value from the rising oceans of data.

Part IV, Society, looks at the societal implications of our increasing dependence on a fragile socio-technologic infrastructure. The discussion begins at the level of the individual, where issues include the psychological significance of creating nontangible works like eBooks instead of printed documents, and the way in which life will change as today's professional knowledge workers are transformed into professional knowledge brokers who are paid for their store of easily transferred data and not for their ability to fill an office chair. The exploration then moves to a much larger scale, and illustrates how, unless adequate safeguards are established, the inevitable fluctuations in the political, economic, and natural environments will result in a massive loss of data and a corresponding total disruption of our socio-technical infrastructure.

Part V, Solutions, explores the solutions available to minimize the likelihood of a second Dark Ages, including efforts underway in parts of the government and in some sectors of corporate America that may scale to a national level. This part also explores ways in which individuals can act now to manage and safeguard their personal data warehouse. Given that cities and towns in America have lost decades of public records because of unreadable digital data stored in nonstandard, undocumented formats and that corporations lose millions of records daily due to viruses and benign neglect, the threat of a large-scale, catastrophic data loss is real. Clearly, the Web and other forms of digital information storage and dissemination may have improved our access to data, but the quality and durability of the record we leave behind—even for the immediate future—must be questioned. It's as though, as a society, we're building an amazing information highway but haven't taken the time to think about, and proactively make provision for, the inevitable parking problems that lie ahead.

The purpose of *Dark Ages II: When the Digital Data Die* is to heighten the reader's awareness of the risks associated with the current practice of entrusting the accumulated personal and public intellectual properties of our society to nameless archivists who work in libraries constructed according to evolving and largely untested architectures that sit on shifting foundations of silicon, rust, and plastic. The aim is neither to create a legion of Luddites nor to disregard the economic and intellectual gains that have been made possible thanks to computerization. Rather, this book should serve as a call to intelligent action through explicit, conscious decisions on how to proceed with the complex socio-technical phenomena that we call the digital revolution. The solutions put forward in this book are offered to readers who are concerned about properly maintaining digital archives, whether for preserving personal data, for securing business, employee, and customer data, or for safeguarding public data in town halls and libraries at risk for catastrophic data loss.

Bryan Bergeron

Acknowledgments

A book can be compared to a meal at a fine restaurant. The author, whose name appears on the book cover, like the chef, is but one member of a team that has a unified goal: that of pleasing the customer. Just as there are numerous roles in the kitchen, from preparing the sauces and tasting the ingredients to washing the pots and pans, there are a variety of tasks—some more pleasant than others—involved in the process of creating a book and bringing it to market. In addition, just as in a kitchen, there is the constant time pressure to move the process along as quickly as possible while not sacrificing quality. That being so, a highly interdependent working relationship forms between the author, editorial assistants, researchers, editors, and reviewers. The quality of the final product is as much a function of the chemistry of this relationship as it is of the art and vision of the author. Similarly, the publisher, analogous to the restaurant owner, adds to the product by creating an ambiance and a quality presentation through the use of a particular cover design, paper stock, and even the font style. The publisher's goal is to create a product commensurate with the readers' expectations, based on the publisher's other offerings.

With this analogy in mind, I would like to thank my editorial assistant and long-time friend, Miriam Goodman, an accomplished artist in traditional as well as digital media, poet, teacher, photographer, and author in her own right. Miriam not only provided much of the insight into the historical and cultural context of the issues discussed in this book, but helped refine the focus of the work as well. Similarly, thanks to my enduring research assistant, Ana Maria du Aljuri, for her exquisite work in providing assistance on this project, and to her husband, Nikolai Aljuri, a research scientist at MIT, for his technical insights and for sharing Ana with me on yet another project. To my readers and reviewers: Rosalind Bergeron, my sister, business partner, and attorney in Silicon Valley; Ron Rouse, author, editor, historian, and Software System Specialist in Educational Computing at Harvard Medical School; and, of course, Gilles, for their time, inspiration, insight, and constructive criticism. I would also like to thank those who contributed to my apprenticeship in the art form, Nancy Mulford and Michelle Williams. Finally, special thanks to Mark Taub and Jennifer Blackwell, my development editors, for allowing me to practice my craft in the kitchen of restaurant Prentice Hall.

Introduction

According to the law of entropy, every physical system naturally decays from order to disorder, and the loss of data through time is expected. As a species, we have fought a battle with entropy—dating back before written history—sometimes winning and sometimes losing. Consider, for example, the period in western culture known as the Dark Ages, the lapse of Europe into five centuries of intellectual silence, between the fall of the Roman Empire in 476 and 1000. This time of cultural amnesia has been attributed to factors ranging from the high levels of lead in the water supplied by the Roman aqueduct system to a variety of complex socio-political and religious forces. Historians presume that life in Europe at that time was comparatively uncivilized, even while centers of art and science flourished in Asia and elsewhere.

Even though there were certainly pockets of original scholarly and artistic thinking in Europe during the Dark Ages, little evidence of it survived the years of wars, famine, plague, religious dissent, and neglect. What did survive is the direct result of the painstaking work performed by monks, the keepers of western civilization during the Dark Ages. Most of their activity was devoted to copying, translating, and otherwise archiving the knowledge of previous centuries.

That is, a few hundred zealots decided which works from the vast libraries of human knowledge would be placed in a time machine for future generations to enjoy and which ones would succumb to the scourges of time. Not only did the monks do their work, but the power of the church and the church's protection by the state helped preserve the libraries in monasteries. The buildings themselves functioned as time capsules.

The United States, one of the most technically advanced nations on the planet, is poised to enter a second Dark Ages—a time when what we leave behind will be viewed as negligible compared to the previous centuries. Although the causes are very different from those that precipitated Europe's Dark Ages, we are gambling with the contributions of our most profound thinkers to the arts, science, medicine, and the insights we've gained through exploration of the sea and stars.

It's important to note that this hypothesis isn't dependent on intense global warming, a wide-scale nuclear attack, an asteroid impacting the earth, a plague, or invasion by a foreign power. Although any one of these events would certainly precipitate a profound change in our society, the projection of a second Dark Ages is based on the natural progression of systems and processes already in place.

The issue is really *when*, not if, over the course of several millennia, most of what we produce as a society will return to the primordial elements from which they were formed. Eventually, the centipede-like integrated circuits, the batteries that power our electronic devices, the skyscrapers, and even Styrofoam coffee cups will decompose and return to dust. However, of more practical concern is the survival of data in the immediate future. Providing a record for some researcher in the year 3020 is of secondary importance.

To the typical American who walks past newsstands overflowing with papers, tabloids, and magazines on his way to work, who deals with mountains of data, then returns home to watch TV on one of 1500 cable or satellite channels while pouring through junk mail simply to locate his bills, it may seem ludicrous to propose that somehow we're poised to lose much of our hard-earned intellectual property. However, anyone who works directly or indirectly with computerized information systems—which includes everyone from professional knowledge workers to bicycle couriers—has experienced digital data loss. Given the exponentially increasing rate at which we are creating data, it doesn't take much to project current losses into the future.

In exploring the assumption that we are on the verge of a second Dark Ages, we can think in terms of analogies: a tipping point, critical mass, or a chemical catalyst. These three analogies highlight the concept of being just at the edge of a major change, where almost imperceptibly small perturbations can result in catastrophic consequences. Consider critical mass, a concept used to explain the workings of an atomic bomb. Two half-spheres of plutonium, each less than critical, sit quietly, decaying and emitting radiation in an orderly and controlled fashion until they are slammed together, forming a larger sphere of critical mass. Within milliseconds, the once quiescent plutonium generates an exponentially increasing flash of deadly heat and gamma radiation that disrupts the atomic structure of everything in the blast zone. Similarly, consider a chemical catalyst. One of the oldest man-directed chemical processes, fermentation, requires more than mashed grapes, sugar, and time to create wine. As Louis Pasteur discovered, without the minute amounts of white powder found on some grapes—yeast—the fermentation reaction doesn't occur. The yeast creates an enzyme that serves as a catalyst, the chemical equivalent of an electric amplifier, that promotes the chemical reactions involved in the fermentation process.

Following the tipping point example, consider that in most social and business situations, the personalities, environment, and marketing can make the difference between a product that sits on the store shelves and the next must-have status symbol. A star basketball player can transform an otherwise ordinary brand of basketball shoes into the latest fashion. That is, the wide-scale propagation of a trend can occur from seemingly minor manipulations of a huge process by only a few individuals. The point is that our seemingly stable socio-technologic infrastructure can be upset by minute changes in a number of factors, many of which may not be obvious.

The precariousness of data stored ephemerally in bits and bytes represented as magnetic fluctuations on a film of rust on a hard drive or as pits on a sheet of aluminum foil sandwiched between two disks of plastic in a CD-ROM is often difficult to appreciate. However, society stands to lose more information than was created during the entire Renaissance period if modern means of preservation fail.

Despite all of the challenges ahead, this book does not mean to argue that a world like the one Ayn Rand depicts in *Anthem*—technologically barren and socialistic, where even basic technologies have been lost—lies inevitably in our future. It is intriguing, however, that *Anthem*'s hero, Prometheus, happens upon a library of books that describe the technologies lost to the centuries and, based on his new knowledge, begins to plan the new renaissance of humanity. The novella succinctly illustrates how selectively archiving the right data can be useful for the survival of individuals as well as society.

The concept of parallel timelines, popularized by science fiction writers, seems appropriate here. The premise is that decision points mark divergent paths in parallel universes, even when the decisions and their associated actions are seemingly insignificant and made by a single person. Suppose that, looking to the immediate future of one universe, a particular person is faced with the seemingly insignificant decision of how to approach the data conundrum. That person decides to ignore the problem and continues along his path, uninterrupted. As a result, twenty years into the future, none of the images taken today with digital cameras exist. The American digital economy will have imploded from the vacuum of meaningful, accessible data, and the monolithic mainframes and millions of personal computing devices will have been reclaimed for their metal and glass content, just as the great pyramids were stripped for building materials. The only records for a real-life Prometheus of the future to stumble upon are personal tax return statements and cancelled checks. As a result, the third-world countries with nonvolatile records are the ultimate recipients and keepers of the knowledge gained in the developed, digital cultures.

Peering into the immediate future of a parallel universe, the same person is faced with the identical, seemingly insignificant decision of how to approach the data conundrum. The fate of society in this universe—our universe—is similarly dependent on the decision of that one individual: you, the reader.

ONE

....

History

1

Language, Writing, and the Collective Memory

What the faculty of reason is to the individual, history is to the human race. By virtue of this faculty, man is not, like the animal, restricted to the narrow present of perception, but knows also the incomparably more extended past with which it is connected, and out of which it has emerged. But only in this way does he have a proper understanding of the present itself, and can he also draw conclusions as to the future.

— *Arnold Schopenhauer*

A pirate's treasure map can be invaluable in the hands of someone who has experience in map reading, a knowledge of the relevant geography, and a knack for digging. Similarly, to an FAA investigator attempting to piece together the events surrounding an airplane crash, the black box that most military and larger commercial airplanes carry can represent a year or two shaved off an otherwise arduous fact-finding mission. In both cases, data that are recorded with the intent of later interpretation are much more valuable than data that are reconstructed from happenstance. For example, knowing that an infamous pirate frequented a particular island in the Pacific is much less valuable than a detailed treasure map showing the exact location of a treasure chest. Similarly, the black box that contains a time-stamped recording of pilot conversations, altitude, and engine status reduces the ambiguity of reconstructing the cause of an accident, even if the wreckage is available for investigation.

Despite the best intentions of the designers of systems intended to record information for posterity, there are inevitable failures. For example, a significant amount of data collected on Jet Propulsion Laboratory computers during the 1976 Viking Mars mission was lost because of decaying digital magnetic tape. Some of the records of the Vietnam War, stored on media designed to run on U.S. Department of Defense computers, can no longer be read. Universities, banks, and other businesses routinely lose data as a result of human error, failure of storage media, obsolescence of the original computer system capable of reading the media, and because the original application software, operating system, and other components of the original computing environment are no longer available.

To appreciate how these seemingly minor events presage the catastrophic data loss waiting to happen, it helps to understand humanity's historical struggle with collecting and preserving data over vast expanses of time, and the fragility of the current information infrastructure and information technologies compared to previous traditions. To this end, this chapter reviews how humanity's store of data—in the form of oral, painted, inscribed, and written data—has either passed from one generation to the next or was lost because of economic pressures, disease, war, religious beliefs, intentional destruction, or benign neglect.

DATA AND SURVIVAL

The practice of assembling natural objects to measure and record time and other data predates the written word. Statues and assemblages of stones that cast shadows on other stones illustrate that prehistoric humanity had an understanding of the cycles in life, of the seasons, and of the importance of keeping track of time for survival. The importance to survival of recording group belief systems or religions is apparent in some of the earliest cultures. The Australian Aborigines, for example, recorded the mythology of their hunter-gatherer lifestyle on bark paintings, on rocks, and on the ground as early as 75,000 years ago. The relative durability of rock engravings allowed a pictorial view of their culture to survive. These engravings depict Aboriginal behaviors, belief patterns, and institutions. Similarly, cave paintings of animals in the Lascaux and Chauvet caves in France, dating back 32,000 years, tell of times of magic, ritual, and religion.

Although images of men hunting animals provide clues as to how early humanity survived day to day and what they may have passed on through an oral tradition, the richest source of data from antiquity is from writings. The modern concept of writing had a humble beginning 15,000 years ago, in the form of number notation in which scratches and notches were arranged in groups of straight lines, each line corresponding to the number one. Writing became more complex when humans finally settled down in Egypt and Mesopotamia. In the area now known as the Middle East, the intelligentsia developed writing to create enduring records of the society's rules, regulations, and cumulative knowledge, including who owed and paid taxes.

The Sumerian cuneiform alphabet, recorded on baked clay tablets, was used to record legal contracts, tax assessments, and sales, as well as religion and the law. Our knowledge of the culture in the Mesopotamian kingdoms is derived for the most part from the 30,000 surviving clay tablets from the Library of Assurbanipal that record the ancient Sumerian healing traditions. For more enduring documents, stone was used in place of clay. For example, The Code of Hammurabi, engraved on a slab of stone in Iran sometime near 1700 B.C., details the 282 laws dealing with society, family life, and occupations. In Mesopotamia, it made sense for attendants to keep the growing collection of thousands of clay tablets in one place in the center of town so that the community leaders could refer to them as needed. In this way, out of simple necessity, the first library was formed in Nippur almost five thousand years ago. Although the cuneiform writing was used as a literary language for almost three thousand years, its use as the basis of a spoken language lasted only about a thousand years. Like the use of Latin during the Dark Ages, the application of cuneiform writing went beyond oral communications and served as a common or intermediary language that could be used to translate between languages.

The first writings in Egypt appear around 2000 B.C., recording a much older tradition reflected in the Egyptian hieroglyphs carved in stone. Early papyri describe ancient Egyptian medicine, and the Ebers papyrus from 1550 B.C. is the oldest surviving medical text.

The papyrus scroll, over 20 meters in length, shows the prominence of magic in treating diseases.

Like Egyptian hieroglyphs, the Chinese written language developed as picture writing, with one character for every object or concept described. The oldest Chinese texts are oracular sayings incised on tortoise shells and cattle scapulae and date to about 1200 B.C. As in Western cultures, the early Chinese rulers often rewrote history to suit their needs. For example, in the third century B.C., Shihuangdi, the first emperor of a unified China, ordered his subjects to destroy all historical works that disagreed with his philosophy, including those by the Chinese philosopher Confucius.

Little is known of ancient Greek civilization before the appearance of eighth century B.C.E. texts written in the new Greek alphabet. The earliest writings highlight the Greek ideals, which are also reflected in sculpture and painting of the period. They describe exercise, bathing, massage, gymnastics, and diet. Not surprisingly, there is also a detailed record of the Olympic games in 776 B.C. The Greek alphabet, derived from the older Phoenician alphabet, allowed the Greeks to record and publicize state laws and decrees as well. The Homeric epics, the *Iliad* and *Odyssey*, dating from 600 B.C. but incorporating a much older oral tradition, provide insight into ideals and belief in their gods. Similarly, our knowledge of Hippocratic medicine dates to writings from 410 B.C., which illustrate a new separation of medicine from religion.

The first library with actual literature, albeit religious and viewable only by the aristocracy, was built by King Ramses II of Egypt in about 1200 B.C.E. Another notable library, built in the palace of the Assyrian King Ashurbanipal in 600 B.C., contained over 25,000 clay, wood, and wax tablets that were indexed according to the shape of each tablet and by keywords. The Alexandrian Library and Museum in Egypt, the largest collection of texts in the ancient world, was a center of learning in the third century B.C.E. The library was dedicated to the Muses, the nine daughters of Zeus, each of whom presided over a different art or science. It contained 700,000 manuscripts, an observatory, a temple, zoological gardens, lecture halls, and rooms for research. Scholars were hired to collect, authenticate, and translate all the known Greek philosophers onto papyrus scrolls and to create a 120-volume catalog of the library's holdings.

The Alexandrian Library and Museum, like most libraries, was stocked with loot from numerous military conquests. In turn, the holdings of the library were eventually lost to zealots fighting in the name of religion. For example, the library was wrecked in 48 B.C.E. by rioters. Later, Christian leaders encouraged destruction of the Temple of the Muses. Christian fanatics beat to death the last scholar at the museum in the fourth century. When Muslims conquered the city in the seventh century, the library was completely destroyed. In a continuation of the cycle of looting and collecting, the zealots that destroyed the Alexandrian library acquired the practice of amassing books into private and public libraries and of recording their own religious beliefs. By 1000, the library in Baghdad held over 400,000 books, mostly Arabic translations from the Greeks, Egyptians, and Romans.

Shortly after the fall of the Roman Empire, during the period referred to as the Dark Ages, networks of monasteries developed a network of libraries. Monks in these libraries translated works into Latin, the standard, universal language at the time. Because it took 20 years to transcribe one book from Greek into Latin, most monasteries had fewer than 100 books in their libraries. As Western civilization withered beyond their monastery walls, the monks toiled away, copying and translating the works they considered key to humanity's history and future survival. Given the thousands of scrolls that had to be rejuvenated by copying and the time it took to copy or translate a single manuscript, monks in England, Ireland, Spain, and elsewhere in Europe had to be highly selective in what they preserved and what they set aside for some future monk to archive. Still, time erased many of these manuscripts. Whether because of religious, political, economic, or cultural bent, some were preserved at the expense of others. In many instances, the monks were fighting more than the slow decay of parchment. When the Vikings attacked Ireland in the eighth century, they sacked the monasteries, which held not only libraries of translations but art and other valuables as well.

The destruction of libraries in Spain in the 12th century and Constantinople in the 14th century marked further significant losses in humanity's knowledge that had survived until that time. One advantage of the sackings was that not all manuscripts were burned, but some documents made it into the hands of others who used the information they found in the books in new ways. Columbus, a pirate and mapmaker, for example, used purloined maps to develop a plan to visit the New World.

Even though war had the effect of spreading data to new cultures, access to the books was restricted to religious and political leaders. Things improved for the general public during the Renaissance, with the 1450 invention of Guttenberg's movable type printing press and the practice of printing in English instead of in Latin. As a result, books became accessible to the literate general public. In subsequent years, libraries throughout Europe grew in size and relaxed their restrictions on public access.

England's first public library opened in the mid-19th century and started a movement that resulted in the formation of the British Library, one of the greatest collections in the world. In Russia, where libraries also evolved out of monasteries, the National Library of Russia, the Russian equivalent of the U.S. Library of Congress, was formed. Libraries developed in Asia as well during the European Dark Ages and also evolved from religious collections.

Unfortunately, the sacking and destruction of libraries wasn't limited to early cultures. For example, there were the looting of French libraries during the French Revolution, the looting of Polish libraries by the Germans and Russians during World War I, and the looting of the German libraries by Russians during World War II. Similarly, during World War II, the Germans were destroying English libraries as Allied bombs fell on German and Japanese libraries.

Although most writings were intended to last, the ephemeral nature of the storage media on which they were recorded, even stone, was understood in ancient times. A well-known example is that of the chief engineer of the original aqueduct system designed to bring potable water to Rome. Apparently proud of his achievement and perhaps not very impressed with the politics of the current ruler, at the foot of his masterpiece, the engineer had his men carve a tribute to the politicians of the time, and their contribution to the project, in a slab of limestone. Behind the slab of limestone, which was worn down by weather after only a few hundred years, the engineer had set a slab of marble, engraved with a tribute to himself and his team of engineers. The engineer, obviously aware of the properties of the materials he worked with every day, knew that the soft limestone would soon succumb to the weather and crumble away, leaving the much harder and enduring marble behind to proclaim his success for a millennium or more before it, too, was lost in time.

....

Knowledge of the Ages

Instinct, the collective data of a species stored in DNA and reflected in the inborn structure of the brain, takes tens of thousands of years to develop and is relatively limited. Most hominids, for example, instinctively fear and react to sudden, loud sounds. Although this startle reflex and other instincts clearly have survival value in the wild, it is the human facility for language that confers the greatest survival value to *Homo sapiens*. Although the debates continue over whether language and speech are learned or inherited behaviors and how speech and writing have evolved, all three have accelerated the dissemination and storage of not only data, but knowledge.

At this point, a few definitions are in order:

Data are numerical quantities or other attributes derived from observation, experiment, or calculation.

Information is a collection of data and associated explanations, interpretations, and other textual material concerning a particular object, event, or process.

Metadata is data about information. Metadata includes descriptive summaries and high-level categorization of data and information.

Knowledge is information that is organized, synthesized, or summarized to enhance comprehension, awareness, or understanding. That is, knowledge is a combination of data and an awareness of the context in which the data can be successfully applied. Although the concept of knowledge is roughly equivalent to that of metadata, unlike data, information, or metadata, knowledge implies a human—rather than a computer—host.

Understanding is the possession of a clear and complete idea of the nature, significance, or explanation of something. It is a personal, internal power to render experience intelligible by assimilation of knowledge under broad concepts. Like knowledge, understanding is currently limited to *Homo sapiens*.

The distinction between data and knowledge is not only one of semantics but lies at the root of our evolutionary advantage. Consider that instinct, unlike knowledge, is context independent. An instinctive fear of the dark is independent of where the darkness happens to be—a cave, deserted house, or under the covers in a bedroom behind a closed door. Fear based on the knowledge of the potential dangers that can be lurking in the unseen darkness, in comparison, can be quieted as appropriate to the situation. Language, both spoken and written, makes it possible for context to be communicated from one person to the next (e.g., parent to child), allowing individuals to modify their behavior within a given environment. In this regard, language serves to communicate exceptions to otherwise instinctive or learned habits. For example, through stories that take place in a forest, it can be communicated, in context, that not all snakes are dangerous and not all mushrooms are poisonous. Language serves to extend meaning through analogy, for example, not all strangers on a dark street are dangerous (knowledge vs. understanding).

Given sufficient motivation, time, and access to information, it's possible for people of reasonable intelligence to assimilate the collective experience of their culture or any other culture, regardless of whether it is in the past or present. Unlike the Borg in the science fiction series *Star Trek*, who assimilate cultures by embedding hardware in the host's body, and unlike the rebels in the movie *The Matrix*, who can download experiences directly into their brains, relatively complete assimilation takes decades. And while it's impossible for one person to completely absorb a culture in a lifetime, a society can distribute the task among its members, with specialists in each area, thereby effectively absorbing all of the traits of the previous generation. In this way, a society can survive without having to reinvent the technologies, social practices, and other traits of the previous generation.

The transfer of data, information, and knowledge from one generation to the next rarely occurs smoothly and without loss. Unlike instinct, data are ephemeral, and our fragile conduit from one time to the next is fraught with limitations. There are shifting recording standards, limitations in the longevity of the storage medium, the inevitable errors and data loss associated with translation or migration of data from one form of representation to another, and even

the eventual obsolescence of the method or machinery used to interpret the data. The focus on speed and portability, as opposed to longevity, also threatens the transfer of data. In more recent times, a
realization that many of our activities threaten the ecology of the
planet has resulted in recording methods that, while more ecologically sound, don't have the archival quality of earlier methods. For
example, although digital photography may obviate the darkroom
full of toxic chemicals, photographic negatives will far outlive the
image data stored on a floppy disk.

The transfer of data through time and across cultures has always
involved loss. While it's difficult to place a relative value on, say, a
Shakespearean sonnet versus a ten-thousand-line computer program that makes it possible for the Space Shuttle to orbit the earth
and return safely, it's obvious that more and more varied data are at
stake today than ever before. Contemporary libraries hold millions
(not thousands) of books and records, and commercial, online digital image libraries offer tens of thousands of images. Similarly, a single digital encyclopedia, such as Microsoft's Encarta, provides more
information on a few CD-ROMs than most people learn in a lifetime. The Web certainly provides access to more information than
any one person could read in several lifetimes.

The point is that much is at risk today, in that catastrophic data
loss would seriously impact our society and way of life. The major
challenges ahead regarding the preservation of contemporary data
are related to shifting standards, the limited longevity of modern
storage media, technical obsolescence of hardware platforms necessary to read the data, and the limitations of modern data migration
methods.

Shifting Standards

Alphabets, languages, and storage media for recording data adapt
over time to take advantage of new technologies. For example, heavy,
relatively fragile clay tablets were eventually replaced with papyrus
scrolls that were not only more portable but also supported a much
greater data density. A single scroll could contain the data once held
by dozens of clay tablets. Similarly, alphabets were changed to support
greater data densities and more complex concepts. They shifted from

one-to-one representation of objects to richer, one-to-many representations capable of efficiently communicating complex concepts.

As data are translated and migrated from one standard to the next, whether because of improvements in the storage media, as in the evolution from clay tablets to more portable scrolls, or because of improvements in the representation used, data are invariably lost. For example, in migrating data recorded in one language to another, because there may not be a one-to-one correspondence to physical objects or concepts, shifts in meaning often occur. Shakespeare's works lose something when translated from his original English into modern Japanese, for example.

Longevity of the Media

The longevity of the storage media obviously limits the ability to transfer data from one generation to the next. A stone engraving generally lasts longer than a newspaper, especially when both are exposed to the elements. However, with the emphasis on speed and portability, longevity is often sacrificed. Early wax tablets, for example, allowed students to take notes with a stylus and then erase the tablet for the next day's lesson. Taking the time to chisel characters in stone or to draw on sheets of expensive wood was not a viable alternative.

Today, speed sells. The facsimile (fax) machine was developed for convenience and speed, with little regard for longevity of the documents. Most first-generation fax documents, transmitted to scrolls of thermal paper that darkened and became unintelligible and unmanageable after less than a year, are long past the point of possible recovery. Although plain paper faxes have largely alleviated the loss of documents due to fading and curling, even the latest fax systems use quick-drying ink and papers optimized for speed, not for the long-term status of the document.

Similarly, consider that the photo labs that dot the streets of most larger cities don't attract customers by advertising the longevity of their photographs, but their one-hour service. As the Polaroid camera and later digital cameras illustrate, customers are willing to pay a premium for instant gratification in visual data capture and display. However, early black-and-white Polaroid prints tend to curl and become brittle after only a few years, and Polaroid color prints tend to darken with time. In addition, since there is no negative, copies must be made from prints. As a result, unlike prints from negatives, copies of Polaroid prints have less data than the original print.

Traditional photographic technologies have their limitations as well. Because of ecological considerations, the chemistries used to develop and print film have changed markedly over the years, often at the expense of the longevity of the film. For example, E-6 chemistry, which is used to develop 35mm color transparency or slide film, was changed to a more environmentally friendly formula in the mid-1980s. While more ecologically sound, the new fixer or chemical used to stop the change in color and density of the film over time is not as effective as the original formula. As a result, slides made with the new chemistry fade sooner than those made with the original fixative. Even so, the images on color transparencies made today, if properly cared for, will certainly outlive most of the readers of this book.

Platform Obsolescence

In the short-term, the decreased longevity of 35mm slides may not be significant, especially with the increased reliance on digital imaging technologies. With the advent of the digital camera and software such as Microsoft PowerPoint, the 35mm slide show is quickly becoming a thing of the past. A business presentation using slides and a slide projector is almost unheard of today, especially in the high-tech arena. A sleek laptop computer and a diminutive LCD projector, which doubles as a wide-screen projection TV system on weekends, have quickly superseded the slide projector. Not only can presentations be tweaked at the last moment, but the new technology supports sophisticated transitions and links to other applications. Similarly, digital images, whether from an electronic image bank or an inexpensive digital camera, can be instantly incorporated into a presentation. As a result, 35mm slide projectors, once a ubiquitous staple in every board room, are virtually obsolete.

Despite the advantages of digital presentations of 35mm slide shows, images that exist only as bits in a digital camera or laptop computer have a relatively limited life span. Given the rapidly evolving computer and camera systems and standards, either the interface between camera and computer or between the camera storage medium and the computer is eventually compromised. For example, the Polaroid digital camera, one of the earliest professional-quality digital cameras, required a special SCSI interface and cable in order to download images from its internal hard drive onto a host computer system. Today, however, SCSI is no longer an assumed standard, having been successfully challenged by both FireWire and USB standards, which are faster and easier to use.

Furthermore, most of the current generation of digital cameras forgo the need for a cable to download images altogether and instead use removable solid-state flash memory, which can be used with a floppy disk adapter to quickly move image data from a digital camera to a desktop or laptop computer. In operation, a postage-stamp sized flash memory card is inserted into a carrier that resembles a $3\frac{1}{2}$-inch floppy disk that fits into a standard floppy disk drive bay. The carrier is read like an ordinary floppy disk, even though it may contain 64 MB or more of digital image data.

However, the once-ubiquitous floppy disk drive standard is threatened on a number of fronts. At least one model of the Apple iMac, for example, uses a writeable CD-ROM for secondary storage, forgoing the floppy altogether. In addition, several manufacturers offer drives that can read and write CD-ROMs and much higher capacity DVDs. Similarly, many PC users rely on high-capacity Iomega Zip disks, which provide the storage space equivalent to about 200 floppy disks. Although Zip disk drives now come as standard equipment on many computers, whether or not adapters for camera memory will be created for the Zip disk standard remains to be seen.

Migration

Even with modern methods of data storage, data can be lost almost as rapidly as it is created. Loss of digital data stored on computer systems and storage media is an everyday occurrence. However, for the same reason that banks don't go out of their way to advertise successful bank robberies, most companies and governmental agencies don't make the losses widely known.

Consider that data stored on $5\frac{1}{4}$-inch floppy disks, the ubiquitous storage media for desktop computers only a decade ago, are now largely unavailable. Even if a professional data recovery and migration service is used to move data to, say, a $3\frac{1}{2}$-inch floppy disk, odds are some of the data will be lost in the migration process. Once the data are stored on media that can be read by a modern PC, the issue becomes one of reading or retrieving them. Consider that spreadsheet data, created on the Apple Lisa, the immediate predecessor of the Apple Macintosh, for example, are not readable or importable by the current version of Microsoft Excel running on either the latest Apple Macintosh or Windows machine.

The migration challenge is compounded if the data to be read have been compiled into an executable computer program. Once the original text or source code have been converted into machine-readable language, it may be impossible to reconstruct the original operating environment. Computer applications, from eBooks to games, are often designed for specific software and hardware environments. Programs designed for the Commodore 64, for example, a popular home computer in the late 1980s, were distributed as cartridges and on $5\frac{1}{4}$-inch floppy disks. Neither of these media is readable on a modern PC. Furthermore, since the Commodore 64 used special graphics and sound hardware, even if the applications could somehow be manipulated to execute on a modern PC, many of the graphics would not look right without a special emulator environment installed on the PC.

Computer applications written within the last five or ten years may not operate properly across platforms or operating systems because of differences in the software or hardware environments. Applications designed to create sounds on the first models of the Apple Macintosh, for example, don't work on current Macintosh models because of fundamental changes in sound generation hardware. Similarly, before the PC standardized on the SoundBlaster sound card, there were dozens of sound cards and "standards" that application developers either adopted or ignored.

The same holds for the evolving video standards on the PC, which migrated from the low-resolution, green font on black background to full-color, high-resolution S-VGA in only a decade. As a result, a spreadsheet program written for the monochrome video standard of the late 1980s won't display properly on a modern PC with S-VGA graphics. Unfortunately, many video cards didn't make it through the evolutionary jungle. Replacement cards and associated documentation are no longer available. Barring a chance encounter with an ancient computer system at an estate sale, applications designed for an extinct video or media standard are effectively lost forever.

The evolution of the computer and digital data handling continue today. Current evolutionary pressures include a pessimistic economy in which once hopeful dotComs are reaching their dead ends. In most cases, the technologies die with the dotComs that created them. The millions of lines of computer code once populating servers and desktop PCs may languish as a few backup tapes in someone's closet for a few years until the economy turns around. When it does, the issue to whoever holds the backup tapes will be whether or not the data are retrievable, and if so, how they can be used. For example, most backups assume a particular operating environment. It's certain that in less than a decade, computers running Windows 98 will be as scarce as those running MS-DOS and using $5\frac{1}{4}$-inch floppy disks are today.

LITERACY AND INTERCONNECTEDNESS

The fiery Arab character in Michael Crichton's *The 13th Warrior* initially won the respect of much larger and stronger Nordic warriors because of his facility with language. Not only did he have the intellect to learn their oral language, but he was able to "draw sounds." His literacy was valued because, like swordsmanship, proficiency with the written word took years of practice to develop fully. And, like knowledge of how to fight in battle, literacy conferred a permanent survival advantage to the holder. Although many students in America today take their education for granted, education or the development of literacy was limited to the ruling class in ancient times. Much of Alexander the Great's success as a leader, for example, is attributed to his years of schooling under Aristotle. When most of the people in a society are living from hand-to-mouth, there simply isn't time for children to spend years learning to read and write, nor is literacy immediately useful for survival. Only when there are rules, laws, belief systems, and other data worthy of recording, such as the time of the planting season or migratory patterns of particular game, and when there is time to use the data, is the investment in literacy worth the effort.

A scroll of sheep's skin containing notes of history, geography, mathematics, and philosophy once represented a scholar's learning. More recently, a paper diploma certifying the holder's successful studies in an academy holds the same weight. Today, the diploma provides a survival advantage, in the form of increased income. Engineers, physicians, lawyers, programmers, and their families have a survival advantage conferred on them through knowledge acquired from their teachers and their readings.

Given a literate population, language and writing can form a bridge that spans and connects time and space. A lifetime of experiences, a philosophy developed over generations, or the history of an entire culture can be gleaned from the pages of a book. This seemingly alchemic reality is possible because of language, a system of arbitrary visual marks that form alphabets, words, and sentences. Even though the marks may have no innate meaning outside the system, rules defining a grammar, the form and structure of words (morphology), and their interrelation in sentences or syntax allow complex concepts to be recorded and communicated.

As noted earlier, the migration of data from one system of representation to another, as in translating a passage from Shakespeare into a contemporary idiom, inevitably changes the meaning, even if only slightly, from the original. Another factor that affects the accuracy of migration from one language to another is the personal bias of the translator, whether intentional or accidental. Considering that most works from antiquity are available today only because of multiple levels of translation—from Greek to Latin to English, for example—it's understandable that something may have been lost in the process. Another potential source of confusion that potentially interferes with human interconnectedness is the differences between the spoken and written word. These differences are especially evident in nonsyllabic, iconic, or pictorial languages such as Chinese and ancient Egyptian hieroglyphs.

THE EVOLUTION OF PREDIGITAL MEDIA

The practice of writing is the intersection of language, a system for recording ideas, and a storage medium. Consider the evolutionary path of the media used to record the predigital written word and the effect of often orthogonal goals of portability, data density, ease of use, and affordability. Book-sized clay tablets were used by the Sumerians, Babylonians, and other ancient people of Mesopotamia. The ancient Greeks and Romans used small, ringed notebooks of wax-coated wooden tablets to write letters, keep accounts, and jot down notes. Papyrus scrolls were used extensively by ancient Egyptians, Greeks, and Romans. Bamboo tablets tied with a cord represent the earliest semblance of a book in Asia. The Chinese, who invented paper, started around the second century to use strips of silk or paper made from a mixture of bark and hemp that was wound around sticks. Scrolls of parchment, the tanned or untanned skin of a sheep or goat, were used for centuries by the peoples of the ancient Middle East. The invention with the greatest impact on the written word is paper, first developed in China in 105. One reason that paper became so valued as a means of disseminating the written word is because of the invention of printing. The process of printing from carved wood blocks, invented in China in the sixth century, advanced to the point that a 130,000-page Buddhist scripture was printed in 972. By the 11th century, the Chinese invented movable type. However, this technology was difficult to use because of the great number of characters in Chinese writing. It was not until movable metal type was independently invented in Europe that the book became an affordable, popular source of knowledge and entertainment.

....

GETTING THE WORD OUT

The dissemination of written information parallels the availability of the book, an affordable distribution medium. Paradoxically, although the appearance of the modern paper book marked the beginning of mass dissemination of data, the personal ownership of books was initially fueled by their relative rarity. This phenomenon seems to repeat the practice seen at the end of the Dark Ages, when collecting rare books came into vogue for the aristocracy that could afford them. More recently, in 19th-century London, where rare books were auctioned, it became a status symbol among the wealthy to have a significant library, if only for show.

Toward the end of the 19th century, the center for private book-collecting activity gradually moved to the United States, where many early book collections formed the seeds for public, university, and private libraries. For example, modest, personal book collections formed the basis for institutions ranging from Harvard University and Brown University to the New York Public Library. The library institutionalized the practice of collecting and managing information for specific groups of people, eventually including the general public.

Although the modern library continues to be a line item in most city, state, and university budgets, the institution now takes a back seat to many other forms of data distribution to the general public. Most people interact every day with disposable and ephemeral data, in the form of newspapers, tabloids, paperbacks, cell phones, radio, and TV. Electronic access to reference books, dictionaries, and the content carried by newspapers, supplemented by millions of documents and sources of information on the Web—including listing of the holdings of many public libraries—either competes for advertising eyeballs or enjoys access to the public coffers.

The popularity of online booksellers, such as Amazon.com, and the new social bookstore chains, such as Borders and Barnes and Noble, highlights the business of publishing to the masses for a profit. These bookstore chains, which encourage browsing and social gathering with their coffee and bakery areas, brightly lit atmospheres, and progressive background music, have converted the staid library where the slightest whisper was not tolerated to a fun and mutually rewarding social event. In addition, despite the popularity of the Web for data gathering, new digital technologies, such as just-in-time publishing, are resulting in more, not fewer printed book purchases.

As shown in Figure 1-1, the various forms of data available in electronic or digital form are a relatively recent phenomenon. Although the commercial availability of the telegraph and the laying of the transatlantic telegraph cable predate the shift of rags to wood pulp for the basis of paper making, most contemporary media and information sources date back less than 75 years.

For example, broadcast and cable TV had their starts in the late-1940s and early 1950s. The now ubiquitous CD dates back only to 1980, only about a decade after the introduction of the 8-track and

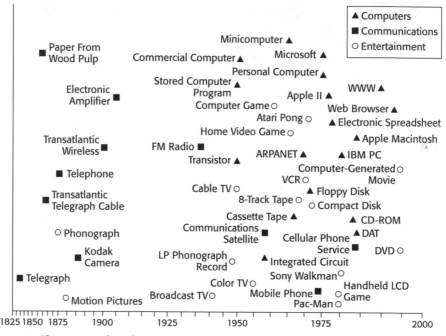

Figure 1-1 The Information Technology Timeline.
Most forms of data available today in electronic and digital form are the result of relatively recent developments. Note that most activity began around the time paper from wood was beginning to be used in Europe.

cassette tape formats, and only a few years after the introduction of the VCR. The Sony Walkman and hoards of competing look-alikes that appealed to a highly mobile society date back to the introduction of the CD. Similarly, in the area of communications, mobile phones became available in the mid-1970s, about a decade after the first communications satellite started operation, and about a decade before the introduction of analog cellular phone service.

It's hard to imagine that the indispensable electronic spreadsheet is a product of the late 1970s, right on the heels of the first personal computer. Similarly, only three decades separate the first computer game, developed in the mid 1960s, and the first fully computer-generated movie, *Toy Story*. Within that brief thirty-year period, not only was the Internet developed from the ARPANET project, but most of what people consider critical to the age of modern computing was born. The IBM PC, Apple II, Apple Macintosh, email, World Wide Web, and the first Web browser were all introduced within a few years of each other. During that time, not only did computer hardware and software evolve but the media and formats followed suit, even within brands from the same companies. No one seemed to notice or even mind the change, given that the industry had yet to crystallize and define the personal computer from the user's perspective. In this regard, the mood was reminiscent of the early days of the automobile, when there was a plethora of models to choose from.

. . . .

A MULTIMEDIA EXISTENCE

Although the previous discussions focus on the written word, most people live today in a digital, multimedia world. As shown in Table 1-1, the typical American is bombarded with data from a variety of

Table 1-1 Data, Data Sources, and Media.

Specialized areas, such as engineering, medicine, and computer science, are associated with greater numbers of data sources and storage media options.

Data Sources		Data	Storage Media	Transport Media
Answering Machine	Modem	Animation	35mm Film	Air
Broadcast Station	MP3 Player	Audio	Cassette Tape	Cable
Camcorder	Interactive TV	Line Art	CD/CD-ROM	Ether
Car Engine	Newspaper	Still Image	DAT	Fiber
Cassette Player	Pager	Text	DVD	Internet
CD Player	PDA	Tracing	Flash Memory	Satellite
Cell Phone	Physiologic	Video	Floppy Disk	Wire
Computer	Monitor		Hard Disk	
Digital Recorder	Radar		Magnetic Tape	
Digital/Still Camera	Slide Projector		Memory Stick	
Digital/Video	Speakers		MiniDisc	
Camera	Spectrum		Paper	
DVD Player	Analyzer		Plastic	
eBook	Telephone		ROM	
Game Console	Television		Cartridge	
GPS	Thermometer		SuperDisk	
Handheld Radio	VCR		X-ray Film	
Instrumentation	Watch		Zip Disk	
LCD Projector	Web			
MiniDisc Player	X-ray Machine			

sources and in different formats for education, entertainment, communications, news and information, business, and military applications. Everything from car engines, telephones, and computers to slide projectors provide multimedia—animations, audio, still images, text, tracings, and video—from a variety of media and through multiple delivery platforms.

Consider a day in the life of a typical professional in America.

PLUGGED-IN

Kathy, the Vice-President of Marketing for a large corporation in New York, wakes to a digital clock radio, with the time displayed in bright green digits as the radio plays her favorite radio station. She gets up, goes to the kitchen to prepare breakfast, where the countertop TV broadcasts the day's weather forecast, together with a global weather map. She picks up the paper from just outside her front door and pours herself a bowl of cereal. Having already read the back of the cereal box, Kathy glances over the newspaper, reviewing the main events of her day.

On her way to work, to make the commute more bearable, Kathy pops a CD into her car stereo, which shows the title and track information in the LCD display. Fortunately, her radar detector warns her of a police speed trap before it's too late, and she carefully brakes to drop her car's speed to just above the limit. Passing by billboards, advertisements in the store fronts, and advertisements painted on the sides of trucks, she makes it to the company parking lot. Once inside, she takes the elevator to her office with the other ten passengers, enduring the elevator music and the advertisements on the built-in LCD panel.

After greeting her secretary, Kathy takes her mail to her office and boots up her PC. Before checking her email and the performance of the company's stocks on the Web, she listens to her voice mail messages. Checking her PDA, she makes certain that everything is ready for her presentation to the board of directors. Picking up her laptop from her desk and the color handouts from her printer and turning off her cell phone ringer, she heads to her first meeting of the morning. In the board room, she plugs her laptop into the LCD projector in preparation for her PowerPoint presentation of her new marketing plan for the company's latest product. She checks the time on her quartz wrist watch and, thinking ahead to the large group expected at the meeting, walks to the digital thermostat and drops the temperature by a half a degree to make the room more comfortable for the board members.

Within her presentation, Kathy has a video clip, with audio, of her latest proposal for a 30-second TV commercial. The concept, rendered in 3D by staff in the company's media department, shows a virtual reality scene in which the company's latest software product is associated with a sporting event. In addition, images of the company headquarters, captured the day before with a digital camera, accent the presentation. After fielding questions, which Kathy captures with her pocket digital recorder for later review, she returns to her office to check her email and answer a page that she received while in the meeting.

In the afternoon, she uses a voice recognition application on her computer to compose a note to her staff, then logs in to an online eBook store to download a book on the wireless Web to her PDA, and then checks the national weather forecast in preparation for her two-hour flight to Chicago the next morning. On her way home, Kathy listens to her favorite news station on her car radio. Once home, she pops a dinner in the microwave and a DVD into her home theater system. After packing for the trip to Chicago, Kathy gets ready for bed and curls up with her favorite magazine. After a few minutes, she sets her alarm, turns out the lights, and is off to sleep.

· ·

In a typical day, Kathy depends on a variety of data sources for information, entertainment, and business. She uses her charge card number to purchase an eBook online, for example, and her PDA to retrieve the telephone numbers of her business associates. At home, she relies on digital video and music for entertainment. Most of the infrastructure from the telephone network, the Internet, and the cable TV is invisible and yet critical to the smooth flow of data between Kathy and devices or other people.

· ·

FILTERING

Even though we live in a seemingly overwhelming flood of man-made noise, the data actually reaching our consciousness aren't necessarily any greater than those experienced by prehistoric man. Part of the human nervous system, the reticular activating system (RAS), acts as a gateway or filter for events attempting to reach our consciousness, whether the event is a TV commercial, a mosquito bite, or the sound of a twig snapping in the forest. For example, professional swimmers don't feel the water unless it's unduly hot or cold, and Olympic-class runners don't feel the wind on their faces unless it's extraordinarily variable or pushing them headlong or backwards. In this way, the RAS allows athletes to acclimate to the barrage of certain types of data and to focus on what's important—winning the race.

Genetically, humans are predisposed to be more alert to some types of data than to others. As every marketing and advertising agent knows, sex and violence elicit predictable primal responses. However, like a muscle tightening, the RAS can be conditioned to respond to certain events and ignore others. For example, most American adults, indoctrinated with TV, stereo, and video games, aren't conscious of the rate, depth, or rhythm of their breathing from one minute to the next, in part because their RAS is tuned to events outside of their body. However, with training in meditation or Yoga, anyone can learn to recognize and control breathing, heart rate, and other physiologic functions.

To a hunter who depends on big game for his family's survival, paying attention to the state of the environment for clues regarding approaching game can mean the difference between eating and going hungry. The snap of a twig, the intonation of a bird's call, and the scents in the air, the state of a hunting dog's tail and ears, all provide a constant source of multimedia information that he must process and respond to in real time. When game finally approaches, the seasoned hunter has to predict the animal's most likely behavior, based on cues he's learned to recognize, to determine when to make the shot. When he does let loose an arrow or pull the trigger of his rifle, he knows to do so between heart beats while holding his breath to steady his shot. When the prey is in his gun sights, he is in the "zone," aware of his breathing, heart beat, stance, and his prey. In the meantime, if a mosquito bites the hunter's arm, his RAS will temporarily block the pain. However, if a snake or other threat enters the hunter's visual field or makes a threatening sound, then the hunter's RAS will allow the danger signals to reach his consciousness.

Even modern city dwellers must train their RAS to respond to some data at the expense of others. Although filtering everything out during a commute can allow time to reflect and to plan the day, failing to notice a red light at a crosswalk while listening to tunes on a Walkman can mean the difference between walking home intact and ending up under a truck. Even with the RAS, in the swarm of data and without proper training, data can be confusing. For example, mistakes with interpreting x-rays have resulted in "wrong side procedures": amputating the wrong limb or operating on the wrong side of the skull. For some people, the flood of extraneous information or noise is so great that they supplement their RAS's natural filtering abilities with ear plugs and active noise-cancelling headphones. Others simply make a conscious decision to limit their exposure to TV, the Web, and other data-dense sources of potential distraction. However, most people realize, as illustrated in the next chapter, that modern information technology is an enabling, if not inescapable, component of modern life.

TWO

Technology

Digital Media and Machines

Give me your intuition of the present and I'll give you the past and the future.

– Ralph Waldo Emerson

he electronic digital computer, like other modern technologies, wasn't the brainchild of a single person, but an evolving product, based on the work of a multitude of inventors, scientists, philosophers, mathematicians, engineers, and entrepreneurs. The 1941 EDVAC computer, for example, was based on binary mathematics and vacuum tube technology. It was one of the first that could accept input, process data, store data and programs, and produce an output. Its binary mathematics, in turn, was the result of work by generations of mathematicians. Its vacuum tube technology, developed at the beginning of the 20th century, was based on hundreds of experiments dating back to early Greek philosophers who explored basic physical properties. Of course, a handful of vacuum tubes and a mathematical system are necessary but insufficient to create a digital computer; the concepts of input, output, storage, and processing had first to be developed. Although a computing machine was sketched out by Leonardo da Vinci over five hundred years ago, it wasn't until 1938 that a fully functional digital computer was put to practical use. The Z-1 computer, used by the Germans in World War II for encrypting and decoding messages, relied on mechanical relays to represent data. Although this fully functional *electrical* digital computer was capable of commanding funding from the German military, for a number of political and business reasons it was unsuccessful in the marketplace. Commercial success took people with an entrepreneurial bent, connections, and capital, the right political environment, and customers who were willing to pay for the technology. The UNIVAC I, the first commercially successful *electronic* digital computer, was introduced in 1951, a full decade after the technology proved viable.

Today, electronic digital computer technology isn't limited to raw number crunching or decoding ciphers for the military but has transformed virtually every field, from scientific investigation and education, to entertainment, medicine, and the military. Computers are routinely used in control applications, from guiding the Space Shuttle to a smooth landing to regulating the rate and timing of fuel injection in a school bus engine. Data mining is becoming common practice in business, where customer relations management (CRM) requires up-to-date information on potential customers, including their buying habits and preferences. Expert systems, computer programs that simulate the decision-making capabilities of human experts, are used in many areas, from medical diagnosis to the automatic focusing of 35mm cameras.

While a relatively small number of researchers are using computers in their original number-crunching capacity, such as deciphering the human genome, many more users are applying computer technology for pleasure and profit to the creation and collection of music, digital animations, and synthetic and virtual environments. For example, special-effects studios routinely use 3D graphic engines to model environments, creating Martian landscapes, menacing dinosaurs, and lifelike stand-ins. The 1995 debut of *Toy Story*, the first fully computer-generated movie, marked the start of a digital movement throughout the movie industry. Digital special effects are now expected in every major movie, to the point that digital artists have their own Oscar category. In a related effort, Hollywood is experimenting with interactive, digital movies that transform the audience experience from passive viewing to active participation.

A theater that shows digital movies rather than reels of film is the natural extension of all-digital movies. Although not yet up to top-tier movies with their resolution of 70mm film format, digital theater has the potential to transform the movie industry by providing titles on demand through a relatively inexpensive distribution mechanism. Consider that a typical movie on a standard 35mm reel of film is only good for about thirty showings before it starts exhibiting obvious signs of wear, and it costs about $2,000 to duplicate. In addition, theaters must contend with the cost of shipping and the logistics of delivery. In comparison, *The Phantom Menace*, a digitally mastered movie, exists as a 342-GB digital file. Unlike ordinary analog film, the entire movie can be sent in a matter of hours from the centrally located archive to dozens of theaters through a high-speed Internet connection, and the audio and video can be duplicated and stored on tape or other storage medium without any degradation—at least in the short term—from one generation to the next. The movie can also be output to tape for archival purposes and for traditional distribution.

Although studios have yet to announce consumer versions of all-digital movies, they are continuing to market analog VHS video tapes and, more commonly, digital video discs (DVDs). However, the common promotional theme, "Own it on video," is misleading. Copyright issues aside, VHS tapes and DVDs are temporary storage media. Not only does each storage medium have a finite life span, but the rapidly evolving playback technology will render each format obsolete in a few years.

This chapter presents an overview of the cornerstone of the digital age, the electronic digital computer, hereafter referred to simply as the computer, along with the associated media, software, peripherals, and network infrastructure. The chapter introduces the hazards in the life cycle of data from its creation to its retrieval, use, and obsolescence, and illustrates how, at any of these points, data can be lost or degraded. The many mechanisms and concepts involved in data creation and storage are defined: analog signals; digital conversion of analog inputs; differences among computers and their application to different tasks; use of input/output devices, storage media, and transport media; network traffic; software controllers; and operating systems. The aim is to introduce the tremendous variability and volatility in the continuing, multidimensional evolutionary process of computing so that the concepts of limited computer longevity, unavoidable obsolescence, and the significant probability of data loss become apparent.

THE DIGITAL AGE

Even though the digital age is often considered to be synonymous with the appearance of the computer, there is nothing inherently digital about computation. Many of the earliest computational engines, like the majority of electronic devices up until the recent past, were analog. In this context, analog systems work with signals that vary smoothly from one value to the next over time, whereas digital systems work with signals that vary in discrete steps. Aside from quantum events that occur at the subatomic level, most natural events and signals are analog, from the howl of a wolf to signal processing by the human brain. Conversely, digital signals and events above the subatomic level are generally manmade.

The first home game console, the Odyssey, introduced in 1971, was an analog system. The cellular phone service, first introduced to the United States in the late 1970s, is still primarily an analog service. The majority of cellular phones sold in the United States are compatible with the analog modulation techniques because of the huge analog legacy systems still in place. Dual-mode devices, capable of working with either digital or analog networks, default to analog services if no digital services are available. However, even analog systems use digital computers for cell switching and billing.

Many modern cell phones and all PCS (personal communication services) phones are completely digital because of the added functionality digital services provide, such as caller ID and lower handset power requirements, and because digital systems are somewhat better than analog systems at maintaining a quality communications channel. That is, digital amplification, unlike analog amplification, doesn't add noise or distortions to the audio signal. Digital signals are less affected by noise than are analog signals because digital error correction and regeneration technologies can be applied to digital signals.

Despite the advantages of digital technology, some types of computation are more suited to analog computational methods than are digital methods. Many forms of machine learning benefit from an analog approach. Machine learning is a branch of artificial intelligence (AI) that deals with creating machines with the ability to collect data autonomously from the environment and categorize them into meaningful patterns. For example, machine learning based on neural networks, simulations of how the human brain functions, is inherently an analog method of computation.

Similarly, voice recognition, the pattern matching of analog voice signals, is easier in the analog domain. The first successful voice recognition system that was capable of responding to specific verbal commands was developed with analog techniques in the early 1950s, about three decades before the same capabilities could be demonstrated with digital techniques. In addition, many audiophiles claim that they can hear the difference between "cold" music produced by digital solid-state electronic systems and "warm" music from analog sources and amplifiers. These same people are willing to pay ten times the price of a high-end digital stereo system for one that uses an analog, tube-type design that predates the transistor.

Despite the niche areas that appear to be better suited to analog approaches, the computer and electronics industries have taken the digital path. In a self-fulfilling prophecy, current digital techniques are now so advanced relative to analog methods that it's more cost effective to take an analog signal, such as a human voice, and move it into the digital domain where it can be processed with digital signal processing (DSP) techniques, and then return the signal to the analog domain. That is, digital computers circumvent the digital versus analog debate by simulating analog operations whenever they are needed.

Translating data from the analog to the digital domain and then back again involves digitization, or digital-to-analog (D/A) conversion, and the mirror process, analog-to-digital (A/D) conversion. The D/A conversion process is used in MP3 (music) players, in the conversion of digital sequences stored in solid state memory to analog waveforms corresponding to, for example, a Bach concerto. CD and DVD players similarly use D/A conversion to translate the binary information stored on the storage medium into a recognizable, pleasing sound. Digital still and video cameras, in contrast, rely on A/D conversion to capture analog images on digital storage media. Similarly, the standard sound capture hardware found in most PCs provides the A/D conversion needed to capture digital audio for manipulation and storage, and D/A conversion to play the audio back.

THE DIGITAL COMPUTER

Although there will continue to be a place for analog methods, the digital computer is here to stay for the foreseeable future. However, given the incessant pace of innovation in the realm of computers and computer software in the two decades since the introduction of the IBM PC, it's unclear exactly what will constitute a standard digital computer in another twenty years. However, it is clear that the concept of standards is a nonstarter. The so-called standards for media formats, operating systems, peripherals, and graphical user interfaces are temporary at best. Despite the best efforts of companies as influential and powerful as Intel, Microsoft, Apple, and Oracle, there is no single computer architecture, no universal storage medium or file format, no universal operating system, and no universal database standard.

Operating systems are constantly being upgraded; desktop and laptop computers are replaced with faster, cheaper models as soon as they're delivered, and the form and content of the Web evolve daily. As a result, a database application or other program that executes flawlessly on a "standard" PC or other computer one day may be completely inaccessible on the same machine after an upgrade of the operating system, the installation of an antiviral program or other utility, or the contention of programs for memory or other resources.

Before delving into these and other realities of modern computer systems, first consider the general categories of computer hardware available today. Supercomputers are highly specialized, one-of-a-kind, hand-built, high-speed computers that are optimized for specific types of computations, from analyzing complex weather patterns, to simulating biological and mechanical events, to competing against world master chess players. Because they are specialized, supercomputers often use custom operating system and application software.

Mainframe computers are typically expensive, room-sized computers found at NASA, the IRS, larger financial institutions, and major research facilities, made by companies like IBM, Honeywell, and NCR. IBM was the first company to offer a line of mainframe computers that used a single operating system, allowing companies to upgrade their hardware without having to translate all of their data to a new operating system.

The minicomputer, ostensibly named after the miniskirt that was in vogue during its introduction in the early 1960s, was an affordable, closet-sized computer. Because dozens of firms were competing for customers, a variety of "standards" emerged for operating systems, media, media formats, and peripherals.

Things really started to get interesting with the introduction of the microcomputer. Desktop microcomputers like the Altair, Commodore 64, Apple II, IBM PC, and Apple Macintosh moved computer technology out of the military and academic laboratories and into the hands of visionary entrepreneurs who saw the microcomputer as more than a programmable calculator on steroids.

In addition to serving as a platform for surfing the Web and running office productivity software, microcomputers in the home took on the popular role of game console. As the popularity of game consoles from Nintendo, Sony, Sega, and IBM game machines attest, computer games are big business. Unfortunately for game developers and consumers, none of these systems are cross-compatible, and game developers must create games to take advantage of the particulars of the hardware.

Today, the fastest-growing market for microcomputers is in the form of personal digital assistants (PDAs) from Palm, RIM (Research in Motion), Compaq, and others. Many people view the PDA, when combined with an appropriate user interface and a high-speed wireless communications infrastructure, as key to realizing the dream of pervasive computing, the anytime, anyplace ability to access, manipulate, and create data. However, like the early desktop microcomputers, palmtop computers are characterized by diversity in packaging, operating systems, and application software. While the majority of palmtop computers are based on the Palm operating system, an increasing proportion of PDAs are compatible with Microsoft's CE operating system. Research in Motion (RIM) uses yet another proprietary system.

Despite its diminutive size, the typical palmtop has more processing power and RAM than the original IBM PC. Palmtops, like desktop PCs, are especially useful when used in conjunction with a network. When connected to a wireless network, palmtops combine email and Web connectivity with mobility. However, for email and messages generated or received on a palmtop to be archived, they have to be moved to a PC for storage on a hard drive, Zip disk, or other storage media.

COMPUTER NETWORKS

Computers, especially personal computers, started out as stand-alone devices. Today, however, virtually every computer is part of a network infrastructure, such as the Internet or a corporate intranet, that supports it in some way. In a corporate environment and, increasingly, in homes, networks allow users to share the expense of an Internet connection and access to printers, scanners, external storage devices, and other networked peripherals. Networks vary considerably in complexity, architecture, the types of signals they handle, the speed of signals they carry, security, and the topology or physical layout of the network. Variations in the supported protocols or communications standards, as well as the variety of applications and devices connected to the network, add to the complexity and fragility of the entire system.

The network architecture describes the physical infrastructure of a network—the cables, copper wire, fiber optic cables, wireless services, and associated electronics—that supports the flow of data between devices connected to the network. The architecture determines how information can be shared among different types of computers and other devices, regardless of their design or operating system.

Most computer networks are fully digital. However, the domestic public telephone network, one of the largest and oldest networks in the United States and the one used by most people to access the Internet, is predominantly analog. One of the advantages of an all-digital network, in addition to the error correction capabilities discussed earlier, is that it offers a level of privacy and security that's difficult to match with analog networks.

The distinction between high-speed versus normal-speed networks is a relative one that shifts with time. For the home and small-business user, the dial-up 56 Kbps analog modem represents a benchmark for normal speed connectivity to the public telephone

Chapter 2 · DIGITAL MEDIA AND MACHINES

network, whereas Integrated Services Digital Network (ISDN), satellite, T1, Digital Subscriber Line (DSL), and cable modem technologies represent the higher-end of speeds possible, ranging from 128 Kbps for ISDN to over 7 Mbps for DSL.

Of the high-speed options, DSL and cable modems represent the most popular means of connecting to the Internet. However, because of the way they attach to the Internet, both DSL and cable modem connections to the Internet are less secure than a connection provided by a standard 56 Kbps analog modem. Although a cable modem normally filters out all content not intended for a particular user account, with the right equipment anyone can monitor all data sent though a cable modem network. Similarly, the security risk associated with DSL is that its connections to the Internet, unlike those of a typical analog modem connection, are assigned a fixed address. Someone with enough patience can determine the DSL address of any subscriber and, with that information, can access and potentially destroy data on any device connected to the network.

As shown in Figure 2-1, networks can be very complex, incorporating the Internet and other networks. Connectivity to external networks comes at a cost, especially in terms of trading simplicity for capability and complexity. As a result, many networks are highly variable in design, implementation, and stability. Applications that assume or manipulate network resources, such as a network-based data archival service, must contend with the complexity and inherent instability of an evolving network environment.

The outage of a single communications satellite, for example, can disrupt network services for hours, or months, depending on the availability of alternative connectivity options. Similarly, as rolling power outages in Silicon Valley and other parts of California in 2001 demonstrate, high-technology grinds to a halt without affordable, dependable power.

COMPUTER MICROPROCESSORS

Long before "Intel Inside" became part of a marketing campaign, the focus in the computer industry was on the microprocessor, the brains of the computer. The evolution of the central processing unit,

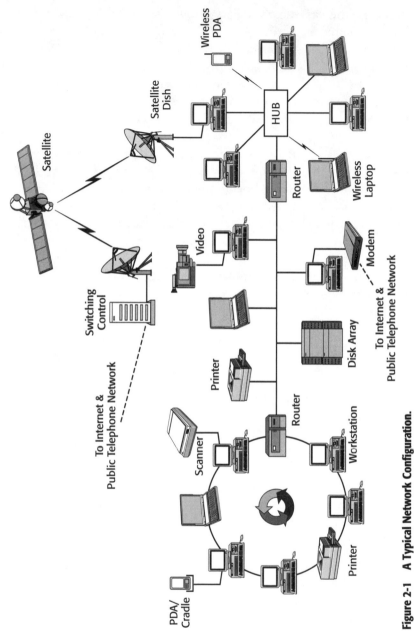

Figure 2-1 A Typical Network Configuration.

Networks are often complex systems that extend beyond the confines of a single business installation to minimally include the Internet and telephone network through a variety of cables, satellites, and microwave links.

the IC (integrated circuit) that directs the flow of data in a microcomputer has been the driving force in computing for over two decades. The often quoted Moore's Law, a prediction advanced by Gordon Moore, co-founder of Intel, is that the number of transistors per square inch on integrated circuits, including microprocessors, will double every two years. Thus far, the prediction has actually underestimated the growth in the capacity—and complexity—of integrated circuits.

The Apple Macintosh caused the evolution tree of microprocessors for desktop computers to branch out significantly. Apple used a microprocessor created by Motorola instead of one from the Intel lineage. Although there continue to be microprocessors manufactured that are incompatible with the Intel standard, because of the popularity of the Apple Macintosh, its divergence probably affects more people than any other. Because of the inherent differences in microprocessors, software written for the Macintosh won't execute on an Intel-compatible PC, and vice versa, without special hardware or software.

Note that compatibility with the Microsoft Windows operating system, initially more or less synonymous with the Intel line of processors, is now more important than compatibility with the Intel microprocessor. It's no longer imperative that a PC use an Intel processor, but rather that the software and data be compatible with the Windows operating system. It doesn't matter if a server or workstation is using a Pentium III or IV or a Clawhammer or Sledge microprocessor from AMD, only that the system is capable of supporting the same version of Windows.

New microprocessor models consistently enter the market every six months or less. More importantly, each microprocessor is typically released with a new chipset, or set of supporting integrated circuits that interface the microprocessor to other computer resources, such as RAM. As such, operating system and application software usually has to be rewritten and recompiled to accommodate the changes. There are always incompatibility issues that arise from unavoidable errors and undocumented features in the new software.

DATA STORAGE DEVICES

All of the microprocessor power in the world is useless without somewhere to store programs and input and output data. Programs and data are stored on a variety of devices, depending on environmental, packaging, dimension, and cost constraints. Storage devices are commonly described as either primary or secondary storage, as a function of how often, and at what speed, the data need to be accessed by the computer's central processing unit. RAM is considered high-speed primary storage, whereas CD-ROM, floppy disk, hard disk, Zip disk, and magnetic streamer tape drives are considered secondary storage.

Table 2-1 lists some of the more common secondary storage options available for microcomputers and their characteristics.

Table 2-1   Data Storage Options.

Technology	Characteristics
Cassette Tape	Linear access, slow transfer rates, antiquated
CD-I	Interactive format no longer supported
CD-R	Write once
CD-ROM	Standard, readable only
CD-RW	Multiple read/writes possible
DVD	High-capacity audio and video distribution
DVD-R	Recordable, but expensive writers and blanks
DVD-RAM	Can act as a virtual hard disk
Flash Memory	Fast, high cost per MB, saves laptop energy
Floppy Disk	Standard, low capacity
Floppy Upgrades	SuperDisk and Zip provide greater storage capacity
Hard Disk	Fixed and removable, fast access
Microdrive	High data density, but uses copy protection
MO Drives	Magneto-optical drives offer high capacity but nonstandard
PROM Cartridge	Resilient in tough environments
Punched Cards	Paper based, outdated
Streamer Tape	Digital tape, high capacity, inexpensive
Tape Cartridges	Multiple standards
Video Disc	Replaced by smaller DVD
WORM Drive	Cannot be erased, high capacity

The most important storage devices today are the floppy disk, floppy upgrades, hard disk, CD-R, and streamer tapes. The ubiquitous $3\frac{1}{2}$-inch floppy disk provides an inexpensive, highly portable means of transporting textual data. It isn't considered an archival medium, however, because of the quality of the oxide coating on the thin plastic disk. In addition, because the standard floppy has a capacity of only about 1.4 MB, floppies aren't practical for storing audio tracks or graphically rich data.

Because of the limited capacity of the floppy disk, floppy upgrades, such as the Zip disk, are increasingly common. The standard Zip disk, much more popular than the similar SuperDisk, is available in 100-MB and 250-MB formats, which are sufficient for storing multi-megabyte image and sound files. The Zip disk is considered an archival-quality medium. Iomega, the manufacturer of the Zip disk, also offers a much smaller 40-MB model that is not compatible with the 100-MB standard Zip disk.

The hard disk, a hermetically sealed version of a floppy disk, is the workhorse of secondary storage. The technology is fast, inexpensive, and capacities from 10 to 60 GB are typical on desktop PCs. Because hard disks provide so much capacity, it's tempting to let all work accumulate on a hard disk, assuming that it will be safe. However, hard disks do fail occasionally, and some means of backing up the data is required. For backing up high volumes of data—on the order of several GB—streamer tape is a popular, inexpensive, high-capacity option. Tapes with storage capacities in the 20- to 40-GB range are common, allowing all or part of a hard disk to be backed up onto a cartridge smaller than a typical PDA.

Whereas the previous storage options rely on altering the magnetic properties of a thin film of metal oxide (rust), the other major storage technology, CD-R, is based on the optical properties of light-sensitive dye. Data are stored as alternating dark and light patches on a disc, created and read by a laser. The advantage of CD-R over a floppy or Zip disk is cost per MB—a 650-MB CD-R blank is less than a dollar. In addition, a CD-R is much thinner than a Zip disk, allowing several gigabytes of data to be archived in a space-efficient manner.

Many other forms of storage are available, but most are fringe products that have a small market share and, therefore, an uncertain future. The most notable is the magneto-optical or MO drive, which combines CD-R and hard disk technologies to create a high-capacity storage device. The MO drive may be useful for a stand-alone system, but the nonstandard format makes it virtually impossible to share the data with others who do not have access to the same make and model of MO drive. Similarly, DVD-R technology, while providing higher storage capacity than a CD-R, is not yet stable enough to compete with CD-R, and many computers are incapable of reading DVD-R media.

Some storage options, such as the cassette tape, CD-I, punched cards, and video discs, passed into and out of vogue. CD-I, or Compact Disc Interactive, combined video and application software on the same disc, allowing stand-alone, microcomputer-controlled players to access the content. However, the format was somewhere between an information appliance and a video game, and the market for CD-I never materialized.

· ·

INPUT/OUTPUT DEVICES

The general-purpose microcomputer can be used in a variety of applications. In this respect, the microcomputer is like a multipurpose hand tool that can accept a variety of attachments, which change it from a screwdriver to a hex-head driver in seconds. A sampling of the parallel in the microcomputer world, the devices located outside of the computer case or peripherals, is listed in Table 2-2. Many of these devices connect to the main computer case through cards inserted into the PC motherboard.

One of the most important output devices is the monitor and associated video display boards or adapters. Monitors have evolved from the MDA (monochrome display adapters) on the first IBM PCs to the full-color, high-resolution SVGA (Super VGA) standard. Specialized adapters for LCD panels and super-high-resolution display and graphics accelerators for more exciting game play are also on the market.

Although low-level variability in devices and components is often shunned, high-level variability, as in the ability to customize a microcomputer, is one reason for the microcomputer's popularity in business, research, and the home. With the appropriate software and

Table 2-2   Common Input/Output Devices.

Each device can be associated with a specific hardware interface, software driver, and application software.

Device	Notes
3D Goggles	Synchronized LCD shutter
Amplified Speakers	Important in game environments
Bar Code Scanner	For inventory control applications
Biometrics	Fingerprint, retina recognition for security
Business Card Scanner	Specialized optical character recognition device
Digital Camera	Still and video
Digital Paper	Uses handheld, wireless pen
Film Scanner	For digitizing 35mm film
Flash Reader	For reading flash memory
Flatbed Scanner	Used with optical character recognition software
Game Controller	Includes game-specific controllers
Handheld Scanner	Optical character recognition and image digitization
Haptics	Force feedback for game and training simulations
Keyboard	Alternative layouts, integrated trackball, function keys
LCD Projector	For electronic presentations
Modem	Standard analog modem operates at 56 Kbps
Monitor	Color temperature a factor, may be LCD or tube
Mouse	Various button configurations, cordless or corded
DSL	High-speed Internet connectivity over phone system
Cable Modem	High-speed Internet access over cable TV system
Network Controller	For LAN connectivity
PDA Cradles	Synchronizing PDAs
Pressure-Sensitive Tablet	Natural interface for artists
Printer	Color, black and white, laser and ink cartridge
Plotter	Large format color and black-and-white prints
Label Printer	Personal, small format, convenient
Trackball	Ergonomic alternative to the mouse
Voice Recognition	Voice converted to keyboard equivalents
Wireless Modem	Popular in small-office settings

changing of a few peripherals, the same microcomputer can be transformed from a home game machine (with a wireless game controller and amplified speakers) to the multimedia center for a marketing firm (with a digital camera, flatbed scanner, pressure-sensitive tablet, and plotter) or to an inventory control system for a warehouse (with a bar code scanner, modem, and biometric security sensor).

Given the variability in computer hardware configurations, it's difficult to compare the performance of two computers configured to simulate a conventional device such as a TV receiver or storage oscilloscope, much less a computer with a conventional device. For example, stereo CD players are typically rated in terms of frequency response and signal-to-noise ratio. Similar figures are difficult to determine for the CD players built in to most personal computers because of potential interference from the monitor, peripheral cables, and the type of sound card used. However, returning to the communications model developed in Chapter 1, one can assess a computer, CD player, or other electronic device in terms of how well it transports data from the source—the CD—to the destination, the speaker.

COMPUTER SOFTWARE

Computer software is the set of instructions that the microprocessor and other components of a computer system must follow. Figure 2-2 illustrates the relationship between software drivers, the operating system, extensions, application software, utilities, languages, and the typical computer infrastructure.

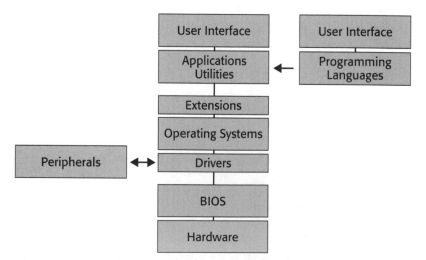

Figure 2-2   Computer Software and Hardware Relationships.

Drivers

The hard drives, monitors, pointing devices, and other peripheral and input/output devices require software "glue" to connect them. Software drivers are the glue that provides the connection, allowing devices to connect and communicate in a controlled way to the main microprocessor. Drivers for popular hardware, such as the Iomega Zip drive, are often shipped with the operating system. Other, less popular devices, and devices released after the operating system, require the installation of specific or updated software drivers. Upgrading an operating system to a later version frequently entails reinstallation of software drivers as well. Occasionally, updated drivers that accompany an operating system upgrade may not work with existing applications.

As illustrated in Figure 2-2, drivers talk to the basic input/output system (BIOS), the collection of software code built into a PC that handles the fundamental tasks of routing data from one part of the computer to another.

Operating Systems

The operating system defines the basic computer software environment. As illustrated in Figure 2-2, the operating system handles communications between an application, such as a word processing program, and the underlying computer hardware. The primary task of the operating system is to convert instructions expressed in application code to BIOS calls that route data from one part of the computer to another.

Proprietary operating systems, such as Microsoft Windows and Mac OS, generally require specific hardware environments. Other operating systems, such as Linux, are designed to run on a variety of hardware platforms with little or no modification. In addition, because every PC make and model is different, most vendors that bundle Microsoft Windows with their systems provide patches for their standard hardware configurations. As a result, the version of Windows that ships with one PC may not work on a PC from another manufacturer or on a different model PC from the same manufacturer.

Extensions

Extensions are to software applications as drivers are to hardware. Software extensions create environments compatible with particular software combinations. An extension can add an advanced memory management feature to a software application, without which the application would not run in all computing environments or configurations. Often, extensions not only ensure compatibility with proprietary software, but they establish the proprietary nature of a software environment. For example, although Microsoft FrontPage creates Web pages based on standard HTML, the code won't execute on a generic Web server environment without the addition of proprietary extensions for FrontPage. With the extensions installed on the Web server, developers can edit Web documents in the familiar FrontPage environment.

Application Software

Applications are task-oriented software, such as word processing, email, games, spreadsheet, database, desktop publishing, electronic presentation, and personal productivity utilities. Although dozens of programs in each category have been developed since the start of computing, the top productivity software category is dominated by giants such as Microsoft, Oracle, and Adobe.

Utilities

Utilities are applications that perform specialized housekeeping tasks, such as disk defragmentation and detection and removal of viruses. Sometimes companies sell utilities that are simply easier to use than those that ship with the operating system. For example, Norton Utilities is a popular set that provides an easier-to-use, if not better, interface to many of the tools contained in Microsoft Windows.

Languages

Computer languages, like human languages, vary from the mainstream to the esoteric. Languages vary from low-level, hardware-specific assembler to high-level, object-oriented languages to suit the applications. For example, game developers, who must squeeze every bit of performance out of a game console, rely heavily on processor-dependent assembly language.

Higher-level languages let the programmer write less. Each instruction the programmer writes in a high-level language is, in turn, automatically translated or compiled into many assembler instructions by another program. High-level languages don't allow the programmer as much control as assemblers and generally don't produce code that is as tight and efficient as possible. However, by insulating the programmer from the details of the microprocessor's internal function, these languages allow programmers to concentrate more fully on the higher-level issues at hand. For example, a programmer writing a word processing application can focus on a more efficient spellcheck algorithm instead of how often the application should check for the location of the mouse pointer on the screen.

The most prevalent language among professional microcomputer programmers today, C, and a variant, C++, were originally developed to write operating systems. In the hands of a skilled programmer, C and its variants can produce tight, efficient code with less overhead—that therefore executes faster—than code written in high-level BASIC. An advantage of C is its popularity, meaning that finding a programmer who can modify or maintain a program written by another C programmer isn't as difficult as finding a programmer who knows MAGIC—a database language used throughout the Virginia medical system, for example.

Some languages were intentionally developed, whereas others evolved from existing tools. For example, SGML, the markup language used by publishers for format-printed documents, evolved into HTML, the language of the Web. Over time, as the Web was transformed from an electronic billboard to an interactive medium, the standard Web authoring languages migrated from simple display HTML to new languages like PHP and XML that support interactivity. Each generation of these newly derived languages provides more power, extensibility, and control over the display and management of data than previous generations.

Trends

Today's applications programmers are tasked with integrating high-level scripting languages with high-level applications. With the scripting language, applications can be extended with custom reporting capabilities, for example. Microsoft Access supports the use of a BASIC-like scripting language for creating custom features not available in off-the-shelf office applications.

Computer software, like the programming field itself, has undergone massive changes in the past few decades. Because hardware and storage tend to be cheap, programmers have a tendency to spend them recklessly, writing "bloatware"—voluminous, inefficient, needlessly complex software. Another trend is the incorporation of utilities, extensions, and even applications into the operating system. Microsoft, for example, bundles its Web browser, Internet Explorer, along with a variety of disk utilities, image and text editors, and communications tools, with its Windows operating system.

The constant market pressure to offer computers with more and better features, and therefore to provide a reason to purchase another computer, even when a customer's existing machine performs adequately, results in a continuous stream of new and "improved" operating systems. New computer buyers have little choice in the matter; it's virtually impossible to buy a new Intel-based computer without also receiving the latest version of Microsoft Windows or Linux installed, for example. This practice of bundling software with hardware, a new practice in the industry, provides software manufacturers with another channel for selling their products and has become widespread. Similarly, many computers come bundled with the latest version of office suites as well—typically Microsoft Office.

As a result of this practice, the new computers are largely incompatible with computers running previous versions of applications and operating systems. A database created with the latest version of Microsoft Access, for example, can't be read by an older version. What's more, without special utilities, it's impossible to remove Access 2000 and install an earlier version of Microsoft Access on a computer's hard drive.

The bottom line is that in a networked office environment, it's virtually impossible to add new Windows-compatible computers to the workgroup without upgrading the existing computers. While this may involve adding RAM and perhaps larger hard drives to fulfill the requirements of the software upgrades, the real issue is the inevitable incompatibilities users will experience with their email, browser, and networking programs. They may lack drivers for printers, scanners, digital cameras, internal CD-ROM burners, and label makers. What's more, some applications, especially custom programs, may not run in the new environment, either because of incompatibilities with the core operating system or because of contention with another application for computer resources.

As a result, computing environments undergo fundamental changes every six months or so, and many older applications may have to be abandoned because the hardware and software environment capable of supporting them no longer exist. Smaller companies without the resources to create product upgrades that are compatible with the latest operating system releases don't survive very long in this environment. Therefore, data that may have been entered into a custom database application developed by one of these smaller software companies may not be retrievable without significant work.

Networks and network protocols are increasingly important in modern computing, especially since the advent of the Web. With the proliferation of software distribution over the Web, it's almost impossible to develop, test, or run an application from a single computer any longer. Often, developing software entails two computers, one as a server and one as the client machine.

The other big trend in computing is from proprietary to open computing systems. For example, the Windows operating system, a proprietary product controlled by Microsoft, has been challenged by Linux, an open computing operating system. Open computing software, like the Linux operating system, is not only free but open— that is, the source code is available as well. As a result, open computing software is more flexible, allowing programmers to adapt each standard to their specific needs.

JUST FOR THE FUN OF IT

No discussion about digital computer technology would be complete without mentioning the most popular class of non-desktop PC microcomputers on the market, the game console. Although desktop PCs outnumber game consoles ten to one, the top game console manufacturers, Nintendo, Sony, Sega, and most recently, Microsoft, are pushing the envelope of what's possible in animated computer graphics and high-fidelity stereo sound effects. A comparison of the technical specifications of the top game consoles is listed in Table 2-3.

Unlike PC manufacturers, game console developers sell their products below manufacturing cost, intending to make money on proprietary games instead. To sell games, game console developers pour research dollars into improving the quality and speed of their graphics, and the power and realism of their sound systems. In addition, game console makers entice developers by offering special development software and hardware at extreme discounts, a practice borrowed from desktop computer manufacturers. The success of the original Apple Macintosh, for example, was due in part to the efforts of Apple at enjoining a group of certified developers who were given access to information and other resources—including pens, coffee mugs, and other memorabilia—for their loyalty.　•

Game consoles, and the entire video/computer game industry, are significant in the context of data archiving and management because they have historically represented the leading edge of the popular computing industry. For example, one of the first commercial uses

Table 2-3　Game Console Specifications.
The top manufacturers rely on hardware-specific software that is not cross-compatible.

Manufacturer	Microsoft	Nintendo	Sega	Sony
Console	XBox	GameCube	Dreamcast	PlayStation 2
Media	DVD	Mini-DVD	Double-sided CD-ROM	DVD
Processor Speed	733 MHz	405 MHz	200 MHz	300 MHz
Processor	Intel Pentium 3	IBM PowerPC Gekko	Hitachi SH4-RISC	Proprietary "Emotion Engine"

of the microcomputer was to control video games such as Pong from Atari. The game industry also provided the raw talent that eventually resulted in the concept of the personal computer. Steve Jobs and Steve Wozniak, founders of Apple Computer, originally worked for Atari as game programmers.

Advances in multimedia, user interface design, processing power, graphical rendering power, and handheld, portable computing in the game industry predate similar capabilities in the general computing world by a decade or more. Unfortunately, the hundreds of early software titles, many of which use technologies not yet available on the PC, can no longer be run because the hardware is no longer available.

Looking to the future of desktop computing, consider that Microsoft's XBox game console uses a graphics processing unit (GPU), that is, a dedicated integrated circuit for creating graphics on the screen. Its IC chip is the most complex integrated circuit ever mass produced.

Of course, the new hardware will require new software to take advantage of the power, meaning that developers will turn their efforts to new hardware, eventually forcing gamers to leave their investment in older games and upgrade to the new, higher-margin titles. If game console developers have their way, their products will not only provide preprogrammed entertainment, but will serve as the center of a family entertainment center, with connections to the Internet, broadcast TV, and other entertainment media.

. . . .

THE MATRIX

Given the virtually mind-numbing possible combinations of software and hardware that can be used to configure a desktop PC, it's amazing that anything runs. It's even more phenomenal that the environment on one machine can be duplicated on another, identical machine, much less a later model running a different operating system. Consider the matrix of potential combinations that can be involved in a "standard" desktop microcomputer, shown in Table 2-4. Note that in cases where hardware is involved, usually one or more software drivers are involved, and there may be both software and hardware contention for microcomputer resources.

Table 2-4   Matrix of Potential PC Configuration Variables.

Other than in highly controlled environments, there is no "standard" PC configuration.

Technology	Examples	Issues
Architecture	ISA, EISA, MCA, VLB, PCI	Overall performance
BIOS	Manufacturer specific	Compatibility with operating system
Bus	AT, IDE, PCI, ESDI, SCSI	Card and operating system compatibility
Coprocessor	Graphics coprocessor	Software driver compatibility, stability
Drivers	Zip Drive driver	Compatibility with operating system
Interfaces	Serial, Parallel, PCMCIA	Nonstandard connectors
Internet Connection	Analog modem, DSL	Security, bandwidth
Local Storage	CD-ROM, hard drive, tape backup	Longevity of media and device, standards
Microprocessor	Pentium 3	Performance, power requirements, backward compatibility, stability, performance of the chipset
Monitor	Silicon Graphics LCD	Color temperature, repeatability of results
Network Connection	ISDN, DSL, T1, Wireless	Security, speed
Network Storage	Storage Area Network	Nonresponsibility for archiving
Operating System	Windows 2000, Linux	Application, extension, and driver software compatibility
Peripherals	Keyboard	Number of keys, layout, functions, drivers available
Power Source	UPS	Power outage protection, line noise filtering
RAM	DRAM, SRAM, VRAM, Flash	Expense, speed, volatility, compatibility, and packaging
Video Card	Matrox Millennium	Bit depth, resolution, color temperature calibration, video RAM, graphics acceleration, operating system compatibility

To add to the confusion, microcomputer resources are sometimes linked in less obvious ways. For example, the integrated circuit responsible for generating sound in the original Macintosh computer also doubles as a controller for the floppy drive. As a result, if the operating system accessed the disk drive while sound was playing, the sound would be intermittently interrupted. Similarly, because of hardware constraints, adding a flash memory card to a laptop can disable, for example, the laptop's internal modem.

To avoid the chaos of multiple operating system versions and different mixes of peripherals, drivers, and applications, virtually all IS departments with larger companies are obliged to enforce strict procurement and operating guidelines. There is typically only one sanctioned brand, model, and configuration of laptop, desktop PC, laser printer, and label maker, for example, and only one version of the operating system, office suite, and Internet browser supported. Installing third-party software may be prohibited as well. As a result, computers in large corporate installations typically lag behind the latest operating system and office software by several versions. Smaller businesses without IS support who rely on third-party software for their day-to-day operations—and the data they produce—don't fare as well because they're forced to upgrade on the vendor's schedule, not their own.

The challenge of controlling complex, interdependent systems can be formidable. As the material in this chapter indicates, creating and storing data is a complex, potentially hazardous activity that requires the seemingly impossible coordination of resources, evolving technologies, and the ever-present human variable. As described in the following chapter, the challenge of configuring and debugging a new computer system, while sometimes daunting, can be trivial when compared to attempting to read data from old storage media on a system that has been out of service for a few years or that is damaged. The constant shifting of the so-called standards, the incessant introduction of newer, higher-margin technologies, and the dumping of software and machines bode poorly for the data entrusted to those systems.

3

Rust Never Sleeps

All my best thoughts were stolen by the ancients.

— Ralph Waldo Emerson

At the height of dotCom fever, anyone with even an inkling of the difference between a keyboard and a keyhole could secure a job at a high-tech firm with stock options and an in-house masseuse. Graphic artists, once happy to accept contract work to create occasional artwork for newspaper advertisements, were suddenly catapulted into high-paying Web designer roles. Even lowly writers, accustomed to scratching for occasional articles, were in high demand as Web content gurus. At one point, warm bodies were so scarce that receptionists were promoted to heads of customer service within a month of starting work. Consider the story below, which details one common side effect of the constant movement of those with computer expertise from one job to the next.

One of the then prominent dotComs managed to entice the head computer technician in a department of a major teaching hospital in the Northeast to join the company. The void initiated a frantic search for a replacement technician. After a month of searching and much negotiating, Ed, the replacement technician, was hired. After a brief tour of the department, Ed was given the keys to his new office—a smallish room filled with cables that snaked along the floor, connecting about a dozen computers mounted in racks and hidden under boxes, and two laptop computers on his desk. Some of the PCs, which were configured as servers for email and a variety of databases, were well over a decade old; a few even had slots for antiquated $5\frac{1}{4}$-inch floppy disks. Unfortunately, there was virtually no documentation on the server hardware and not even a description of which computers were used for particular clinical, administrative, and research data. There was also no time to hunt for answers. With the pent-up demand for service and training, Ed was working sixty plus hours per week, dividing his time between learning the existing system, meeting the staff, and putting out fires.

Less than a month after taking the job, sleep-deprived from working most of the previous night, Ed found himself on his hands and knees. He was moving boxes of parts and books and servers in order to trace the path of a cable that he suspected was the root of the crisis of the day. One of the servers that had to be moved was a two-hundred-pound behemoth equipped with a six-disk RAID system. The handles on each of the six hard drives, intended to facilitate swapping hard disks during routine maintenance, thereby minimizing power-off time, were the only obvious holds for moving the server. In his haste to trace the cable and lacking any other obvious means of moving the server, Ed tugged on one of the drive handles, assuming that the drive bay mechanism was locked. It wasn't.

Less than a minute after the hard disk dangling from Ed's hand screamed to a halt, his phone began ringing. Representatives from the two dozen research labs in the department were complaining that the connection to their server was out. After powering down the server, Ed reinserted the drive in the drive bay, locked the drive bay mechanism, and powered the unit back up. As he feared, the server wouldn't boot. Information critical to the boot process had obviously been destroyed or severely corrupted when he pulled the disk out. With the department's research data for the past four years at stake and irate callers taking turns demanding that their data be made available to them, Ed located a crash recovery company in California. He crated up the server and shipped it to arrive the next morning at the company.

Meanwhile, in a frantic search for the archives that he knew had to exist, Ed discovered a few dozen tape cartridges of various makes and models at the bottom of one of the boxes of computer cards in his office. The only markings on the tapes were cryptic notations of what appeared to be the archiving (backup) date. Ed quickly determined that only three of the tape cartridges were physically compatible with the tape drive in the crippled server and that the latest backup, according to the tape cartridge labels, was almost three months old. A few more phone calls and emails later, Ed was on his way across town to visit a colleague who ran an Information Services department for a large bank. His contact happened to have a computer connected to an operational tape backup unit. However, the three tapes, while physically compatible with the unit, were not readable. Without other equipment, Ed couldn't determine if the tapes were defective, if the data were formatted with a compression utility or other format not recognizable by the tape drive, or even if the tapes were blank.

Two days later, Ed received a call from the crash recovery company informing him that the hard drive was physically destroyed and that the heads had scraped the disk surface at a velocity of several hundred miles per hour, instantly vaporizing the iron oxide coating—and encoded data—over a wide swath of the disk surfaces. The technician with the recovery service also discovered that the RAID assembly, which was designed to survive mishaps such as disk crashes, was improperly configured. The data that were lost on the dislodged disk were not mirrored or backed up on any of the other hard drives. Furthermore, because all of the directory information was on the ruined disk, the other data were rendered unreadable. In short, unless Ed's nonprofit hospital department was willing to pay CIA rates—dollars per byte—then the data were practically not recoverable. The server was returned with a charge on Ed's personal charge card for more than the original cost of the server.

In a meeting with the department administration, it was agreed that the only thing left for Ed to do was to recover the data from the existing archival tape cartridges. After a phone call to another data recovery company, also in California, Ed had a quote of $2,000 plus an hourly labor fee per tape to transfer the contents of a tape to CD-ROMs.

After express mailing the tapes to California and two weeks of phone calls, Ed finally spoke with the technician from the recovery company. It turned out the one technician who was familiar with the antiquated tape drive worked part-time, only came in on Thursdays, and had been on vacation. Three weeks after receiving the tapes, the technician called to tell Ed that the tapes were unreadable because the tape data tracks didn't line up with the heads in his tape drive, but changed relative position on the tape every few feet of tape. Apparently, and unknown to Ed's predecessor, the tape drive in the departmental server had been defective, and the mechanism laid out random, zigzagging tracks instead of straight, parallel ones. The previous chief technician had obviously never attempted to recover files from tape backups. The practical implication was that there never was a real archive for the department's research data.

The technician informed Ed that there was a way to capture data from the tape, but that it was time consuming and expensive, with a cost per megabyte of recovered data and an hourly labor charge. He could capture data from tape if he realigned the tape head by hand every few feet, following the zigzag tracks with an oscilloscope to monitor signal strength. What's more, there was no guarantee that the data would be useful, or even what Ed expected, until the data were fully recovered. With the clinical research teams clamoring for their data, Ed didn't have much choice in the matter. He gave the go-ahead and promised the research committee that all of their data would arrive any day now, neatly laid out on CD-ROMs that could be distributed and copied as needed.

Back at the recovery company in California, some major corporate clients had cases of tapes that had to be processed, and their multimillion dollar projects were given priority over a few dusty tapes from some hospital. In short, despite daily calls, it took eight weeks and $34,000 to get copies of less than a quarter of the original data that once resided on the research server. The tape backups were only incremental, and the data on the tapes only reflected new data added to the system from about six months to three months before the accident.

To the dismay of everyone involved in research in the department, there was no full backup. As a result, at least one research group was unable to compete for federal funding on their project because they couldn't prove that their preliminary findings came from actual clinical data. Other labs hired students to rekey and scan data from printed and published reports.

The ordeal took Ed almost three months, over $40K of departmental money, some deft political maneuvering, lots of lost sleep, dozens of phone calls, and fending off three hundred clinicians and researchers from the department. In the end, he had to confront the department with the plain truth that three years of research information and years of archived email and miscellaneous applications, personal calendars, and other files were lost forever.

· ·

On the bright side, Ed was able to secure the funds for replacement servers with built-in tape backup units that automatically performed an incremental and full backup on a predetermined schedule. In addition, primed by the previous event, Ed taught one person from each of the research labs how to back up data onto the lab's own CD-ROM writers.

This true account illustrates how modern knowledge-based businesses depend on technologic devices and processes. The story also shows how data loss can result not only from ever-present human error, but from obsolescence and deterioration of media and hardware. In Ed's case, not only was the hardware defective, but because the media was outdated, he was totally reliant on external resources for help in attempting to read data from the tapes. It turns out that the selection of a tape format, perhaps a decision that Ed's predecessor based on cost or capacity issues alone, unnecessarily complicated the data recovery process. As discussed below, the various types of media available for data archiving provide a range of features and characteristics that should be considered before media are selected for a particular archiving project.

· ·

MEDIA

The medium is the physical material, whether in the form of a disk or a tape, used to store computer data. The material, whether it is a thin layer of iron oxide sprayed on a paper, plastic, or metal base, or whether it is a thin sheet of aluminum foil sandwiched between disks of plastic, or whether it is a paper card punched full of holes, imparts

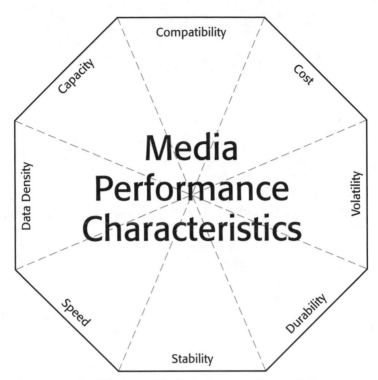

Figure 3-1   The Eight Axes of Media Performance Characteristics.

certain characteristics to the media. These characteristics, together with the major types of media and how these relate to the longevity of data they contain, are described in more detail here.

Media Performance Characteristics

The actual media that a storage device uses can be characterized along the eight axes shown in Figure 3-1: compatibility, speed, capacity, data density, cost, volatility, durability, and stability.

Compatibility is the ability of media to function within a particular software and hardware environment. For example, the surface of a floppy disk that is specially prepared or formatted for the Windows 2000 operating system is generally not readable on a system designed expressly to run Unix. Conversely, some formats are standardized among operating systems. The ISO 9096 manufacturing standard, which specifies how data are stored on a CD-ROM, makes it possible for computers running Windows as well as those running Mac OS to read the same CD-ROM.

Speed is a multifaceted performance characteristic. It encompasses both the time to locate data (seek time) and the time to write to or download from the media (data transfer rate), all of which are functions of the construction of the media as well as the supporting hardware and electronics. Seek time may be several hundred milliseconds for a CD-ROM, a few milliseconds for a hard drive, and a few microseconds for a flash memory card. Similarly, the data transfer rate supported by a CD-ROM drive varies considerably, depending on whether the drive is rated at 2X or 32X, where X is the speed of the original CD-ROM standard. The highest data transfer rates are available from solid-state memory devices such as IC chips.

Capacity, the maximum amount of data the media can store, is a function of the media construction, the tolerance of the casing or cartridge for tape- and disk-based media, and the technology used to read and write the data. Typical data capacity ranges from about 1.2 MB for a standard $3\frac{1}{2}$-inch floppy to around 250 MB for a Zip disk and 10 GB for a double-sided DVD (see Table 3-1). Niche products, such as the DataPlay disks, which are about the size of a quarter, have a capacity of up to 500 MB.

Data density, which affects capacity, is a function of the media used, the drive mechanism, and the error coding and compression technologies. That is, error-control and compression schemes used in CD-ROMs, hard drives, and other media allow higher practical densities than the raw media would support otherwise. For example, the checksum technique, in which a number is assigned to each letter and number in a word or sentence and the total is used to determine if the word or sentence has been received correctly, can be used to determine whether a string of data has been correctly read from a disk or tape surface. If the checksum doesn't match the data, then the area on the disk can be reread. Ideally, the effects of dust, scratch, or other impediments to a clean read can be circumvented on subsequent attempts.

Cost is a function of the raw materials involved in the creation of media but has more to do with what the market will bear and what the competition has to offer. In general, the cost per megabyte is less for optical media than for magnetic media. For example, a 250-MB

Table 3-1 Typical Data Storage Capacities for Common Digital Media.
The values listed here assume no disk compression, which can more than double the listed capacities.

Medium	Capacity	Note
CD-ROM	650 MB	Higher-capacity versions are available but are not standard.
DataPlay	500 MB	This is an example of a niche product with uncertain market survivability.
Digital Tape	2–200 GB	Digital tape is available in a variety of formats and form factors.
DVD	10 GB	Double-sided DVD has more capacity, but few DVD players can access it.
Flash Memory Card	2–128 MB	This has nonvolatile, solid-state memory, it's fast, and it's especially popular for use with battery-powered devices.
Floppy Disk	1.2 MB	The formatted capacity varies slightly, depending on the operating system and the quality of the media.
Hard Disk	20–60 GB typical	The "typical" drive capacity increases with each new computer model.
Hard Disk Cartridge	2 GB	Typically slower and more expensive per MB than hard disks, but total capacity is virtually unlimited. The Iomega Jaz cartridge is an example in this category.
Zip Disk	40, 100, and 250 MB	A popular magnetic media format, the 250-MB hard disk is backward-compatible with 100-MB disks.

Zip disk, which uses magnetic media, generally costs at least 10 times more than a 650-MB writeable CD-ROM blank. However, the Zip disk drives are typically faster, that is, they provide better performance on storing data than CD-ROM writers, which tend to be relatively slow.

Volatility, a characteristic normally ascribed to solid-state memory, refers to the status of the data when external power is removed. Dynamic RAM, for example, loses all data when the power is removed, whereas flash memory retains data without power applied. Removing the batteries from a Palm Pilot results in the loss of all data after the electric charge has drained from the capacitors supplying the RAM—about five minutes. Flash memory, the type of memory used in digital cameras and MP3 players, is considered relatively nonvolatile and can hold data for years without loss.

Durability refers to the physical properties of the media that contribute to the longevity of the surface, mechanisms, and housing, if any, during normal use. The housing, although separate from the media surface, can add significant durability to an otherwise fragile storage medium. For example, the $5\frac{1}{4}$-inch floppy is much less durable than the contemporary $3\frac{1}{2}$-inch floppy. Although both floppy designs use the same type of magnetic media dispersed on a plastic disc, the hard shell of the $3\frac{1}{2}$-inch floppy provides much more protection in a hostile briefcase or a postal carrier's backpack. For example, although cardboard mailers were mandatory for shipping $5\frac{1}{4}$-inch disks in the U.S. mail, the current generation of $3\frac{1}{2}$-inch disks can be mailed in an ordinary envelope and arrive unscathed by either the mechanical handling or the low-radiation x-ray equipment.

Tribology, the science and technology of interactive surfaces in relative motion, including the study of friction, lubrication, and wear, is especially relevant to high-speed hard drives, which typically operate at 10,000 revolutions per minute (rpm) or more. Normally, the device—the head—that reads and writes data to a hard drive flies just above the disk surface and never actually makes contact with the thin surface coating. However, the bearings and other components in the rotational system undergo wear and tear over time. Even flash memory cards are subject to wear and tear each time they are inserted and removed from a camera or laptop computer. Eventually, the metal pins providing electrical connectivity wear or corrode, rendering the memory card useless.

Stability, the static equivalent of durability, reflects the physical properties of the media, in a given environment, that contribute to the longevity of the media and therefore the data, in a dormant state. For example, a hard drive that isn't in use, a flash memory card sitting on a shelf, and a floppy disk stored in a shoe box in the bottom of a closet all have different stabilities.

As noted earlier, metal contacts corrode, for example, rendering RAM and ROM chips inserted in sockets of a computer motherboard unreadable. In this regard, gold-plated contacts are more stable than those composed of pure copper or nickel. However, even gold contacts can corrode, especially in high humidity. Under the right conditions, fungus grows on the gold, which excretes an acid that dissolves the metal, breaking the electrical contact.

A hard disk, a complex electro-mechanical device with greased bearings and other lubricated metal and plastic parts, is subject to the same problems that beset a car that has been stored for years in a garage. Lubrication dries out, leaving bearings dry and without protection, rubber becomes brittle, and plastic parts deform. Furthermore, the magnetic patterns induced in the iron oxide coating on the disk platters fade over the years.

The environment has a major effect on the stability of a storage medium. For example, plastic-based optical media are susceptible to damage from high humidity, rapid and extreme temperature fluctuations, and contamination from airborne pollution. Over time, skin oils can also damage the plastic surface of a CD-ROM or DVD or ruin photographic prints and negatives. Fluctuations in temperature and humidity can also cause shrinking and expansion of magnetic tape, distorting the position of data tracks, resulting in data loss. In this regard, the one- or two-week transit that CDs, DVDs, tapes, and other prerecorded and blank media make through the mail system exacts an unknown and variable toll on the lifetime of the media. Eggs are graded at the point of origin and are expected to drop at least one grade by the time they arrive at their destination, and media that have been shipped should be considered degraded as well. The question is how much. Blank CDs in a case that has been sitting in a postal delivery truck for three days in Arizona in midsummer are likely to undergo much more degradation than CDs in a case in a truck parked in an air-conditioned warehouse.

Media Type

Virtually all PCs, like many other electronics devices, use several types of media to store data. For example, most PCs use one or more of several types of solid-state media and some type of magnetic or optical media, and most PDAs use both volatile and nonvolatile solid-state memory. Multifunction devices, such as portable CD players that also function as CD burners and MP3 players, are increasingly popular in home computing environments. Common media types and their characteristics are summarized in Table 3-2 and described in more detail here.

Table 3-2 Common Media Types and Their Characteristics.
Not shown are more esoteric or outdated media, such as those based on magnetic bubble, core, phosphorous, or punched paper.

Type	Characteristics	Note
Magnetic	Inexpensive, available in tape and disk formats, susceptible to stray magnetic fields, nonvolatile	Ubiquitous. The cartridge, if any, adds significantly to the longevity of the media
Optical	Inexpensive, high capacity	Soft plastic face susceptible to scratches
Magneto-Optical (MO)	Durable, glass and metal construction	Special, nonstandard hardware required, more expensive than pure optical
Solid State	Fast, no moving parts, expensive, volatile and nonvolatile designs	Ubiquitous. ROM, RAM, and flash memory cards

Solid-State Memory. The most common type of memory used in microcomputers from PDAs to supercomputers is solid-state memory based on high-density integrated circuits. For short-term memory operations, usually lasting on the order of a microsecond to a few seconds, data are usually stored in solid-state random access memory, or RAM. All modern microprocessors have some amount of RAM or cache on the same chip substrate to support high-speed calculations. This cache is used to hold the intermediate results of calculations; final results are sent a much larger—but more remote and therefore slower—array of external solid-state RAM.

RAM comes in a variety of flavors, and each is suited to different applications. For example, Dynamic RAM (DRAM) is relatively slow, but very inexpensive. Static RAM (SRAM), in comparison, is very fast, but expensive. Although hard drives and even floppy disks can be configured to simulate RAM for background printing and memory-intensive applications such as image editing, solid-state RAM is much faster.

Another major category of solid-state memory is ROM (Read-Only Memory), which, as the name suggests, is normally read but not written to. ROMs, storehouses of nonvolatile data, are sometimes referred to as firmware, intermediate between the software that can be loaded into or erased from a computer at will, and the hardware, including the hard drives, microprocessor, and motherboard, that constitute the computer. ROM is commonly used in the BIOS, described in Chapter 2, to provide data for the operating system and computer hardware during the boot-up process, before any data can be read from a floppy, hard drive, or CD-ROM.

ROMs can be created for each make and model of computer, but this requires the manufacturers to maintain an inventory of ROMs that has to be disposed of when the hardware configuration of the computer changes. To save production time and avoid wasting money on unused inventory, computer manufacturers commonly use a variant of ROM called PROM or Programmable Read-Only Memory. The most popular forms of nonvolatile ROM that can be reprogrammed after they are attached, either permanently or in sockets, to the PC motherboard are the EPROM (Erasable Programmable Read-Only Memory) and EEPROM (Electrically Erasable Programmable Read-Only Memory).

EPROMs are a type of PROM that can be erased by exposure of the microchip circuitry, which is covered by a transparent quartz window, to UV light. However, for computers intended for consumer use, modifying EPROMs is unreasonable, and even hobbyists usually resort to swapping one EPROM out for another. Reprogramming is more easily accomplished with EEPROMs, which can be erased and modified electrically, either with an automatic utility program or with a few keyboard commands, without the need to open the case and hassle with a UV light or even swap chips.

PROMs can be accessed without the reading of data from a powered peripheral, such as a disk drive, minimizing boot-up time. PDAs, which don't have disk drives, typically use PROMs to store the operating system software and application code. In the game world, storing data on an EPROM cartridge has a number of advantages over magnetic or optical media. As millions of very young video game users have demonstrated, EPROM game cartridges are almost physically indestructible. EPROM cartridges can be dropped or handled with dirty hands, and as long as the contacts are kept clean, their data can be quickly loaded into a game console. But EPROMs, like all other solid-state components, are susceptible to catastrophic damage from static electricity discharges.

The durability and size advantage of EPROMs has also contributed to the popularity of pocket reference guides, such as those used by physicians to look up drug dosing information. Changing to a different electronic book is simply a matter of swapping out an EPROM module the size of an ordinary 9V battery.

One of the more recent types of solid-state memory is flash memory, an innovation that makes digital cameras and pocket digital recorders practical. Flash memory is very much like an EEPROM designed for rapid read and write operations; it provides much faster data access and transfer capabilities than does a hard disk or floppy drive memory. Flash memory, which can be manufactured in paper-thin modules the size of postage stamps, is nonvolatile in that, unlike RAM, it doesn't lose data when the power is removed. In this regard, flash memory combines the read/write capabilities of RAM with the nonvolatility of ROM. The projected life span of data stored in flash memory is on the order of ten to one hundred years.

The primary use of flash memory is as a solid-state volume or disk in laptop computers, usually in the form of a flash memory card, about the size of three or four plastic charge cards stacked on top of each other, that fits into a standard PCMCIA slot. An advantage of using flash memory instead of a laptop's hard drive to store working documents is that flash memory is faster and consumes less than 10 percent of the battery power needed to keep a hard drive spinning. The speed advantage of flash memory is related to the ability of the memory to support simultaneous read and write operations. That is, unlike a typical hard or floppy disk, data can be read from a flash memory card while data are being written to another part of the card.

Magnetic Media. The second most popular form of media on the PC is based on a thin film of metal oxide, typically a mixture of iron, cobalt, chromium, and other elements, deposited on a plastic or metal disk. The metal oxide film can also be deposited on a paper base or, more often, plastic tape. Whether part of a marketing campaign or grounded in reality, a number of magnetic media manufacturers periodically announce different coating processes for magnetic media that supposedly increase the reliability, capacity, and speed of their tapes and disks.

The now pervasive magnetic disk was developed because of the long access time associated with tape. As a sequential media, tape has to be rewound, like the early papyrus scrolls, when particular data are to be located. On the other hand, magnetic disks, like books, allow random access to tracks of data, corresponding to a reader rapidly flipping the pages in a book. Magnetic disks are also now relatively resistant to travel hazards such as mailing and can be safely carried through airport metal detectors without danger of erasure. This is true of floppies and the higher-storage-capacity Zip disks.

Magnetic disks typically have oxide deposited on both sides to double the effective data storage capacity compared to a single-sided disk. The density figure often ascribed to floppies, either high density (HD) or double density (DD), is a function of the density of the magnetic coating on the disk surfaces as well as the accuracy and precision of the disk drive mechanism. Double-density disks, no longer in general use, provided 360 KB of storage, double the storage of the single-density 180-KB IBM floppy disk. The modern $3\frac{1}{2}$-inch floppy disk is a high-density disk, capable of storing up to about 1.4 MB. In operation, distinct areas of the film are magnetized in specific orientations, with one orientation corresponding to 0's and the other to 1's in digital data. Before formatting, the magnetic orientation of the film is random. All disks, and most digital magnetic tapes, must be formatted before use. The formatting process establishes parts of the media that will hold directory information, as well as the tracks and sectors, corresponding to the table of contents of a book, chapters, and pages, respectively. During the formatting process, areas of the media that are not usable are identified and blocked off in the directory. For this reason, the formatted capacity of seemingly identical floppy and hard disks can vary from each other after formatting.

The process of erasing a magnetic tape or disk has a different effect, depending on the type of erasure process used. A true erasure of a disk or digital tape involves orienting every potential bit on the surface in one direction. A partial erasure, in contrast, involves simply removing the reference to particular data in the disk directory. Partial erasure, while less secure, leaves the opportunity to recover data that is still on the disk or tape, a feat usually accomplished with the aid of a utility that builds directory information based on data it finds on the medium.

As shown in Table 3-2, magnetic disks, whether fixed or removable, are similarly marketed according to a particular standard, capacity, and size. Size is especially critical in laptop computers, where a half-inch-high hard drive can seem huge. So-called microdrives are an increasingly popular means of moving data from one laptop to the next. They are so small that complete 64-MB microdrive assemblies can actually double as key chain baubles. In fact, avant-garde jewelry made of circuit board components and media drives has been available for several years.

Magnetic tape cartridges are sold by width, length, capacity, and cartridge size. For example, 4mm, 8mm, and $\frac{1}{2}$-inch widths are common, in lengths from 90 to 160 meter lengths. Capacities of 2 to 50 GB are common, with cartridges made according to a variety of manufacturing or quality assurance standards, such as DDS, DLT, LTO, and Travan.

PCs configured as servers, whether for serving Web content or email, typically employ several independent hard drives configured as a Redundant Array of Independent Disks (RAID system). The idea behind a RAID system is to provide real-time backup of mission-critical data by increasing the odds that data written to a server will survive the crash of any given hard drive in the array. As Ed's experience illustrates in the chapter opener, however, RAID technology is not foolproof if hardware performance is not monitored and regularly maintained. Computer peripherals, like cars, require regular maintenance. More than one computer system has been brought to its knees because of overheating due to lint clogging its ventilation fan. Alas, lint and dust, like rust, never sleep.

Optical Media. CD-ROMs and DVDs of various varieties, along with a few other, less common formats, are based on a technology in which data are represented by the presence or absence of nonreflective pits in a reflective film, typically made of aluminum. The film is sandwiched between sheets of polycarbonate or other plastic in order to provide rigidity and protection from the environment. One of the advantages of optical media is that there is no physical contact with the surface during the read operation, so there is less chance of physical wear.

Compact Disc Recordable (CD-R) technology uses dual-power laser beams to read and write data. In the write mode, a stronger beam is used to turn a dye dark; the weaker read beam later responds to the dark area as it would to a pit on a CD-ROM. The difference is significant in that the pits sandwiched between plastic sheets in a commercial CD-ROM are more stable than the dye used in recordable CDs.

Write-Once-Read-Many (WORM) drives, as the name suggests, can record data once, but read it indefinitely. Unlike CD-ROMs and DVDs, WORM media are usually based on glass, not plastic discs. DVDs, which provide over ten times the capacity of standard CD-ROMs, are a popular means of distributing digital videos. Working with the recordable version of the technology, DVD-Recording (DVD-R), is more complex than working with the more standardized recordable CD-ROM technology. For example, the user must choose the video standard as well as the type of compression to use during the recording process. DVD-RAM and other DVD variants promise to be easier to work with in the future.

Magneto-Optical Media. Magneto-optical (MO) discs and cartridges combine laser and magnetic technologies to provide a different kind of recordable, high-density storage medium. In operation, a high-power laser beam heats the disc surface, making it susceptible to a magnetic write-head. In a way that parallels the recording of data on a hard disk drive, the write head alters the direction of crystals on the disc surface, which changes the reflectance of the disc surface. To read data from an MO disc, a lower-power laser reads the disc according to changes in reflectivity, similar to the process used with standard CD-ROMs. As a result of the combined technologies, MO discs can provide a higher data density than disks of magnetic media. They are also relatively immune to the effects of stray magnetic fields that they might be exposed to while in transit.

Trends

Data storage encompasses much more than raw media and typically includes some form of transport mechanism. The ultimate performance of the combination therefore defines the performance and usability of the technology. Sometimes the potential of media is intentionally crippled by the transport and data interface because of intellectual property concerns. For example, the electronics used with commercial MiniDisc technology prevents the copying of one MiniDisc to another. Similarly, the DVD-R devices available on the market allow users to create DVDs from a variety of sources—except commercial DVDs.

Another trend is to use network-based storage to supplement or replace local storage. Two prominent network-based storage technologies are Storage Area Networks (SANs) and Network Attached Storage (NAS). These and other database management technologies are discussed in more detail in Chapter 4.

....

HARDWARE

A CD-ROM or Zip disk isn't very useful if there is no hardware to read it or write data to it. In this regard, the life span of media is inextricably linked to that of the supporting hardware. In cases where the media and hardware are inseparable, such as in an internal or fixed hard drive, the data die with the hardware. Even when the media and the hardware that read it are separate, as with DVDs, CD-ROMs, magnetic tape cartridges, diskettes, and Zip disks, the ultimate fate of the data on the media can be tied to the hardware.

Consider that if the hardware required to read the media is obsolete, two obstacles arise. The first is locating operational hardware, whether in someone's basement or in a company that happens to be using the antiquated technology. The second, and often more vexing, task is to locate someone who is an expert at configuring and using the hardware. As Ed's dilemma illustrates, working with old media is often a problem of people's knowledge, not available technology.

As listed in Table 3-3, computers and their related peripherals have very limited life spans. Sometimes computer hardware simply wears out. More often, however, some new technology comes along to make what was the latest technology only a few months ago seem immediately antiquated and slow. Whether it's a larger display and faster, more powerful microprocessor, or a flat screen and ergonomic keyboard for more user comfort, there seems to be continuous pressure to upgrade to the latest hardware.

Table 3-3   Defunct Microcomputer Hardware Platforms.
This list is limited to notable microcomputers only. Hundreds of laptop, handheld, and desktop models, especially clones, are no longer in common use or in production.

Platform	Notes
Apple I, II, IIe, IIc, III	II series bolstered by the electronic spreadsheet
Apple Lisa	Too expensive but ahead of its time
Apple Macintosh (original)	No hard disk, limited RAM, small screen
Commodore 64	Popular alternative to the Apple II, superior graphics
Game consoles	Dozens of consoles introduced in the 70s and 80s
Osborne	Innovative portable designs
PC-AT	Set the standard in business computing
PC-JR	Failed to take the home market from Apple
PET	Popular in Europe
Portable PC	Luggable, tiny screen
Radio Shack TRS-80	Popular with hobbyists and BASIC programmers
Sinclair	Laptop-sized system popular with hobbyists

Given this reality, part of the challenge in preserving computer data is that the hardware and standards quickly come and go. In the period of five years, a once ubiquitous format can become obsolete. For example, before the introduction of the popular Zip disk, the most popular removable magnetic media was the SyQuest 45-MB cartridge system. Because the Zip disk offered over twice the storage in a package about a quarter of the size, a tenth of the weight, and less than half of the price of a SyQuest cartridge, its sales and use immediately replaced the SyQuest.

Often the challenge of keeping data alive is compounded because of the way hardware and software standards are linked. Consider the fate of the analog videodisc, which at first glance looks like a CD-ROM the size of a vinyl LP record. With the introduction of the videodisc came several incremental standards, each attempting to add some degree of interactivity to the video experience. Whereas the earliest version relied on a separate computer and software to control the playback, later versions mixed computer code with the analog video signals on the same disc. The hybrid videodisc required a videodisc player with a built-in microprocessor for self-contained control, but also worked on a standard player with an external computer and associated software. In this environment, keeping current with the data meant not only upgrading to new hardware every six months but also maintaining at least two versions of the controlling software for each videodisc title. In the end, constantly transferring the content to new formats and upgrading the supporting hardware became too expensive compared to alternative technologies, and the videodisc format died.

INFRASTRUCTURE

Modern computing extends beyond the confines of a single PC to the Web and beyond. That being so, the fate of data depends on the long-term integrity of the worldwide data communications infrastructure. As illustrated in Figure 3-2, the key components of the data infrastructure include the satellite communications systems, microwave links, the network of fiber optic and copper cables, and the network electronics that tie it all together.

Today, satellites carry about five percent of all telecommunications, including direct-to-home TV and Internet service, digital radio, and the Global Positioning Service (GPS), and the volume of data handled by satellites is expected to increase significantly in the near future. However, despite the versatility and functionality provided by satellites, including the ability to provide Internet access to remote, relatively unpopulated and underdeveloped areas of the world, satellites have relatively limited lifetimes. The useful satellite lifetime for modern satellites is on the order of twelve to fifteen

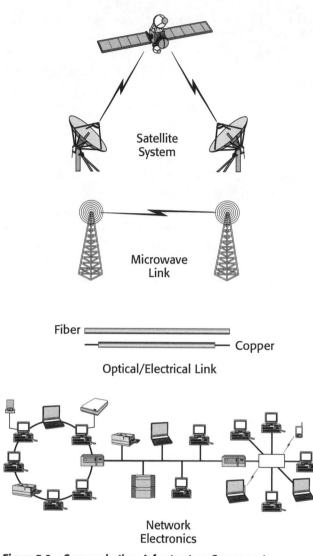

Satellite
System

Microwave
Link

Fiber 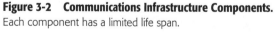 Copper

Optical/Electrical Link

Network
Electronics

Figure 3-2 Communications Infrastructure Components.
Each component has a limited life span.

years, owing to improved fuel efficiency and improvements in electronic components. In other words, if something—economics, war,
or natural disaster—prevented satellite launches for a decade or
more, the satellite component of the communications infrastructure
would be useless.

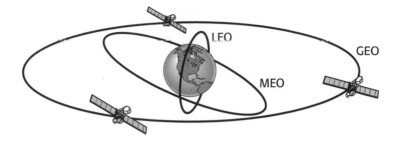

	Altitude	Visibility	Cost	Footprint
GEO	36,000 km	Continuous	Low	13,000 km
MEO	10–20,000 km	2–4 hours	Medium	8–10,000 km
LEO	500–2000 km	10–20 minutes	High	1–5 km

Figure 3-3 Communications Satellites and Their Characteristics.
GEO: Geostationary Earth Orbit; LEO: Low Earth Orbit; MEO: Medium Earth Orbit.

All else being equal, higher orbits are associated with longer life spans, given that a satellite in a high orbit is less affected by the friction of the earth's outer atmosphere. The height of the orbit also defines the communications coverage area, usually referred to as the footprint. As illustrated in Figure 3-3, communications satellites are commonly placed into one of three orbits: Geostationary Earth Orbit (GEO), Low Earth Orbit (LEO), or Medium Earth Orbit (MEO). The orbit not only affects the footprint, but also the reliability and availability of communications, terrestrial antenna and power requirements, and the latency or time it takes a signal to travel from the earth to a satellite and back to earth again.

For example, a satellite in a Geostationary Earth Orbit has a footprint of about one-third of the globe, covering virtually the whole planet with only three satellites. The first geosynchronous communications satellite, placed into service in 1963, has long since ceased operation. LEO communications satellites, such as the 66-satellite Iridium system, have the lowest orbits, smallest footprints, and largest number of satellites. The planned Teledesic network, promoted as the "Internet in the sky," is designed with 288 primary LEO satellites and 12 spares. Eventually, the system is designed to extend the terrestrial fiber network to anywhere on the planet. When the Teledesic system becomes available, the number of Internet users worldwide is expected to increase rapidly. While this growth bodes well for people in sparsely populated countries and in remote locations, it also means that the data communications of millions of Internet users will depend on the continued integrity of hundreds of satellites that must be continually monitored and maintained.

Sputnik, the first orbiting manmade satellite, a product of great human ingenuity, was short-lived. It operated for only days before the batteries supplying the transmitter died. As the intentional decommissioning of the Russian space station *Mir* in early 2001 demonstrated, even orbiting systems that have had years of attention and repair eventually fail. Communications satellites are so expensive and so important to keep operational that several Space Shuttle missions have been devoted to repairing communications satellites.

Although satellite communications systems are often taken for granted, it's a system at the edge of chaos. As several disastrous attempts at launching military communications satellites in the late 1990s demonstrated, each launch failure has disastrous consequences. Not only does the loss of a billion dollar satellite require years of unexpected development to replace, but the capacity of the entire communications infrastructure is crippled in the meantime.

Despite the risk of relying on satellite communications, the economics of satellite communications are such that it's often the least expensive method of providing communications between points separated by more than a few hundred kilometers. The distance covered by terrestrial microwave hops is limited by the curvature of the earth. A hop of 1700 km (1000 miles), for example, might require a network of 20 terrestrial microwave dishes and associated hardware. The same distance might be covered by a single satellite hop (see Figure 3-4).

However, for short hops across town, from one building to the next, or even across a river, microwave links are an economical, easily established, secure method of data communications. Depending on the frequency of the link and the construction of the antenna system, however, communications may be adversely affected by weather and seismic activity. Like satellites, microwave links require a constant source of power for continuous operation.

The copper and fiber optic cables, while not as exciting as communications satellites, provide the core interconnectivity for the

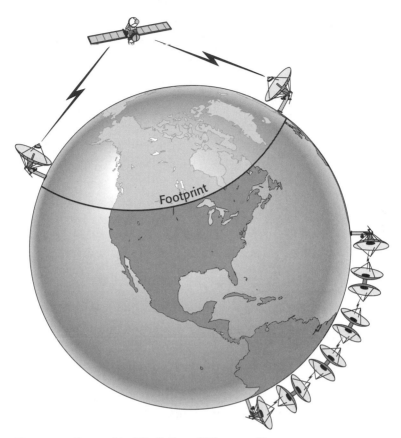

Figure 3-4   Geographical Limitation of Microwave Hops.
The earth's curvature limits the length of a microwave hop to line-of-sight, which is only a few hundred kilometers under best conditions.

Internet and other communications systems. The wired component of the data communications infrastructure is more stable and reliable than satellite or microwave communications. Millions of miles of copper wire, in the form of coaxial cable and twisted pair, feed phones, faxes, TVs, and computer modems throughout the United States. Fiber optics, touted for its bandwidth carrying capacity, also criss-crosses the United States and much of Europe and Asia as well.

Data traveling over the wired communications infrastructure are not impervious to disruption. As the "do not dig" signs suggest, one of the most common fates of copper and fiber cables is accidental disruption. A misdirected backhoe can take out the main trunk for an entire city in one swoop. Corrosion over time is another disruptive factor, especially for copper wire run in damp underground tunnels of the big cities. For copper as well as fiber, the problems tend to be at the splices or junctions, where the protective plastic sheath is disrupted, laying bare the copper wire or fiber optic strand. Rats, squirrels, and other rodents can disrupt the protective cable sheaths as well, accelerating the normal aging process by allowing water to seep into a cable bundle.

Although the cables and microwave hops provide the backbone for data communications, the electronics, in the form of routers, firewalls, terrestrial and satellite repeaters, servers, bridges, and a variety of computer-controlled devices provide the global intelligence that holds the communications system together. The apparently ephemeral communications network works most of the time because of standards and, of course, paying customers.

However, standards are as fleeting as microprocessor designs. A decade ago, digital cellular systems were anomalies in an analog network; today, digital communications, whether through wireless PDAs or PCS phones, is the standard. Similarly, up-and-coming digital communications standards, such as Bluetooth, promise to change everything, ushering in a new generation of electronic infrastructure hardware and related standards. The risk of introducing these new technologies into the communications infrastructure is increased complexity, decreased reliability, decreased security and privacy breaches, and other forms of data loss.

. . . .

DETERIORATION

In the late 1920s, a grandmother by the name of Violet Shinbach started the uniquely American tradition of bronzing baby shoes. Although the bronze shoes that result from the process are reasonable facsimiles of the original leather, plastic, or rubber shoes, they aren't usable as shoes anymore. However, unlike a pair of leather baby shoes that will eventually rot and crack and be attacked by puppies, kittens, and moths over the decades, bronze baby shoes will likely outlast the baby—and his or her grandchildren. However, at some point, the bronze shoes will crumble to dust as well.

It turns out that, despite the heroic efforts of chemists, physicists, physicians, and priests, sooner or later, everything dies. The effects of the passage of time are inescapable. Everything on the planet undergoes continuous physical and chemical changes. The human skeleton, for example, is completely replaced by new minerals every few months. As illustrated in Table 3-4, many of these changes are accelerated by rapid swings in temperature and humidity, by extremes of temperature and humidity, by light, pollution, biological infestation, wear and tear, contamination with chemically reactive substances, and the innate chemical composition of materials.

Table 3-4 Deterioration Accelerants.

Factor	Effects/Examples	Targets
Biological Infestation	Insects, rodents, molds, and bacteria destroy organic materials and some plastics.	Books, tapes, cable coverings
Bright Light	Sunlight or artificial light bleaches pigments and accelerates photochemical deterioration in plastics.	Photographs, printouts, CD-R, DVD-R, microfilm
Contamination	Glue oxidizes paper, acid-containing paper deteriorates prints and documents, gases from untreated wood cloud plastic surfaces, impurities promote oxidation of metal films.	Book bindings, CD-ROM, CD-R, DVD, DVD-R, tapes
Temperature (below freezing)	Stone, plaster, and glass fracture; plastic becomes brittle; metals contract.	Glass WORM discs, tape and hard drive cartridges
Temperature (high)	Metals expand and deform, tapes delaminate, plastics deform and melt, wood and paper char and burn.	All digital media

Table 3-4 Deterioration Accelerants. (Continued)

Factor	Effects/Examples	Targets
Humidity (high)	Wood swells, paper becomes limp and self-adhesive, organic substances develop mold, plastic swells and clouds, metals oxidize.	CD-ROM, CD-R, DVD, DVD-R, magnetic disks
Humidity (low)	Wood and ivory warp and crack, leather and paper become brittle, static charges develop and can discharge through media.	EEPROM, RAM, flash memory disk
Pollution (particulate and gases)	Paper, plastic, wood, and stone oxidize; plastics cloud; metal contacts corrode.	All digital media
Temperature Swings (rapid/wide)	Metal films, plastic, and glass crack, buckle, and tear or break; electrical contacts within ICs and between ICs and their sockets separate; read and write heads in hard disks become misaligned.	All digital media

One difference between theoretical physics and applied engineering is that engineering is concerned about creating what's good enough, within established parameters such as cost, time to market, and quality. Theoretical physicists, on the other hand, are more interested in whether or not something can be done at all, regardless of cost or performance requirements. In the world of business, engineers rule, and their liquid crystal displays (LCDs), integrated circuits (ICs), and storage media are manufactured to a variety of specifications, such as accuracy and tolerance, as well as long-term stability, sensitivity to ambient moisture levels and temperature variations, and shelf life or stability.

The multitude of factors that contribute to the life expectancy of a device or system can be expressed in the Mean Time Between Failure or MTBF rating. The MTBF, an estimate of the failure rate of a device during its expected lifetime, is one metric that can be used to determine relative resistance to deterioration. Typical MTBF ratings for CD-ROM drive recorders are around 100,000 hours, compared to 250,000 hours for a tape drive and 500,000 for a hard drive. Assuming the expected life of each of these devices is one year, then, after running 1000 of each device for 1000 hours (1,000,000 hours total), one would expect to see 10 CD-ROM drives (1,000,000/100,000), 4 tape drives (1,000,000/25,000), and 2 hard drives (1,000,000/500,000) fail.

Another metric for the expected lifetime of a device is the warranty. A disk drive or computer system with a longer warranty suggests that the manufacturer expects it to last longer before failing. Most device failures occur during the first few hours or days of operation, hence the practice of a burn-in period at the production facility before a computer system or peripheral is shipped.

As discussed earlier, failure rates of magnetic, optical, and magneto-optical media are a function of the design and composition of the media, the amount of wear and tear associated with the drive mechanism, if any, and the environment. For example, unlike the magnetic pickup and write heads of a floppy or hard disk drive, the heads of a magnetic tape system may make contact with the tape. In addition, a tape is repeatedly wound and unwound during normal operation. As a result, the cumulative physical wear on a tape is generally greater than for a hard disk of the same capacity. The tape wear can be minimized by a thicker magnetic coating, special drive mechanisms, and special, low-friction coatings.

As shown in Table 3-5, the expected lifetimes of media vary considerably, depending on the environmental conditions. These expected lifetime figures are obviously only estimates based on simulations of accelerated time, for example, created by subjecting a magnetic tape to abnormally high temperature and humidity. However, many factors are difficult to model. For example, air pollution is a complex phenomena and varies daily with wind conditions, time of day, weather, and traffic. Scientists do know that magnetic and optical media, battery connections, metal connecting pins on memory modules, and magnetic disc media are very sensitive to airborne contaminants.

Under ideal conditions of constant low temperature and humidity, freedom from biological agents, static electricity discharges, and other factors, data stored on magnetic tapes should be accessible for

Table 3-5 Expected Media Lifetimes Under Ideal and Typical Conditions.

Ideal conditions include constant, controlled, low humidity and low temperature, no airborne gases or particulate matter, and no physical handling or jarring. Typical conditions assume media of variable quality, in seasonally varying temperature and humidity.

Medium	Ideal Lifetime (y)	Typical Lifetime (y)	Note
CD-R	5–100	2–30	Dye used to represent data less stable over time compared to pits used with commercially recorded CD-ROMs
CD-ROM	30–200	5–50	Uses actual pits and lands on a metallic surface to encode data; fragile surface
DVD	100	20	Higher-density media more susceptible to environmental changes
DVD-R	20–30	10	Like CD-R, less stable than commercially recorded media
Hard Disk	<100	10–20	Lifetime a function of the integrity of the electro-mechanical assembly
Hard Disk Cartridge	<100	20–40	Lifetime a function of the integrity of the media
Magnetic Tape	30–100	5–20	Should be rewound periodically to release tension
Microfilm	500	100–200	The standard for archival purposes
MO	5–100	2–30	Multiple format standards
Paper– Newsprint	200	5–20	Acidic, high-wood-pulp paper degrades more rapidly in light and higher humidity
Paper– Rag	500	10–100	Can be deacidified to extend the typical lifetime
Paper– Buffered	>500	50–500	Lifetime extended because of high rag content
Photographic Negative	300	>100	Color negatives and positives (color slides) faster fading than black and white
Photographic Print	>200	>100	Assumes nonacid paper and minimum light exposure; Polaroid prints darken much sooner
WORM	30–200	5–50	Format less standardized than CD-ROM or DVD

several decades. Under ideal conditions, CD-ROMs, EPROMs, and flash memories should retain their data for up to a century; hard disks, floppy disks, and disk cartridges should retain data for thirty or forty years.

In some cases, the deterioration of media is more a function of the composition of the media. Stability of media requires a medium that is chemically inert and impervious to oxygen. Eventually, even within a controlled environment, and over a hundred years, hard disks and floppy disks will become demagnetized and lose their data.

TECHNOLOGICAL OBSOLESCENCE

The first few models of PCs from IBM and other manufacturers were built to last, with all-metal cases, mammoth power supplies, and more than adequate airflow management systems. However, the manufacturers soon discovered that they didn't have to build a PC like other office equipment that was intended to be in service for twenty years or more. With the rapidly evolving technology, standards for hardware, software, and media shifted every few years. In the evolving environment, it became obvious that the PC was being overengineered.

Today, PC manufacturers almost have the reputation Detroit did in the 1990s for producing automobiles and components with life expectancies of only a few years. Lightweight, putty-colored plastic has replaced metal as the structural element of choice, and few computer models are in production for more than a year without major modifications and improvements. Furthermore, with the exception of the most popular laptop and desktop PC models, parts are available for only a year or two after each model is introduced.

A constant stream of operating system and office suite releases makes previous versions incompatible in workgroup settings, forcing upgrades. Whether or not the current state of affairs is a planned obsolescence orchestrated by the computer hardware and software industries, the reality is that the greatest threat to the longevity of data isn't the lifetime of the media or durability of a particular PC design, but technological obsolescence.

To use an example from the hardware realm, consider the technologies surrounding the MiniDisc, a storage medium with the capacity of a standard music CD. Although the MiniDisc uses a digital format, unlike CD recording equipment, the MiniDisc system uses a lossy compression algorithm, which means that a copy of a CD isn't a perfect digital copy but has added noise compared to the original. Copying a CD to another CD, in contrast, normally results in an identical copy. In addition, the MiniDisc standard is designed in such a way as to prevent duplication. A MiniDisc can serve as the basis for a cassette recording, but with added loss of data and introduction of noise. Although the MiniDisc doesn't strictly fit the definition of planned obsolescence, it's an example of an intentionally crippled system, and one that is designed to lose data from one generation to the next. The overall effect is to create an evolutionary dead end for digital data that makes it to the MiniDisc format.

It's often said that developments in computer hardware lead corresponding innovations in software by about five years. This delay is in part because it takes programmers years to master the nuances of a new hardware configuration and the concomitant versions of its operating system. To appreciate the constantly evolving software development environment, consider the list of defunct operating systems shown in Table 3-6.

Table 3-6   Defunct Microcomputer Operating Systems.

Rapidly evolving operating system environments not only force end users to constantly upgrade their computer systems, but they pose major development challenges to software developers as well. Note that the many supercomputer, minicomputer, and handheld operating systems are not shown.

OS	Notes
CP/M	Predates DOS
DR-DOS	Digital Research's alternative to Microsoft's DOS
Mac OS	Pre-X versions now outdated
MS-DOS	Versions 1–6x supplanted by Windows
NeXT OS	Associated with hardware that never caught on
Novell DOS	Short-lived attempt by Novell
OS/2	Promoted as successor to MS-DOS; lost to Windows
ProDos	Apple's version of DOS for the Apple II series
Windows 3.1/95	Supplanted by various flavors of Windows 98
Windows NT 3.51	Outdated by NT 4.0 and a series of service packs

Programmers are hard-pressed to keep up with the rate of progress. Although the rapid increases in speed, address space, and other internal workings of the microcomputer bode well for power-hungry multimedia applications, they also complicate the cross-compatibility issues with peripherals and software. Programmers, to take advantage of the new hardware and operating system features such as the ability to access more RAM, must recompile applications and often must add code to check for earlier versions of micropro-cessors and operating systems. If an earlier version of a microproces-sor is detected, exceptions can be made so that features present in advanced microprocessors, such as an onboard multimedia copro-cessor, can be bypassed.

In addition to dealing with the increasing complexity of applica-tion code, programmers depend on the availability of compiler upgrades, the applications that convert code written in high-level languages to low-level machine instructions. That is, taking advan-tage of the new features of an operating system or microprocessor requires a new software compiler. Compilers, like other software, often have problems or bugs, and sometimes the microprocessors themselves have bugs hard-coded into their designs. A notable example was the bug in the first release of the Intel Pentium micro-processor that caused errors in some types of calculations. Intel pro-vided a free replacement for owners who requested a debugged Pentium chip, a move that cost Intel millions of dollars up front, but saved their public image in the long run.

While programmers wear many hats, dealing with issues from hardware compatibility to compiler upgrades, they are primarily the authors of the applications that give PCs their usefulness. In this regard, the source code they generate is a type of literature. Similarly, game developers can be likened to novelists, in that they deal with character development, conflict, and entertaining conflict resolu-tions. Although programmers have to deal with varying software environments and backward compatibility with microprocessors, like other authors, they primarily work with languages. However, unlike English, source code is meant to be read and interpreted by machines, not humans. Exceptions are explicitly made for com-ments within the code so that human readers have a clue as to what is really happening.

In the relatively short history of the computer, dozens of languages have been devised, utilized, and lost. A few languages, such as LOGO, Ada, and MUMPS, managed to survive in niche areas like education, the military, or medicine, but most have been replaced by variants of C, Java, and HTML. Computer science students learn to use C and C++ for creating applications, and Java, HTML, XML, and similar languages for Web development. As a result, applications written more than a decade ago in a language such as PROLOG or FORTH or FORTRAN might as well be written on punched cards for all their readability now. Even if compilers compatible with modern microprocessors and operating systems could be developed, without a pool of programmers who are fluent in a language, the code and the thinking behind an application written in something other than a contemporary language is, for all practical purposes, lost.

An approach taken by the U.S. military is to train programmers in obsolete languages so that they can maintain programs that are still in use. Similarly, the VA medical system runs on a variant of MUMPS, a language virtually unknown in the general programming community. To support ongoing development of the system, the VA hires programmers—and sometimes interested nonprogrammers—and sends them to an intensive training program to make them proficient in MUMPS. The increasing popularity of open standards in the field of programming promises to increase the efficiency of application development. Open standards make it possible for programmers to mix and match software tools to suit their needs. With the source code for Linux readily available, for example, a software development group can create its own variant of the operating system to suit particular needs. However, like variations in the dialect of English or other language, custom development environments may lead to new languages or to evolutionary dead ends.

To be fair, sometimes customization is unavoidable. Consider, for example, that Windows NT is notorious for not handling sound very well, compared to a PC running some version of Windows 98 or to even the most rudimentary Macintosh computer. However, with special hardware cards and software patches, an NT machine can be configured as a formidable music processor. Although the solution may work on a case-by-case basis, the custom environment may be expensive and difficult to replicate widely, especially since the environment may be tied to a single sound card manufacturer, a particular software developer, and other factors. In this regard, custom computer applications and hardware are no different from custom clothes, houses, or appliances. The prices go up, and the availability of spare parts and reparability goes down. Resale value may be diminished as well, unless the seller can locate a buyer with the same needs and tastes. Over time, as the available hardware and software evolve, replicating the customized environment or repurposing the data and associated software may well be impossible.

....

CHAOS HAPPENS

According to complexity theory, physical systems with many independent variables that interact with each other in complex ways have an ability to balance order and chaos. The balance point, the edge of chaos, will spontaneously self-organize and adapt to changing circumstances. Most importantly, from the perspective of maintaining a repository of data, complexity theory suggests that not all systems tend toward disorder or entropy.

However, whether or not there is a unifying balance in the world, it's clear that chaos happens. In the same month that IBM announced a new chipset that promises to sharply reduce the size, power requirements, and cost of a new line of Internet appliances, religious fanatics in Afghanistan razed a statue of Buddha that had endured for more than fifteen centuries.

War, floods, earthquakes, and everyday accidents are unavoidable. That said, it's prudent to take reasonable steps to mitigate the consequences of a disaster, especially if the precautions don't take much energy or time to put in place. For example, one can spare a megabyte of data on a floppy disk the risk of accidental erasure by simply sliding the write-protect tab on a disk to the locked position. As described in the next chapter, more advanced precautions and processes have been developed expressly for managing and maintaining digital data.

Digital Data Management

Managing digital data isn't a job that can be left to chance. In an organization of any significant size, managing data is usually a full-time responsibility, and one that's so complex that it can't be done effectively in an ad hoc manner. A data management policy that calls for making backup tapes "whenever there's free time" simply won't do in the fast-paced world of corporate computing—or in a busy household. Unless the process for managing digital data is completely and explicitly defined, debugged, and enforced, data are going to be lost. Often, as the story below illustrates, challenges to a data management plan come when they're least expected.

Around 2:00 A.M. on Monday, the day after New Year's Day, Roger, the assistant director of a major computer research laboratory in the Northeast, was awakened by a phone call from one of his staff. The programmer, who lived a few blocks from the laboratory, said that there was some sort of accident at the laboratory because the building was surrounded by fire trucks, police cars, and at least one ambulance. Twenty minutes later, Roger found himself standing ankle-deep in freezing water, staring in disbelief at the walls in his office in the second floor of the three-story office building. The walls were covered with uniform, glass-like sheets of water, like the marble fountains that grace many city squares. The glaze didn't even look like water until he disrupted it with a fingertip. The effect was repeated in the thirty other offices on the floor, which was normally home to his thirty-person programming team.

One of the dozen or so firemen dressed in their yellow slickers told Roger that apparently a New Year's Eve party was held on the top floor of the building, and that someone had opened—and left open—a window in one of the rest rooms in order to provide everyone with a better view of the fireworks. With no one in the building on the following day, the rest room door remained closed, and the ceiling temperature matched the subzero temperatures outside. In the frigid temperature, the two-inch water main for fire control that ran along the ceiling for the length of the building froze and burst.

The water level on the third floor, one floor above Roger's area, rose to over three feet at one point during the night. When the firemen arrived, the flood on the second floor was about a foot deep, enough to drown the dozen or so PCs that happened to have been left on the floor beside the programmers' desks, a copy machine, a large document scanner, a cluster of four servers, a disk array, and a high-speed tape backup unit. In addition, the sheets of water running down the walls had torn down posters and inundated books, manuals, and disks, sweeping them off the wall-mounted bookshelves to the floor in each office. Working quickly in the surreal emergency lighting, Roger, with the help of three of his staff who had arrived at almost the same time he did, began covering the desktop PCs and other equipment on desks and tables with plastic garbage bags to protect them from water damage.

It was immediately clear to Roger that it would not be work as usual for the next few weeks. Not only was most of the computer hardware inoperable and potentially damaged beyond repair, but the networking cables in the walls, the network electronics, the servers, scanners, and entire communications infrastructure was down as well. The firemen told him that it would probably be a week or more before they could turn the power back on in the building and that the carpet would have to be either pulled up and replaced or dried immediately with blowers.

As luck would have it, Roger's company was in the last phase of a major software development project for the government, and 60 percent of the payment was contingent on the successful completion of the project within the next six weeks. Failure to deliver on time could mean the loss of a major source of funding for the company and could even prove fatal for the long-term economic health of the company.

Fortunately, Roger's team had a data management system in place. One of the programmers was assigned the task of monitoring the nightly backup of the servers and of taking the tape home with her the following day, to add to the library of tapes she kept in a company-supplied fireproof safe in her home office. In addition, there was a company policy in place that any work during the day had to be saved to one of the servers before the worker went home at night, ensuring that there was at least one backup of all work in the department. Since the company encouraged flexible work hours and several programmers worked a day a week at home on company-supplied computers, many programmers also had copies of their work at home, using Zip disks as the transport medium. Finally, Roger made a habit of making two full backup tapes of every project in his department every six months. He took one home for safekeeping and sent one to his sister (who had signed the appropriate nondisclosure agreements) on the west coast—just in case.

• •

Although it was logistically challenging at first, Roger set up a temporary server cluster in his home office. Within a week of the flood, a replacement tape backup unit had been purchased, and one of the undamaged desktop PCs was configured as a server and loaded with the last backup tape. A second phone line and a dedicated modem were installed, providing dial-in access to the server. Roger used his home PC's CD-ROM burner to make copies of larger files for distribution to employees. Most of the programmers enjoyed working at home and meeting at Roger's home once a week. Cell phones, email, and the online server made for a productive virtual department. In short, the project was finished to specification and on time. After the project was finished, the staff moved back into the office space, which had been repainted, recarpeted, and rewired. The insurance paid for replacement servers, PCs, and the intranet electronics. To guard against a similar mishap in the future, all of the windows in the building were alarmed, and the pipe supplying the sprinkler system was wrapped in insulating foam. However, fresh paint and new servers wouldn't have helped if Roger's team hadn't safeguarded their most important asset—the data.

This true account of an unfortunate New Year's Day in Boston illustrates how one can avoid a potentially disastrous data loss by developing and following a well-thought-out data management program.

This chapter explores the software, hardware, and process technologies related to digital data management and makes recommendations for minimizing data loss. In particular, it looks at the typical data life cycle, from the creation and use of data to archiving and disposal, as well as the key issues to consider when instituting a data management program, from cost and ease of use to security and the most appropriate media to use.

THE DATA LIFE CYCLE

To illustrate the issues related to data management, consider the typical data life cycle, shown in Figure 4-1. The data life cycle, including the processes associated with each stage, is outlined in Figure 4-1 and described in more detail in Table 4-1.

Data Creation

Data creation encompasses the process of acquiring, capturing, or creating images, text, and other data that are of some value to the organization or individual. Depending on the difficulty in creating the data and the intended use, the creation process may be trivial and inexpensive or extremely complicated and costly. For example, random snapshots taken at a work-related party may be inconsequential, in terms of the creation process, compared to medium-

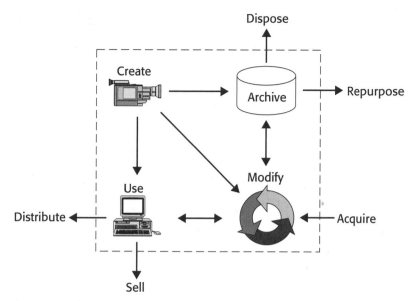

Figure 4-1 The Data Life Cycle.
Data are created, used, repurposed, saved in various states, and, at some point, discarded.
The choice of processes, hardware, and software systems involved in the life cycle can
make the system manageable or utterly useless.

Table 4-1 Characteristics of Each Phase of the Data Life Cycle.

Stage	Issues
Creation	Standards, tools, version control
Modification	Tools, intermediate stages, standards
Use	Intellectual property rights, duration, media, versions, distribution format (e.g., print, Web, or CD-ROM)
Archiving	Indexing (vocabulary, metadata, language, completeness, efficiency), space requirements, completeness, scalability, hardware, database design, process, media selection, location (local, server, or network), infrastructure, support for ad hoc queries, value of data vs. overhead
Repurposing	Search time, sensitivity, specificity, false positives and false negatives, user interface, language, security, free text, searches by example and keyword, original indexing, intended users
Disposal	Time or quality of databases

format, black-and-white images of a wedding taken by a professional photographer. Although the digital snapshot may be invaluable to a man on trial for murder who needs the image to prove to the jury that he wasn't at the scene of a crime, in general, the more resources invested in the creation process or the timeliness or uniqueness of the data, the more valuable the data.

The major issues in the data creation phase of the data life cycle include tool selection and format. For example, in capturing image data, the resolution of the film used in a 35mm camera or of the charge-coupled device (CCD) in a digital camera limit the resolution of the final image. In addition, the quality of the lens affects the distortion or amount of noise that will appear in the image. A similar situation exists in the audio domain, where the resolution and format of the capture hardware limits the quality of the final product.

A professional sound engineer with high-quality microphones, wind screens, and digital multitrack recorders will normally create a cleaner, higher-quality sound track than someone with a modicum of experience who uses a pocket microrecorder. Of course, the best device won't produce optimum results in the hands of someone who doesn't know how to use the equipment. Great photographers don't necessarily have the best hardware, but they always have an eye for composition, lighting, and the mood they create.

Data Modification

Raw data are rarely used without some amount of formatting or editing. If the data are textual, then modification may entail spell checking, formatting, rewording, and combining the text with other text, images, and sounds. Similarly, audio and image data may need to be processed for a particular application or variety of applications. Images intended for the Web and four-color printing need to be processed differently so that colors are represented accurately in each medium and the resolution is appropriate for the capacity of the display medium. Typically, a much lower resolution image is created for the Web, compared to an image for high-quality print reproduction.

The key issues in the modification stage are selection of tools and formats and identification of the key points within the modification process at which intermediate data should be archived for future use. To appreciate these issues, consider the modification process illustrated in Figure 4-2, which assumes that the data are digital images from a variety of sources. The computer graphics and digital photograph represent first-generation data and should have less noise than the second-generation data acquired through scanning a print.

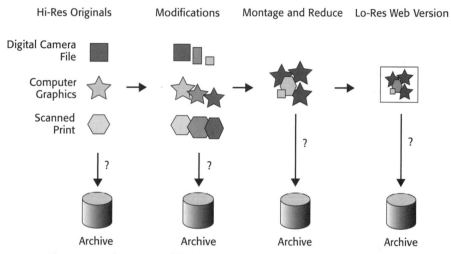

Hi-Res Originals   Modifications   Montage and Reduce   Lo-Res Web Version

Digital Camera File

Computer Graphics

Scanned Print

Archive   Archive   Archive   Archive

Figure 4-2   The Data Modification Process.
In this example, high-resolution images, created with a variety of means, are modified through several versions, combined, and then reformatted to suit the Web. The tools used during the editing and combination, and processing stages affect the quality of the final output. At issue is which versions of the data should be archived for future use.

Depending on the intended use of the data, images are typically resized, cropped, recolored, or distorted in some way, usually through a multistep process. A typical still image might go through twenty iterations of processing before it's ready for the next stage of the modification process. Each iteration typically has a different value for later repurposing. Repurposing typically involves taking data originally intended for one application and using them as-is or, more often, modifying them in some way, for a second application. The Web is a common target for repurposed data, especially images that were originally designed for print publications. Images designed for print that are repurposed for the Web are typically reduced in size—and therefore resolution—so that the Web pages containing the images will download rapidly.

In addition, because the color of images is affected by monitor characteristics, the operating system, and the Web browser environment, the palette or range of colors used in an image has to be chosen carefully. For example, the Web browser within the AOL service compresses the range of colors available for display; subtle changes in colors may not be visible, and images may take on a cartoonlike appearance. Similarly, because of differences in operating systems and hardware, colors are displayed differently on a Macintosh computer, compared to a PC running some version of Windows, and many multimedia developers who repurpose print graphics for distribution on CD-ROM or the Web commonly use both a Macintosh and a PC to review images.

Because images must be processed—often considerably—before they can be repurposed and the alternative future uses are difficult to predict, images, like other data to be repurposed, should be archived in the highest resolution available and with minimal additions or reformatting. For example, the image from the scanner that has been color corrected and cleaned up may have more value than the original, but an image with text labels may have much less value for repurposing. Adding text labels to an image, for example, not only destroys some of the data by hiding it behind a label and pointers, but the text may be inappropriate for a particular publication because a different language or typeface may be required.

Unless the volume of data is relatively low, it usually isn't practical to store every iteration of data during the modification process. For example, if a photographer's entire image library fits comfortably on one CD-ROM, she'll have a much easier—and shorter—time locating a particular image. However, if the library entails hundreds of CD-ROMs, then the time involved in locating the correct CD-ROM, much less the appropriate image file on the CD-ROM, can be prohibitive. Data management technologies designed for huge amounts of data don't scale infinitely. At some point, adding a few data items disproportionately increases the access time for all data in the archive.

It's important to note that a major reason for modifying data after its creation is to prepare it for storage, without an immediate plan for use. For example, a satellite might collect images of a planet that may serve as the basis for scientific investigation for several years. However, the data may be "dirty" and in need of processing to remove extraneous noise. Processing may also be required to change the format of the data so that they can be accessed by standard tools. If satellite image data are compressed for more efficient transmission, they may be uncompressed before being archived, negating the need of the end user to use what may soon become an outdated compression method. Similarly, if the satellite data are in a proprietary or one-of-a-kind format, then they can be converted into an industry-standard image format that can be read by researchers using a variety of off-the-shelf tools.

Another critical issue related to preserving data for future applications is the naming convention used. Proper naming, a high-level defense against data loss, is much easier since the advent of "long" file names, first introduced on the microcomputer with the Macintosh operating system. Compared to the early Microsoft DOS naming restrictions, where file names were limited to eight characters plus an extension, for example, AUTOEXEC.BAT, modern naming conventions are much more powerful. Useful file names, such as Family Photo 02_03_2002, allow users to search for and locate files based on obvious file names.

The power of long file names is best employed if some form of naming convention is established and followed. For example, a simple naming convention for images would be subject name followed by the date, as in the example above. A series of images undergoing several modifications could be named Family Photo 02_03_2002 ver n, where "n" is the version number, from 1 to the number of versions created.

In addition to establishing a standard naming convention, the search feature in modern operating systems allows searching for files not only by name, but by location, file type, modification date, size range, and date or date range. For example, all Word documents (specified by *.doc, where "doc" is the file extension restricted to Microsoft Word documents) in a particular folder or hard drive can be located with the standard search feature within Windows.

The search feature within Windows 95 and above also supports searching on properties assigned to files. Through the properties panel, available through the Windows operating system, a file can be assigned a title, subject, author, manager, company, category, keywords, and comments—all of which are searchable from within Windows.

Data Use

Although there are exceptions, most data are created with an intended use in mind, if only to remind the data creator of an event, place, or thought. In the commercial arena, use normally involves distribution of some sort, including publication of data on CD-ROM, the Web, or in print. In some instances, use may also involve the sale of data, including the intellectual property rights in all or some forms of expression. For example, a poem may be sold to a greeting card company that plans to use it in an advertising campaign on the company Web site. If the company purchases print rights as well, then the data are effectively out of the original data management cycle and enter the data life cycle of the greeting card company.

One of the major issues relating to use is the intellectual property rights of the data creator. Photographers, like book authors, for example, typically retain the intellectual property rights to the work but temporarily assign them to a publisher or other client in exchange for payment of some type.

Data Archiving

The data archiving stage of the data life cycle usually involves several decisions on the most appropriate software, hardware, storage medium, and archiving process to use. There are the obvious issues of media cost and longevity, security standards, the type of hardware to use to store the data, and the best way to store the data to facilitate later retrieval. For example, selecting the optimal storage medium for the archiving process is a function of the frequency with which archived data are accessed, the budget, and the volume of data involved (see Figure 4-3).

The hardware involved in the archival process may include a PC-based CD-ROM burner, a large database server that's networked to a number of workstations and routinely backed up onto magnetic tape, or a network-based storage that may be located offsite. As discussed later in this chapter, each option has security, cost, and per-

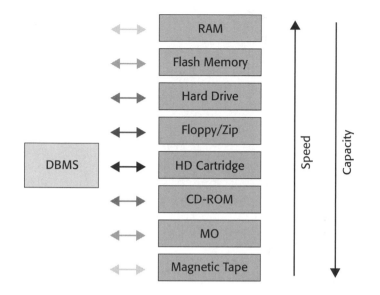

Media	Note
RAM	Volatile, limited capacity
Flash Memory	Fast, expensive, limited capacity
Hard Drive	Fast, moderate to high capacity
Floppy/Zip	Low to moderate capacity and speed
HD Cartridge	Slower than fixed HD, higher total capacity
CD-ROM	Slower than magnetic, inexpensive
MO	High capacity, but nonstandard
Magnetic Tape	Slow, sequential, high capacity, inexpensive

Figure 4-3   Optimum Storage Media.
The ideal medium for archiving data depends on the frequency of access, with fast hard drives used for frequently accessed data and magnetic tape for infrequently accessed, but much larger, volumes of data.

formance issues. The software tools selected for archiving data also define the usability and performance of the data archive, especially regarding data indexing and retrieval functions.

After data have been created and, if necessary, modified for use, and before they can be archived, they are typically named, indexed, and filed to facilitate finding them in the future. That is, the filing system, naming conventions, and accuracy and specificity of indexing limit the efficiency with which the data can be located later. For example, each document can be assigned one or more keywords, but if the keywords aren't appropriate, the keyword vocabulary is undefined or not enforced, or too few keywords are used, then a document may be effectively lost in the system. Not only the choice and number of keywords, but the indexing hierarchy can make data hard to find.

Indexing is usually a time-limited process, in that significant time may be involved in creating a relatively complete, accurate index. As the volume of data increases, added indices are needed to maintain selectivity in later searching, which increase indexing time. Arrows indicate addition of index terms. Indexing is a time-intensive activity, and one that is defined by the value of and the quantity of data. For example, high-value data are usually indexed more carefully and completely than low-value data that has questionable or low future potential. With larger quantities of data, indexing has to become increasingly complete in order to create a reasonable degree of granularity in the searching process. For example, a single keyword index may be appropriate for a collection of a few hundred images. However, with ten thousand images, one or two keywords will probably be extremely ineffective in the search for a particular image in the archive, because hundreds of images may fit within the same indexing terms.

To highlight the issues involved in indexing data, consider a graphic artist who is looking for a digital image she once saw of an older woman on a swing, and she thinks that it was taken by a photographer in Mexico. The image is indexed with the keywords "woman" and "swing." In a diverse collection of a hundred images, using an unspecific query with keywords "woman" and "swing" might return two or three images of women and swings. With only a few results, it would take only seconds to determine if the desired image was included in the returned set of images. However, if there are hundreds of images or documents that are indexed under woman and swing, then it may be impossible to locate the desired image in a reasonable amount of time. This is a common scenario on the Web, where simple keyword searches may result in tens of thousands of "hits," many of which are false positives—that is, unwanted results. In addition, simple keyword-based indexing may be insufficient or inappropriately executed for the intended users of the data. For example, data creators may be interested in indexing images by source, such as particular model of digital camera, scanned photograph, or original artwork, so that they can locate the original print or identify the artist, for example. However, end users may be concerned only with the image data. Furthermore, if the indexes are in English but the users are fluent in German, there may be a language barrier to deal with as well.

One way to address the limitations of simple keyword indexing is to create higher-level descriptions of data (metadata) that can be of use in retrieving the data later. These metadata include contextual information that requires some form of human interpretation. For example, the image of the woman on the swing can be assigned keywords of "play," "summertime activities," "exercise," "elderly," and "Hispanic."

Data Repurposing

Like the process of indexing, the process of locating data once it's been incorporated into some sort of storage system can be simple or complex, depending on the volume of data involved. Efficient retrieval is a function of the hardware and database management software used, the effectiveness of the user interface, and the way the data were originally indexed. That is, the granularity of retrieval is limited by the granularity of indexing.

Returning to the example of the image of the elderly Hispanic woman on the swing, if the original index for the image doesn't contain an entry for her hair color, then it will be impossible for a typical keyword-based search engine to locate the image by hair color. Similarly, although concepts can be mapped from one vocabulary to another and from one language to the next, the original indexing affects the language or vocabulary that can be used during retrieval.

As the search engine portals on the Web demonstrate, alternative vocabularies and even free-text searches can be used to locate data that have been automatically or manually keyword-indexed. For example, natural language searches, based on Natural Language Processing (NLP) technology, allow users to search for the data in the form of:

"Find an image of an elderly Hispanic woman on a swing"

NLP breaks up or parses the sentence and uses "elderly," "Hispanic," "woman," and "swing" to create a keyword search that resembles:

FIND "Format = Image" WHERE SUBJECT = "elderly" AND ("Hispanic" AND "woman") AND "swing"

NLP is one of several practical technologies that can be used to create a more user friendly front end. However, the effectiveness of the NLP technology depends on the implementation. For example, the previous search for an image of an elderly Hispanic woman on a swing could be expressed by the user in a variety of ways, such as:

"Find a picture of an old Mexican woman swinging"

"Get a photo of a Hispanic senior citizen on a swing set"

"Find an image of a Latin grandmother swinging"

"Get a picture of an old Mexican swinging female"

Obviously, each of these searches could be interpreted in a variety of ways. A "swinging grandmother," for example, could return images from a Web site that specializes in adult entertainment. Similarly, a "swing set" may return images of tools used in automobile racing. Given the multiple interpretations possible for all but the most carefully constructed query, it's not surprising that the queries produced through natural language processing of the above queries can take on a variety of forms. For example, consider a few of the possible interpretations of the original search:

"Find an image of an elderly Hispanic woman on a swing"

FIND "Format = Picture" WHERE SUBJECT = "elderly" AND "Hispanic" AND "swing" AND "woman"

FIND "Format = Picture" WHERE SUBJECT = "elderly Hispanic" AND "woman" AND "swing"

FIND "Format = Image" WHERE SUBJECT = "old" AND "Mexican" AND "female" AND "swing"

FIND "Format = Image" WHERE SUBJECT = "ancient Mexico" AND "female swing"

FIND "Format = Photo" WHERE SUBJECT = "ancient Mexican" AND "woman" AND "swerve"

The various NLP implementations handle each of the above queries in different ways. That is, the search engines behind the user interface create different search terms and combinations of terms and use these in different ways to search a database. For example, one search engine might search on synonyms for "elderly," including "old." A second search engine might search on multiple synonyms of "Hispanic," including "Mexican," perhaps resulting in many more unrelated search results. The major differences in back-end or behind-the-scenes processing are highly guarded secrets and account for the differences in the effectiveness of the various search engine portals.

Because of differences in how search terms are parsed and how the data on the Web are indexed, the same search terms posed to different search engines usually result in very different results, regardless of whether NLP or manual searches are used. For example, depending on the search engine, combining terms in quotes, such as "elderly Hispanic," may provide more specific results than using "elderly" and "Hispanic" separately. In the former example, "elderly" and "Hispanic" must occur together and in the specified order to be returned by the search engine. In the latter, the search engine decides on the relative proximity of the terms, as well as the order. For example, one search engine may require the original sequence, but separated by no more than five words. Another engine may ignore the sequence of the words and require that the two search terms occur in the same paragraph.

In addition to NLP, a variety of technologies under development may eventually be useful in locating data in a large database as well. One of these is image-based query by example, where the user selects from a library of images to create a search. Using this technology, the user would select an image of an elderly woman, one of Latin America, and then one of exercise equipment or an image of a swing, depending on the depth of interface and the extent of the database.

All of these technologies get at sifting or filtering through large databases in some way, and there is no one best filter technology. For an analogous example, consider trawling. In trawling, the shape, construction, and use of the net affects the composition of the catch. A more closely knit net takes longer to drag across a given distance and brings up smaller fish along with larger catch. A net with a looser knit not only offers less resistance to the water and therefore takes less time to drag across a given area, but also traps only the larger fish, and smaller fish pass through the net. Similarly, some nets are designed to sink and drag the bottom, returning shrimp and bottom-dwelling fish, such as flounder. Conversely, fishing nets designed to float near the surface generally return smaller fish.

The best—and most humane—nets are designed for a particular type of fish. For example, gill nets are designed to capture fish of a specific size, allowing both larger and smaller fish to escape unharmed. These nets have a mesh size that just allows a fish to poke its head through far enough for its gill flaps to fold over the mesh. The fish can't move forward because its larger body won't fit through the mesh, and it can't back out of the net because its gill flaps expand over the mesh, effectively trapping it. Smaller fish and shrimp simply swim uninterrupted through the relatively wide mesh. Larger fish are funneled through to the end of the net, where a large door in the net allows dolphins, sharks, sea turtles, and other inhabitants of the sea to escape. Larger fish aren't trapped in the mesh of the net because they can't insert their heads far enough through the mesh for their gills to flap over the mesh. A few of the desirable fish make it to the door near the end of the funnel-shaped net and escape, but the vast majority become trapped in the net on their way to the opening.

Of course, the net technology is only one component of fishing. Other factors, such as the skill of the captain steering the trawler, the depth of the body of water, the water temperature, the season, the quality of the water—fresh, brackish, salty, clean, or polluted—and

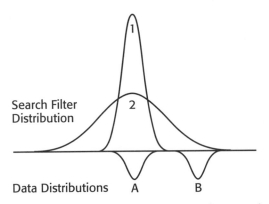

Figure 4-4   Selectivity versus Accuracy of Data Retrieval.

the population of fish in the body of water all affect the efficiency and effectiveness of the catch.

As in the fishing example, searches can fail in two ways: They can retrieve too much data, so that the time it takes to look through results isn't worth the trouble, or they can retrieve the wrong data because the search criteria were not specific enough. That is, if the search terms are too general (corresponding to a net with a tight weave that captures everything), the desired results may be lost in the ocean of unwanted data. Similarly, using specific but incorrect terms, such as "swinging female" from the example above, is akin to trawling the bottom of a lake with a gill net in an attempt to capture fish that live near the surface. The best searches are highly specific, akin to using a gill net when trawling for fish, and accurate as well. As shown in Figure 4-4, a highly selective but inaccurate search, while returning only a few results, may miss the desired data.

Using the most selective search (filter 1) for desired data with distribution A is both selective and accurate, and extraneous data (B in this example) are completely excluded from the search result. However, if B represents the desired data and filter 1 is used, then none of the desired data will be returned. When the exact search terms are uncertain, it is often better to use a less selective search (filter 2) to identify some of the desired data, and then refine the search with more accurate terms.

Regardless of the search technology used, the retrieval process is a tradeoff between selectivity and accuracy. A nonselective search using only general terms normally returns a large number of false hits. In addition to using the proper search terms, the most common means of adjusting the selectivity and accuracy of a search is to use quoted phrases and Boolean operators, such as "A" AND "B" or "A" NOT "B" or "A" OR "B", where A and B are search terms. For example, a Boolean search that provides higher specificity than simply searching for "woman" and "swing" might be:

("Elderly Woman" AND "Hispanic") AND "Swing" NOT ("Young" OR "Caucasian")

Filtering out images of children on swings assumes that the images are indexed in terms of age and that "child" and "elderly" are valid vocabulary terms for indicating age range. For example, if the images are indexed by age, but the classification vocabulary requires "child," "adult," or "senior" for indexing terms, the terms "elderly" and "young" may not be recognized by the system, and images of children on swings, if they're present in the archive, may appear in the search results.

Data Disposal

Eventually, some data are disposed of, either because the value of the data has decreased to the point that it is less valuable than the cost of maintaining it, storage space is limited and more valuable data must be archived, or the data are extremely time limited, such as the local weather forecast. Similarly, the data may have been archived because of legal reasons and have no intrinsic value to the company or person making the archive. Tax records and bank account statements more than twenty years old fall into this category.

Earmarking data for disposal is normally based on the quality and relevance of the data, as opposed to the age of the data. For example, many large corporations have a policy of maintaining email communications while employees are active and then deleting their records after they have left the company for a year or more. However, since some email communications are more important than others, such as personnel complaints that may show up in court later, technical memos that detail important processes, or email from the corporate executives that may have historic value to the company, someone within the company usually reads through the data before it is deleted from the archive. Because email generated at work belongs to employers, employees have no legal say in the fate of their email. Once an email message has been sent, it can generally be used like any other corporate asset. For this reason, several companies have attempted to commercialize utilities that are in effect "unsend" buttons, allowing employees to recall that inflammatory note that was sent off in haste but that they regret as soon as they hit the Return or Enter key. Unfortunately, many corporate environments prohibit loading private software, including external utilities, on corporate machines. In certain government positions, email becomes part of the public domain and can never be destroyed. For example, email from the President of the United States becomes part of the public record as soon as it's generated. For this reason, recent presidents have shunned email for routine communications because they don't want the data of private communications as part of the National Archives.

Data Life Cycle Management Issues

Managing the data life cycle isn't about achieving perfection but is rather an exercise in compromise between several factors. They include speed of storage, speed of retrieval, completeness of the archive, cost of archiving, capacity of the archive, longevity of the data, the usability, and security. For example, the media selected for archiving will affect not only the cost but the speed of storage and longevity of data. Similarly, using an in-house tape backup facility may be more costly than outsourcing the task to a networked vendor, but the in-house approach is likely to be more secure.

These tradeoffs are reflected in the implementation of the data management process. For example, backing up files from a PC every so often onto floppy disks and tossing them into a shoebox that's kept under a bed is a low-cost option. However, searching through a few dozen floppies for a particular file may be a very time consuming way to locate what may be incomplete data. As Roger demonstrated in the story of his flooded office, there are proven methods of systematically protecting data and making it accessible and usable at some point in the future. The following section explores these technologies in detail.

DIGITAL DATA MANAGEMENT TECHNOLOGY

As reflected in the data life cycle model, data archiving entails a complex process of indexing, selecting the appropriate software to manage the archive, and choosing the type of media to use, and the choices made about archiving are a function of frequency of use and expected longevity of the data. From an implementation perspective, the key issues in selecting a particular archiving technology over another depend on the size of the archive, the types of data and data sources to be included in the archive, the intended use, and the existing or legacy archiving systems involved.

In this regard, the size of the archive is measured in terms of the number of items and the space requirements per item. Text-only archives present challenges different from those containing images, sounds, video, and other multimedia. Similarly, a single source of data is generally much easier to work with than data from multiple, disparate sources in different and often incompatible formats. The hardware and software used in the archiving process should reflect the intended use of the data. For example, seldom-used data can be archived with a much less powerful system, compared to data that must be accessed frequently. Finally, it's rare to have the opportunity to initiate a digital archiving program from scratch. Normally, some form of existing or legacy system is in place and has generated data that must be considered in any new archive.

The simplest approach to managing digital data is to establish a database server, as illustrated in Figure 4-5.

To use the hardware most effectively, everyone connected to the server copies their files from their local hard drive to specific areas on the server's hard drive daily or nightly. The data on the server are in turn archived to magnetic tape, CD-ROM, or other high-capacity media. In this way, if the hard drive on a PC fails or data are inadvertently erased from a PC, a relatively recent copy of the data exists on the server. Users can copy the file from the server to their local hard drive as needed. Similarly, if the server hardware fails for some reason, then the tape backup can be used to reconstitute the data on a second server. Software developers favor this data management approach, where the different contributors to a software project check in their parts of the project daily or more frequently. Software

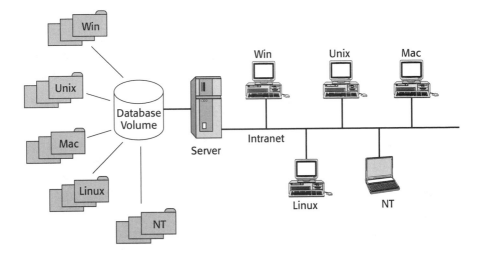

Figure 4-5 Database Server Configuration.
The simplest approach to managing data in a workgroup is to employ a database server
based on the client-server architecture. Users connected to the database server by an
intranet access private and public folders (left) on the server database, typically
grouped by operating system. For example, users of Windows NT work with a disk
section or partition compatible with the NT operating system.

management tools, such as versioning systems, automate the task of
locating the most recent version of a file or program.

Although database servers are popular in smaller organizations,
this approach has several limitations. The expansion capability is
limited by the server hardware; adding more disk space usually
requires installing external storage devices or replacing the internal
hard disks with higher-capacity devices. In either case, the server has
to be shut down and reconfigured, usually at the expense of users'
time. In addition, space on the server is static, in that it can't be automatically shared by another server when one server becomes full. In
addition, anything that hinders the operation of the server, such as
an administrator shutting the server down to add RAM or a new
microprocessor board, interferes with the data management process.
Migrating the data over to a new server because of the availability of
higher-performance, lower-priced technology also requires the
server to be brought down during the process.

Another problem with the database server approach, from the
data life cycle perspective, is that the data are not easily repurposed

at the organizational level. Because the data are created by different applications, perhaps using different formats and operating systems, there isn't a way to search through the data from a single interface. Although the existence of, for example, a PowerPoint presentation may be known to a few people in marketing, someone in R&D who may need the slides for a presentation has no way of knowing that the slides exist. Not only are the contents of the database server typically unknown, but security procedures often actively discourage searching for data in private directories. However, for a small organization or a workgroup of perhaps a dozen users, process can overcome technological limitations. For example, it can be agreed that all electronic presentations are to be saved in a publicly accessible folder on the server for group use and reference.

Most developments in the field of database technology for larger organizations don't focus on archiving per se, but rather on data capture and rapid, easy data retrieval. In particular, the focus is on providing decision makers with views of the entire organization, even though data from within a large organization may come from disparate, incompatible computer systems.

For example, consider the challenge of working with data within a large hospital. There are typically one or more clinical systems that store patient information, such as height and weight, in some form of electronic medical record. There are also administrative systems that encompass the accounting information for various departments, and there may be research systems that generate data from clinical studies. Each of these systems is traditionally separate, running different software and hardware, and the data are of different types, saved in different file formats on incompatible hardware.

To appreciate the challenges involved with managing the data in a large hospital environment, consider that the radiology department may have a digital imaging system that ships radiographs to special viewing stations within the hospital, and the accounting department stores financial spreadsheet data in the administrative systems. Without combining the clinical and administrative data, it is difficult for someone to quickly determine, for example, the actual cost of a procedure, the cost of patient care for particular physicians, the cost of pharmaceuticals for a patient for a given surgical procedure, and other business-related decisions. From a clinical research perspective, it would be impossible to determine, in near-real time, which procedures are associated with the most complications and patient return rates, and which therapies result in the best long-term patient results. These approaches focus on use and short-term storage, not necessarily long-term archiving.

Before the advent of the Web, the two most common approaches to providing access to all of the data in an organization were centralized and integrated. The centralized approach may be based on a single, central archive or database that is used by all applications in an organization. More common, however, is for the data from several disparate databases to be combined in a second, centralized database that can be searched.

The integrated approach shares a select subset of data among several disparate databases to increase the efficiency and accuracy of data management in the organization. For example, customer data can be entered in one application in the system, which then propagates the data to every other database in the organization, eliminating the time and error involved in rekeying customer data.

With the appearance of the Web as a network standard, the networked or federated approach to data archiving has become increasingly popular. In the federated model, data are stored in network-accessible hardware that can be accessed by every properly configured database application on the network.

A Centralized Approach: Data Warehousing

Although a shoebox full of floppy disks might do in the short-term for keeping track of a few personal text documents, someone with a home office, a small business owner, and all large businesses must have some means of rapidly accessing and keeping track of data in a way that supports reuse at some later date. This is especially critical in large businesses, where large, comprehensive customer databases support data mining and other methods that extract meaningful patterns from millions of records. One approach to managing the data life cycle is through a centralized model, broadly termed data warehousing, which involves hardware, software, and a defined process that ties it all together.

A data warehouse is a central repository of data that combines data from a variety of application-oriented databases into a single database. As such, it reflects activity within all applications running in an organization. This is no mean task, however, since it requires cleaning, encoding, and translation of data before they can be included in the single database. Furthermore, unlike most transactional databases, a data warehouse is time-variant in that the data stored are associated with a point in time. By contrast, transactional data, such as the record of a sale, are typically valid only at the moment of capture and access. Another characteristic of data within a data warehouse is that the data are nonvolatile in that new data are appended to the database and never replace existing data.

Data warehouses are distinguished from application databases in how the data destined for storage in the data warehouse are selected, prepared, and loaded into the data warehouse and in how the underlying database is optimized for use. Once data to be included in a data warehouse have been identified, the data from each application are cleaned (typos and other errors are identified and removed or corrected) and merged with data from other applications. Like any other database applications, there are the usual issues of database design, provision for maintenance, security, and periodic modification.

The data warehouse is architecturally different from a simple database used to track the contents of a wine cellar, for example, in that the design can accommodate data that exists on different machines and that comes from different applications and sources, such as text from a word processing application, digital images from a digital camera, or sound from a CD. The goal of the data warehouse design is to keep the right information flowing to the right people in the most intelligent form as quickly and efficiently as possible, which includes making provision for the storage of both frequently accessed and seldom-accessed data. That is, a tiered archival system is typically put in place to accommodate access time, cost, and data longevity constraints. When properly implemented, data warehousing automates the transfer and translation of data from disparate applications to a central database in near-real time.

Although the data warehouse is one of several models of centralized data management, it illustrates the issues and technologies that are part of virtually every data management initiative, including the selection of database hardware and software, the dependence of the hardware and software on a well-planned process, and the use of metadata, controlled vocabularies, and other techniques to make the technology tenable. Let's explore these concepts in more detail.

The Process. In 16th- and 17th-century Europe, the toque or chef's hat took on a variety of shapes, from stocking caps to berets and pointed hats with tassels. During the 18th century, the current custom of the tall white hat came into being, where the relative height of the hat indicates the wearer's relative importance among the kitchen staff. Unfortunately, the relative worth of data are rarely as obvious as the height of a chef's hat.

Data warehousing can be time consuming and expensive without proper planning. The most important task in the planning stage is to identify the data to be warehoused. This challenge represents a classic sensitivity-specificity dilemma, where the tradeoffs are usually between time and storage capacity. One of the most challenging aspects of the data warehouse process, therefore, is selecting what to include in a data warehouse and what to leave out.

The planning stage also includes the time to specify database design, provide for maintenance, security, backup, authorization, and periodic modification. Warehouse planners must also estimate future storage requirements, data expansion rate, and other factors that may affect computer hardware requirements (see Table 4-2).

Table 4-2   The Stages of Data Warehouse Development.
These are planning, data consolidation, data transformation, selective archiving, data distribution, and ongoing maintenance.

Stage	Key Issues/Tasks
Planning	Decide what data to include; decision affects cost, resource requirements, and performance.
Consolidation	Restructure data from individual application databases to be compatible with the data warehouse design.
Transformation	Summarize and package data.
Archiving	Move older or infrequently accessed data to tape, optical, or other long-term storage media.
Distribution	Develop user interfaces for specific types of users.
Maintenance	Continually redesign and evaluate to allow for changes in individual applications feeding the data warehouse.

Once data to be included in a data warehouse have been identified, the next step is to create a process in which the data from the various applications in an organization are checked for errors, such as misspelled names and duplicates, transformed if necessary, merged, and then stored in the central database or warehouse. Data transformation involves, for example, conversions such as inches to centimeters, degrees Fahrenheit to degrees Centigrade, and date in MM/DD/YY format to DD/MM/YY.

Data Warehousing Issues. A properly constructed warehouse takes care of timing and consistency issues, automatically performs any conversion in data representation, and populates a central database in a way that supports subsequent data access. One goal is to simplify the tangled web of application data in an organization that resides on multiple machines and in often incompatible formats to the point where someone can access current data created and originally stored anywhere in the organization by interacting with one central database system.

After data are translated onto physically compatible media, loading the data into a single database that can be queried typically presents additional challenges, for example, timing and synchronization. Ideally, all data entering the central database of a data warehouse represent a snapshot—an instant in time—when all transactions are frozen, and data edits and modifications are halted. However, even if the data are downloaded from each application database at the same instant, the data may be out of sync because of how the individual applications are written. For example, a sales reporting system might save data to its database only periodically, whereas a billing system might write the data to disk immediately after each transaction.

Standards for vocabularies and protocols are other areas of contention in the field of data warehousing. For example, the process of mapping data from individual applications to the central database is hindered by the lack of a universal vocabulary. The difficulties of adopting universal vocabularies and other standards are linked to human limits in foreseeing future needs and to human inability to maintain design consistency across a group of contributors to a project. Human resistance to change and tolerance for variation has always been at odds with a computer's demand for consistency.

Although data mapping and transformation can be accomplished effectively through a tool such as a data dictionary, which serves as a synonym list, the vocabulary that results is typically not standardized. It's more likely to be an ad hoc vocabulary, modified as necessary to minimize translation from the individual application databases. Although this approach may be adequate for getting data into the warehouse, without a standard vocabulary someone searching for data in the warehouse may be thwarted because he used the term "hypertension" instead of "high blood pressure," for example. In some instances, the fault lies external to the data warehouse, in areas such as gene data, which have no standard vocabulary or format.

Another issue is the time and resources required to develop the interfaces between individual applications and the data warehouse. Every legacy and operational application database that is destined to feed data into the data warehouse represents a unique set of challenges. Each database usually requires special tools for the extraction and transformation of data, and in many cases these tools may need to be developed in-house. In addition, a key issue in tool selection or development is how the tool will perform a year or two after initial implementation, when the data swells to hundreds of thousands of megabytes. A particular database design might work well on a single application and with limited data, but when the system is extended to cover an entire enterprise, poor performance of the database may render the system useless. Even the largest systems have scalability limits.

Finally, as Roger's experience of restoring systems after an office flood illustrates, the success of any data warehouse project is a function of the people and the processes in place to work with the system. The organizational dynamics are as much a key to maintaining the integrity of data as are the capabilities of the technology.

The Integrated Approach: System Interfaces

The integrated approach to data management supports the use of the "best of breed" applications in an organization, allowing each group within an organization to select the software package that would make their lives easiest, while allowing a subset to be shared throughout the organization. Separate applications, often running on separate machines and using proprietary data formats and storage facilities, share a subset of information with other applications.

Individual applications share subsets of their data through interfaces. Archiving is a separate procedure performed on each application.

The challenge of using an integrated approach is developing the interfaces between each application. Different industries have developed standard interfaces that vendors can develop for allowing applications to share industry data. For example, in medicine, a standard interface protocol is HL7, which allows the admission, discharge, and transfer system of a clinic or hospital to send patient insurance and demographic information to clinical systems. In this way, when a patient walks into the radiology clinic for a chest x-ray, the patient's name, address, age, diagnosis, and billing information are already entered in the radiology system's database, saving the patient from filling out yet another form and saving the receptionist from rekeying the data into his terminal.

An issue with the integrated approach, from an archival standpoint, is that data management is the responsibility of individual application managers, so in a given enterprise, dozens of systems administrators may be creating archives to fit varying standards that suit their budgets, staffing, and perceived needs. Of course, an enterprise-wide process standard can be established, where all systems administrators are required to abide by the same archiving standards.

The Federated Approach: Network Databases

The federated approach, in many respects, is the evolutionary extension of the integrated approach. However, instead of aiming to handle a small subset of the data from each application, the approach aims to provide access to all data through a single interface. Federated systems, like federated governments, join independently functioning, separate systems for the good of all involved. In the case of federated database systems (as pictured in Figure 4-6), the goal is to facilitate data exchange and storage.

The two major network database storage technologies are Network Attached Storage and Storage Area Networks. (See the discussion of network architecture in Chapter 2.) Network Attached

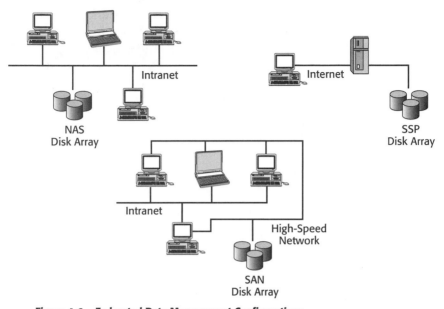

Figure 4-6   Federated Data Management Configurations.
Common configurations include Network Attached Storage (NAS), Storage Area
Networks (SAN), and Storage Service Provider (SSP).

Storage (NAS) is the easiest and most economical way to add storage
to a networked system of PCs. Like a printer or any other device
added to a network, an NAS device is simply attached to the network. To users on the network, the NAS acts like a second hard drive
on their PC. However, the speed of the NAS is limited by the bandwidth of the LAN, which is also used by other devices on the network, and each NAS device must be managed and archived
separately.

By contrast, a Storage Area Network (SAN) is a separate, high-
speed network that provides storage under one interface. It is a dedicated network that connects servers and SAN-compatible storage
devices. SAN devices can be added as needed, within the bandwidth
limitations of the high-speed network. As such, SANs are usually
implemented on high-speed fiber networks. The limitation of a SAN
is that for a device to use it, the device must be connected to the
high-speed network through the appropriate adapters and cables.

A third approach to adding storage to a networked system of PCs is to use an external service, or a Storage Service Provider, which functions as an Application Service Provider (ASP) with a database as the application. Like the other federated approaches, the issue is ultimately one of network bandwidth, in that slow connectivity to a remote storage system may be intolerable, regardless of the cost and local space savings.

The Database

At the core of every database management system (DBMS), whether centralized, integrated, federated, or simply a database server, is a set of tools for accessing, manipulating, and sharing data. In addition to data management, the DBMS provides for security, data integrity, synchronization, failure analysis, failure recovery, and efficiency.

Security — A properly constructed DBMS allows only users with the right to know to have different types of access to specific data, normally down to the level of individual files. Multilevel user password protection schemes can be used, for example, to allow only graphic designers to view intermediate graphic data and those in marketing to view only final versions. Using intranets that limit data communications to within a predefined group of PCs can add greatly to the security of a database.

Data integrity — A DBMS imposes data consistency constraints, such as requiring numeric data in certain fields, free text in others, and image data elsewhere. A user isn't allowed to store his social security number in the space assigned to a proper name, for example.

Synchronization — A DBMS can guard against data corruption that might result from two simultaneous operations on a given data item. The most common example is prohibiting one user from altering a value that is being manipulated by someone else.

Failure recovery — A DBMS should support quick recovery from hardware or software failures.

Efficiency — A properly configured DBMS provides efficient storage that maximizes performance on a given hardware platform. For example, a DBMS should recognize a server with large amounts of free RAM and make use of that RAM to speed serving the data.

Database Abstraction. Perhaps the most important role of the DBMS is to allow users to interact with data in abstract, meaningful terms. That is, the DBMS shields the user from the details of the underlying algorithms and data representation schemes.

A DBMS is often described in terms of three levels of abstraction: the physical database, the conceptual database, and the views. The point of using these abstractions is that they allow humans to manipulate huge amounts of data that may be associated in very complex ways by shielding database designers and users from the underlying complexity. The *physical database* is the data and framework that reside on media, such as disks and tapes. This low-level abstraction is most useful for users who deal directly with data and files.

The *conceptual database*, at a somewhat higher level of abstraction than the physical database, is concerned with the most appropriate way to represent the data. Two methods of representing the conceptual database are the entity-relationship model and the data model.

The entity-relationship model focuses on entities or things and their relationship to each other. It's a useful abstraction because it's a natural human way to categorize the world. For example, database entities are the people, places, things, and events about which data are recorded. Similarly, every entity has some basic attribute, such as name, address, color, height, or size. A particular person may be tall and blonde, for example. Relationships within the model are classified according to how data are associated with each other, such as one-to-one, one-to-many, or many-to-many. For example, a woman may have one pair of shoes (a one-to-one relationship) or many pairs of shoes (a one-to-many relationship). These and other relationships can be used to maintain the integrity of data about each entity. For example, a woman may have more than one pair of shoes, but she shouldn't have more than one social security number (a one-to-one relationship).

Data models, like entity-relationship models, are abstractions of data that can provide an easily understood means of representing and manipulating large amounts of data that may be interrelated in potentially confusing ways. For example, in one data model, a small group of related items is referred to as a record, and each item within the record is referred to as a field. A particular record is identified by means of a key or label, making it easy to search for the record that contains the particular value of the key.

Different database management systems organize their data according to different data models, such as network, hierarchical, relational, or object-oriented data models (see Figure 4-7). Object-oriented data models, which are based on a modular approach that is used throughout the software development industry, have yet to gain widespread acceptance in the database community because of poor performance compared to other models.

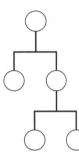 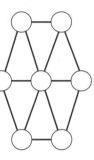 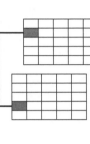 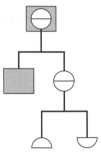

Hierarchical   Network   Relational   Object Oriented

Model	Characteristics
Hierarchical	Hierarchical connections are defined when the database is created and remain fixed for the life of the database.
Network	Many-to-one relationships with multiple connections between files are maintained.
Relational	Data are populated into rows and columns in a table; tables are associated with one another by the joining of matching fields.
Object Oriented	Complex data structures are represented by composite objects, which are objects that contain other objects. This model is best suited for multimedia.

Figure 4-7   **Hierarchical, Network, Relational, and Object-Oriented Data Models.**

These and similar data models allow users to manipulate and organize data by using a variety of metaphors or abstractions that are easier to work with than the bits and bytes on disks and other media. Some models fit some kinds of tasks better than others. The relational model is ideally suited to manipulating tables of textual data, such as accounting data. The hierarchical model is often used in medicine, especially in assigning text codes to different diagnostic procedures, since these codes are derived from a hierarchical naming scheme, where certain diagnoses are grouped under one heading or hierarchy. The object-oriented model is considered optimum for handling multimedia because it allows combinations of text, images, and sounds to be treated as single entities. That is, instead of thinking about a movie with subtitles as a separate sound file, a separate video file, and a separate text document, users can simply work with the movie object.

Views are high-level abstract models of portions of the conceptual database that are optimized for particular users. Views are analogous to the user interface of typical applications.

Metadata. A key issue in database design is the use of metadata, or information about data contained in the database. Views are one use of metadata, which is a collection of information about naming, classification, structure, and use of data that reduces inconsistency and ambiguity. The use of metadata is one reason the centralized data management approach is easy to maintain and control. In contrast, metadata is typically not used in database server systems and federated data management systems, but may be used in integrated data management systems.

For example, while potentially any data can be located in a centralized data management implementation, such as a data warehouse, someone would be hard-pressed to locate a particular file on a database server that supports several dozen active programmers. And someone with administrator privileges would have to perform an exhaustive search of the server hard drives to locate a particular file.

What's Inside? Another issue when considering data management through a DBMS or other database technology is what is being stored in the database. Is it pointers to data or the actual data? For example, the Web is a network database in which Web pages in one location can store pointers to the actual data, with all of the text, images, and other media located elsewhere on the Web. A given page on the Web might be composed of data from a variety of sources collected in real time. An image might come from an image server located in Brazil, the text might come from a news server in Boston, and the sound or music from an MP3 server in Singapore.

Similarly, a typical library has a card file that serves as pointers to books, newspapers, perhaps a few videos, cassette tapes, and maps. The card file is an index to the data but isn't the data itself. Computerizing the card file can greatly improve the ability of a patron to locate a book on a particular topic. For example, a card catalog may be arranged in alphabetical order by subject, but computerizing the card catalog could empower the patron to instantly view the catalog by copyright date or publisher. If the card catalog or the computerized versions of the catalog are lost, the "real" data aren't lost, and the books and other materials could be automatically or manually reindexed if needed.

At the other extreme, the database would contain the card catalog as well as digital versions of the actual books, videos, and maps contained in the library. In this all-digital library, the issue is the size and composition of the collection. Digitizing more than, say, a hundred books, a dozen video tapes, a few dozen audio tapes, and a handful of maps is rarely cost effective, outside of special military applications, because of practical time and budgetary constraints.

. . . .

HARDWARE

From a hardware perspective, implementing a data management system requires more than the obvious—servers, large hard drives, perhaps a network and the associated cables and electronics—to safeguard the integrity of the data. Power conditioners and uninterruptible power supplies protect sensitive equipment and the data they contain from power surges and sudden, unplanned power outages. Providing a secure environment for data includes the usual use of username and passwords to protect accounts. However, for higher levels of assurance against data theft or manipulation, secure ID cards, biometrics, and dongles may be appropriate.

Secure ID cards are credit-card-sized pseudorandom number generators that are synchronized with a similar generator on the server. To gain access to the system, users enter as their password the

16-digit number displayed on the secure ID card. Biometric security systems use personal biological characteristics, such as a fingerprint, voice, or the pattern of capillaries on the retinae to verify the identity of a user. Dongles are hardware keys that applications look for, either on the serial or USB port of a PC, before users can access their data and applications. In one regard, dongles can be considered a form of hardware-based encryption. Dedicated, high-speed hardware capable of high-speed encryption and decryption are available options as well.

Personal Data Management

Although large-scale data management technologies, such as data warehouses, have formidable resource and time requirements, some of the same technologies can be scaled down to work at the personal level. For example, a professional photographer who wants to manage a growing portfolio of traditional and digital images can decide to use a DBMS to contain pointers to her collection. She could assign a unique number to each image and enter a description and two or three keywords in the database for each image.

Time permitting, she may eventually migrate all of her images to the digital realm. Such an archive can serve to supply content to a changing Web portfolio, for instance. If she intends to access her growing collection frequently, then she should elect to keep as much of her collection as possible on local hard drives, archiving to DVD, photo-CD, or tape on a regular and preplanned basis. A variety of off-the-shelf multimedia management software is available to help her maintain control of her collection.

Fast Forward

This chapter ends the Part on technology. The chapters in this Part highlight the fragility of the evolving technology available to create, capture, and archive data. Roger's experience with a flooded office emphasizes the importance of having the appropriate hardware, software, and, most importantly, a process in place to ensure that everything works as expected. This chapter also illustrates the importance of the human element in creating indexes for data and scaling the appropriate database technology so that the data are not only archivable, but retrievable as well. As the Web has demonstrated, if the desired data can't be separated from all of the other data in a database, all of the efforts of archiving are wasted.

With the promise of the Web as the most often used database on the planet today and virtual documents as the most often viewed content on the Web, astonishingly, there remain significant barriers to archive and retrieve Web-based documents and their contexts. Consider that none of the technologies discussed thus far can retrieve, for example, the initial version of Amazon.com's Web site, or the front page of *The New York Times* online version from three years ago. The indexed data elements—the individual images and text—may exist online, but these data are effectively lost because they are out of context.

The initial Web page with pointers provided context as well as a means of viewing the content. So, pragmatics, the interaction between language and the contexts in which it is used, seems particularly important in archiving and later retrieving data, especially if one takes the stance that data cannot be separated conceptually from the form and means of communications. The next Part, Economics, continues this exploration of data and meaning in the context of the economics of data gathering and management.

THREE

Economics

5

The Digital Economy

From Europe to the Pacific Rim, competence in the English language is considered a prerequisite to success. The reason is that English is the language of international commerce. Although the export of English language U.S. films and music may have something to do with the popularity of American culture overseas—a popularity limited by law in France—the driving force behind proficiency in English is economic. Even in the midst of the fallout from the dotCom debacle, the English-language-based American economy still affects virtually every major business in the European Union, Asia, and Africa.

The United States is a consumer nation, with an insatiable appetite for the latest news from around the world, cars and electronics from Japan and Germany, clothes from Hong Kong and China, computer hardware from Mexico and Taiwan, beef from Argentina, and drugs from South and Central America. Although the American economy is bolstered by the export of military weapons and agricultural goods, much of the New Economy is increasingly devoted to intangibles, namely, services and data and entertainment. In today's service economy, where information—and the knowledge it confers—is both power and money, digital data is the currency. Continuing with the focus on business, this chapter explores the basis of the digital data economy, from the perspectives of the inherent and extrinsic value of data in a variety of applications in the private, government, and business sectors. It also examines the economic value of data over time and at various points along the data value chain.

It's not surprising that the vast majority of textual content on the Web, from online journals, business reports, company portfolios, to games, are written primarily in English. Of course, not all of the business activity in America is concerned with creating intangibles, and the Web is becoming recognized as nothing less than a *touch point* to a business's core competency. Touch points, or points of data exchange between the customer and the company, include the telephone, fax, personal contact, email, a retail outlet, and, more recently, the Web. That is, as illustrated in Figure 5-1, the Web is often part of a 360 degree view that customers have of a modern click-and-mortar company—a company with both a physical and Web presence.

Every point of customer contact or *touch point* is critical in providing service and potentially increasing customer loyalty. In this regard, email, the Web, fax, telephone, personal contact, and even the messages that accompany bills influence the customers' perception of a business and their desire to deal with the business in the future. Furthermore, customers expect a business to recognize and remember them regardless of how they interact—that is, exchange data—with the company. Customer service representatives and others who interact with customers at a given touch point must therefore be able to access historical data. Such data include every customer interaction with the business through every other touch point. In other words, there has to be some form of data archive that each touch point can contribute to and access. For example, within the customer relationship management system for American Express, the agents who handle flight changes for customers must have access to airline, hotel, and car rental data in order to better serve the customer—and ensure that the customer uses an AMEX card to pay for the services.

Customers expect a business to provide the same service through every touch point. If they interact with a business through the Web, for example, they should be able to verify the status of an order placed on the telephone or in person. Businesses accomplish this verification by establishing a customer data archive that is accessible from every part of the company.

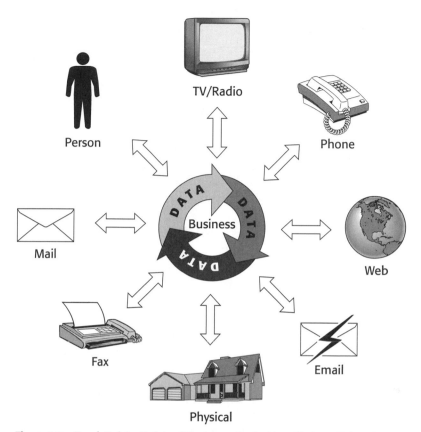

Figure 5-1   Touch Points–Points of Customer Contact in a Modern Click-and-Mortar Company.

Virtually every employee in every business sector is involved in the exchange of digital data in some way. To illustrate how the digital data economy is changing the business landscape, consider how the traditional photo imaging and digital printing industries are co-evolving. The convergence of image science and information technology are giving rise to a burgeoning info-imaging business, where companies that traditionally compete on the basis of either information services and supplies, photographic equipment, or imaging infrastructure find themselves competing with one another. Today, companies involved in document imaging, photographic processing, digital cameras, flat panel displays, photofinishing systems, and networks compete for the same customers.

Kodak, traditionally a camera, film supply, and processing company, now offers digital alternatives to its chemistry-based image film processing and printing, with archiving products and in-store machine services such as cropping and enlarging from original prints. Xerox, known primarily as a copier company, is offering digital kiosks that enable customers to design custom greeting cards in stores. Camera dealers now sell printers and computer supplies for digital cameras. The traditional camera and film companies—Nikon, Cannon, Fuji, AGFA, Minolta, and Olympus—now compete for customers in the digital camera market. They compete not only with each other but also with companies from the copier, print, and consumer electronics areas—companies like Hewlett-Packard, Sony, Ricoh, Panasonic, Casio, Epson, Intel, Logitech, and Toshiba. Similarly, film suppliers like Fuji and Kodak compete with manufacturers of flash memory cards, the media of digital cameras. Traditional photographic paper companies like Ilford, Kodak, Oriental Seagull, and AGFA now share the market with printers and supplies from Epson, HP, Konica, and Sony. Similarly, the flatbed scanner industry, once ruled by Microtek, Epson, Umax, and HP, now competes with AGFA, Cannon, and other camera companies. In addition, the printer and paper companies face competition from new, paperless display technologies, such as digital photo albums made of LCD panels.

The photographic chemistry market has been transformed by digital technology as well. Instead of spending hours in a darkroom with toxic chemicals, virtually every professional photographer works with image editing software, such as Adobe's Photoshop. Kodak offers a digitization service, PhotoCD, as an alternative or in addition to standard prints or slides. PhotoCD is a CD-ROM-based archive of up to 100 images, in four different resolutions. Copy chains, such as Kinko's and Copy Kop, offer high-quality color laser printing directly from computer media, with value-adds such as extra wide format prints. In this way, amateur photographers have access to the same digital equipment used by professionals.

As a result of the convergence of digital imaging and conventional photography, amateur and professional photographers can create digital portfolios by using traditional 35mm camera systems. Once the film is exposed, many photofinishers provide an option of posting the images to the Web, delivering images on PhotoCD, or making traditional prints. The prints can be scanned on a flatbed scanner, the scanner prevalent on many home systems. Another way to get prints is to use a digital camera and either download the images to a home PC for printing or use a printer that prints directly from flash memory cards.

Clearly, everyone involved in the image industry, from the couple taking pictures of their newborn with a digital camera to the developers of software used to edit images, is in the midst of a major change. However, as the new info-imaging business demonstrates, the economic success of players in the New Economy follows the rules of the Old Economy. For example, the five factors that contribute to profits—market, money, methods, management, and metrics—still apply.

MARKET, MONEY, METHODS, MANAGEMENT, AND METRICS

The Five M's of a successful company in the Old Economy hold in the New Economy, as discussed here:

- *Market* — Successful companies differentiate themselves and create a market for their products. For example, flash memory card manufacturers compete in the info-imaging market by offering multiple, incompatible standards, including Compact Flash, SmartMedia, ATA Flash, and Sony's Memory Stick to store digital still images. Similarly, aligning with different camera companies, manufacturers of each competing media standard hope to win out over the other manufacturers in the end. For example, the makers of Compact Flash align themselves with Nikon and Cannon, whereas the makers of ATA Flash work with Kodak and Minolta. There is similar activity in the market for digital video imaging, where the market is segmented by manufacturers that offer everything from 8mm digital tape cassettes to flash memory, standard $3\frac{1}{2}$-inch floppies, and recordable CD-ROM for media.

- *Money* — Companies must have sufficient capital for normal business operations and a source of revenue—such as a sufficient number of customers willing to part with their cash in exchange for the company's digital products and services.

- *Methods* — The appropriate business model should be in place and must be viable. New digital products and services generally require a reworking of traditional methods.

- *Management* — The management, especially upper-level management, must be experienced and capable in the area of competition. For this reason, many of the traditional camera companies have hired senior-level managers from the digital imaging industry, and vice versa.

- *Metrics* — The results of business activity must be measurable and must be regularly measured to assess progress. Such metrics also test the viability of management's assumptions and methods. For example, in the digital imaging industry, output might be measured in terms of the number of files or megabytes of data produced per hour, instead of the number of prints made per hour.

. . . .

THE DIGITAL DATA ECONOMY

The state of the U.S. economy is a reflection of the degree of success that businesses have in competing for customers and resources, both home and abroad. In addition, as demonstrated by the Japanese recession of the 1990s and the bursting of the dotCom bubble in 2000, the world economies are highly interdependent and changes in one economy are propagated almost immediately to another. Increasingly, this economic interdependence is influenced by the constant flow of data between individuals, business, and governments.

As discussed below, the value of data can be appreciated from several perspectives. As a commodity, data can be considered the raw material that moves along a value chain, increasing in value as the raw data are processed for particular markets and consumers. In this regard, data, like tangible products, have both inherent and extrinsic value, and this value depends on the perspective of the producer and potential consumer. The value of data can change from personal, enterprise, and governmental perspectives. That is, each sector has its own value chain and scale of ascending values.

The Digital Data Value Chain

The data value chain is a metaphor for the coordinated processing of data from a raw state to a salable form, where each successive stage in the chain represents value added by the process involved. As shown in Figure 5-2, the digital data value chain begins with the processing of raw data and ends with context-specific data, yielding products at various value points along the way. The processing and value-added for each of these points along the digital data value chain are described below.

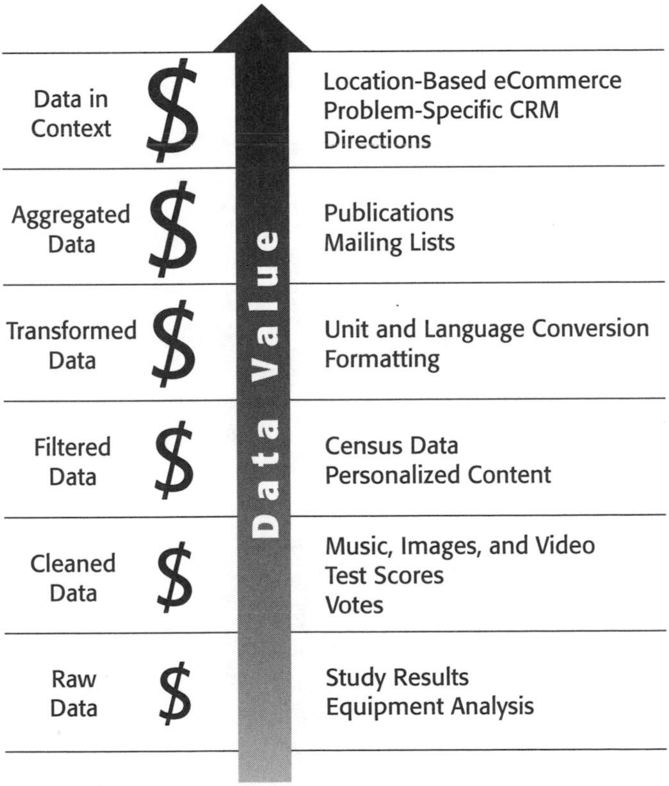

Data in Context	$	Location-Based eCommerce Problem-Specific CRM Directions
Aggregated Data	$	Publications Mailing Lists
Transformed Data	$	Unit and Language Conversion Formatting
Filtered Data	$	Census Data Personalized Content
Cleaned Data	$	Music, Images, and Video Test Scores Votes
Raw Data	$	Study Results Equipment Analysis

Data Value →

Figure 5-2   The Digital Data Value Chain.

Data become more valuable—and their loss is more expensive—as they move up the value chain. For example, cleaned data—raw data that has been processed to remove various types of errors—is generally more valuable than the raw data, which may contain errors.

- *Raw Data* — This category includes study results, equipment analysis, unprocessed data from Web-based forms, customer email, automatically recorded transaction records or records keyed in manually, and instrumentation data.

- *Cleaned Data* — This category includes data that have been statistically processed to remove obvious errors and extraneous data or noise; it includes test scores, commercial music, processed images and video, and votes. For example, raw test scores modified to reflect questions thrown out of the test because analysis after the test was administered showed that the discarded questions were invalid in some way. Similarly, some votes in an election may be discarded because of machine errors or because they were improperly cast in some way. A variety of statistical tools can be used to clean data by identifying outliers or data that fall far outside the normal distribution of data and removing them from consideration.

- *Filtered Data* — This category is a subset of cleaned data selected to highlight a particular population of users or customers, such as U.S. Census data and personalized content. For example, the distribution of males under the age of 50 in a given voting district or the results from a search on the Web in response to a query for "IBM PC" are both filtered data. Because of the methods involved, the former result is more likely to be more highly filtered than the less selective Web search. Raw data can be filtered without first going through the cleaning process, but these data are generally of less value than data that have been cleaned.

- *Transformed Data* — This category is a subset of filtered data, reformatted for a particular medium (such as from paper to CD-ROM) or translated in units or language for a particular viewer population. For example, text and images formatted for a Web site are considered transformed data, as are data converted from metric to English equivalents (centimeters to inches, kilograms to pounds). More advanced transformations include the use of mathematical operators on multiple data values, such as area and volume data computed from container dimensions, or acceleration computed from speed and time data.

Transformation is generally, but not necessarily, a reversible process. For example, enhancing the color saturation of an image may not be a reversible process because some of the image data are lost in the process of transformation. Enhancing the contrast of a black-and-white digital image also may not be reversible, because, while data in the midranges will be shifted or transformed toward black or white, data already at the extremes of black or white will remain at the extremes. Decreasing the contrast of an enhanced black-and-white image will shift data from the extremes of black and white back toward the midrange, including the data originally at the extremes. As a result, the data originally at the extremes of black and white will be lost; the original deep blacks will become grey, and the original bright whites will dim.

- *Aggregated Data* — This category includes data that have been cleaned, filtered, transformed if needed, and then packaged or aggregated for specific uses, such as mailing lists and online publications. For example, an online newspaper, such as the online version of *The New York Times* or *The Wall Street Journal*, aggregates data that have been cleaned, filtered, and transformed for a particular audience. On any given day, *The New York Times* may have more data on arts and politics, whereas *The Wall Street Journal* may have more data on international and national business. The value these online publications bring to the reader lies in timesavings. News is formatted in an easily digestible form and aggregated into a package that is easy to navigate.

- *Data in Context* — At the top of the data value chain, this category includes data that have not only been aggregated, transformed, filtered, and cleaned, but made context specific as well. Directions to the nearest restaurant for a hungry driver, data on the location of a FedEx package, and data on sales in a shopping center while a customer is shopping are all examples of context-specific data.

Similarly, just-in-time online and CD-ROM-based education is another form of context-specific data, in that data are available when they are needed most. For example, F-16 technicians can review the maintenance procedures in the field by accessing data from a built-in LCD panel in the fuselage of the aircraft. Similarly, military physicians can review procedures just as they prepare to perform them in the field with multimedia review data available on CD-ROM. Manufacturers of complex medical imaging systems, such as ultrasound machines, increasingly include CD-ROM-based training materials that can be viewed on the equipment monitor as they are needed.

In addition to the incremental value of data along the value chain, there are secondary economic effects. For example, as data move up the value chain they need to be stored somewhere. As the growing $44 billion digital data storage industry indicates, the amount of digital data involved in modern business is staggering. In response to the onslaught of digital data, massive server farms, some with dedicated power, are being built to supplement those already used to store data destined for the Web and elsewhere. There are even commercial ventures intent on turning the Internet into a vast hard drive to handle the bits and bytes thrown off by the digital data economy. The database software industry, dominated by companies such as Oracle and IBM, is nearly an $8 billion industry in the United States.

Extrinsic versus Inherent Value

As suggested by the digital data value chain, data have variable value, depending on how the data are processed and how closely they suit the customer's needs. The value of data can be characterized as primarily inherent or extrinsic, as shown in Table 5-1. Data that have inherent commercial value include personal health care information, records of banking and financial transactions and balances, music on CD or MP3, videos on DVD or video tape, computer games and other forms of electronic entertainment, and data such as mailing lists from a particular demographic.

The list of data and the associated extrinsic and inherent value shown in Table 5-1 assumes a single perspective. For example, a per-

Table 5-1 Extrinsic versus Inherent Value of Digital Data.

Data have inherent economic value and extrinsic or secondary value. The designation is a matter of degree and assumes a perspective of data creator or consumer. In general, consumers are willing to pay for data with inherent value—a music CD, for example.

Data	Example	Extrinsic	Intrinsic
Business Processes	Recipe for corporate products; manufacturing process descriptions; trade secrets	X	X
Computer Games	Game cartridges and discs for Sony, Microsoft, Sega, and Nintendo		X
Financial Data	Bank account balances; stock prices; stock ownership		X
Health Records	Electronic medical records, including drug interaction history, previous surgeries, and previous diagnoses	X	X
Music	Titles on CDs, MP3 files, and MiniDisc		X
Personal Data	Blood type; driver's license number; social security number; business contact information; to-do list		X
Tax Records	Federal, state, and city tax payments; federal and state returns; sales receipts from business	X	
Video	Home video; commercial programming	X	X

son's social security number has value to that person, in part because of the time and energy cost of contacting the social security administration to obtain a new number. As the $6 billion U.S. game industry suggests, some data have more inherent value than others. A $13 music CD and a $60 computer game CD, both distributed on media worth only a few cents, command significantly different prices because of relative inherent value of the data they contain.

In the inherent data value category, consider the economic impact of online music distribution, patterned in some manner after the Napster model, which allowed users to freely share music files through the Internet without copyright restrictions, a distribution that was roundly destroyed by the music industry. In the wake of Napster, the five largest record labels have announced online music subscription services, and computer hardware vendors, such as Sun Microsystems, are rushing to fill the vacuum. Although a few logistical hurdles remain, such as how to combine the music lists from multiple services, it's clear that the inherent value of data is driving all kinds of companies, from Web portals to database servers, to invest in the digital music distribution market.

Often, digital data have both significant inherent and extrinsic value. For example, CNN, together with IBM and Sony, is in the process of creating a digital video archive system that will allow customers to create their own broadcasts. Part of the five-year project, which began in mid-2001, involves converting 115,000 hours of videotape collected over a 21-year period to digital form. For CNN, the digital video archive has inherent value as an internal resource for creating new broadcast material. In addition, CNN will be able to distribute video to a variety of new customers—those who perceive that the data have an inherent value.

For most business owners and most of the working public, tax records, including records of purchases and funds transferred in exchange for goods and services, have primarily extrinsic value. Tax data has relatively little inherent value to the individual or business reporting the income and tax receipts to the government. In other words, without laws requiring archiving of tax-related business activities in the event of an IRS audit, few people or businesses would bother maintaining records beyond their use for current or future business.

Useful Data Lifetime

Every business transaction creates data, and some of this data is worth keeping for some period of time. In some cases, not keeping a record of a business transaction long enough is frowned upon by the IRS. Table 5-2 lists some of the major types of digital data and their useful lifetimes.

Some data should be maintained indefinitely. For example, electronic medical records and prescription history may have a bearing on public health research to determine the effectiveness of a particular therapy over several decades. The medical data may also have a bearing on the health of a patient's siblings and children. A woman whose siblings and mother died of breast cancer, for example, has a

Table 5-2 Useful Lifetimes for Digital Data in the Digital Economy.

Useful life is not considered to include historical research. "Life+" = significantly more than the life of the individual; "Employed+" = term of employment plus several years, depending on the employee.

Data	Lifetime (years)	Note
Business Correspondence	2+	Indefinite for proprietary information
Charge Card Bills	7	For warranty (1–2 years) and tax purposes
Credentials	Life+	University degrees, professional licenses
Criminal Records	Life+	For local police records
CRM	5	Customer profiles (change over time)
Demographics	Life+	For government, medical, and legal purposes
Email	Employed+	Maintenance after discharge for legal issues
Images	Life+	Digital video and still images for business and personal reference
Insurance Premium Payments	Life+	For survivors
Legal Rulings	Life+	For inheritance, malpractice records, contested property
Mailing Lists	5	Rapid decline of accuracy
Medical Records	Life+	Includes surgical procedures, drug history, past diagnoses, family medical history
Personal Calendar	2	For tax records and personal reflection
Personal Contact Information	5	Phone numbers, email addresses (must be refreshed periodically to maintain accuracy)
Personal Records	Life+	Memoirs, manuscripts, letters
Social Security Payments	10+	For retirement planning and retirement
Tax Records	10+	For audits
Telephone Bill	5	Shorter if not for business purposes
To-Do Lists	1	For review of accomplishments
Travel Records	7	Hotel, plane, and related business expenses
Utility Bill	5	Shorter if not for business purposes

much greater risk of developing the disease than someone without a family history of breast cancer. Having these data available to a patient's clinician and public health researchers can help the patient and others at risk for breast cancer by suggesting more frequent mammograms, for example.

Similarly, other, not so obvious, diseases are passed genetically from one generation to the next, and these data may not be obvious or even known to relatives, who may benefit indirectly from it. Legal rulings also fall into the category of data that should be archived indefinitely. Inheritance, malpractice claims and rulings, and contracts of various types have significant inherent value to the beneficiaries of the judgments, as well as to those who are compelled to abide by them.

Data Value and the Individual

Everyone views and values data a little differently. What someone reads or watches on TV or on the Web is largely a matter of personal taste, modified somewhat by advertising campaigns. Data can be very personal, such as one's taste in music, images of friends or places, and to-do lists. That said, Table 5-3 lists some sources of data and their value to the individual.

Some data are more valuable than others, typically as a function of their replacement value to the owner or originator and not of their inherent value to anyone else. For example, private email or digital images from a summer vacation may be worth very little on the open market, but to an individual, they may be priceless. As noted earlier, however, some personal data, such as medical records, or celebrity data have value to others as well. For example, pharmaceutical companies and third-party payers have a great deal of interest in prescriptions, diagnoses, and costs associated with a particular diagnosis. Obviously, for the individual, electronic medical records are valuable from the perspective of proactive health care and for ensuring that their health care provider is aware of their complete medical history, including drug reactions.

Table 5-3 The Value of Data to the Individual.

Data	Value
Business Correspondence	Tracking resolution of problems with goods and services
Business Licenses	Proof of compliance with legal requirements
Credentials	Employment
Domestic Contracts	For revenue determination for local, state, and federal governments
Email	Personal records; communications
Images	Personal records; sharing; documentation for insurance
Insurance Records	Health care coverage; premium payment verification
Medical Records	Proactive health care; current and future medical conditions
Personal Calendar	Personal effectiveness; planning
Personal Contact Information	Timesavings in locating friends, relatives, and associates
Property Sales/Leases	Legal records for challenges
Sales Receipts	Tax records; write-offs; warranty claims
School Records	For employment, admission to advanced schools
Tax Records	Proof of payment of federal and state taxes
To-Do Lists	Personal effectiveness
Travel Records	Reimbursement; personal keepsakes
Vehicle Registration	Legal requirements for sale or transfer of vehicle
Visa/Passport	Foreign travel; work permits; identification

Data Value and the Government

Local, state, and federal governments, charged with developing programs, collecting taxes, and maintaining the social infrastructure, are highly data dependent. Although the government is involved in

Table 5-4   The Value of Data to the Government.

Data	Value
Assessor Records	Established tax base
Birth/Death Certificates	Census; public health; city planning
Business Licenses	Tax base
Car Taxes	Tax base
Census Data	Business planning; public health
Corporate Records	Tax base computation; fraud prevention
Criminal Records	Tracking of past criminals for the public good
Health Status	Public health; communicable disease control
Income Statements	Tax base
Library Records	Management of holdings; budget; use tracking
Police Records	Public safety; identification of repeat offenders and threats
Property Sales/Leases	Tax base
Pubic School Records	Student records; teacher qualifications; test scores
Sales Receipts	Establishment of tax base
Tax Base	Revenue determination for local, state, and federal governments
Visa/Passport	National security; population control; inhibition of organized crime
Voter Registration	Basis for juror duty roster, voting dates
Voting Records	Method for tracking elected officials and for electing officials

the construction of everything from public facilities to military armament systems, for the most part, it works with data—especially records of funds owed, collected, and spent. Table 5-4 lists data types and sources that are of value to the government.

In addition to data related to taxes, consider the value of personal and population data on controlling communicable diseases and improving public health. Sometimes probing seemingly unrelated government data can reveal public health issues. Consider that records from 18th-century London relating the outbreak of diseases relative to the water distribution system showed that water from one pump was contaminated. Outbreaks of disease often followed the distribution of the water supply, leading government officials to establish standards for sewage control and waste disposal in the city.

Contemporary parallels include tracking the health status of the public through government institutions such as the Center for Disease Control (CDC) in Atlanta and the National Institutes of Health (NIH) in Bethesda. Together with other governmental agencies, the CDC and NIH also monitor health-related issues that may affect the health of the U.S. population and, when needed, take appropriate actions. For example, with the prevalence of hoof-and-mouth disease in Europe during 2000, beef products from Europe are, in 2001, virtually illegal to import into the United States.

Data Value and the Enterprise

Businesses, like the government, live on digital data (see Table 5-5). These data can be grouped into four general areas: those that result from customer interactions, dealings with the government, interactions with employees, such as payroll, and research and development efforts. That is, virtually every enterprise in the United States must communicate with local, state, and federal governments on a regular basis, if for nothing else than to verify tax status. Employer-employee interactions, from payroll to lawsuits, all generate and depend on a constant flow of data. Similarly, research and development generates data from all its diverse activities, from perfecting a cooking recipe to establishing a new project management schedule.

Data Mining

According to reports from the U.S. government, about 1 percent of retail sales in the United States in 2000 were through eCommerce. More significantly, most domestic business transactions were recorded in transactional databases. Some of the transactional data were recorded to abide by federal, state, or local laws. In other cases, the data were used to serve as a basis for improved customer service, marketing, or long-range planning. In this regard, consider that the

Table 5-5 The Value of Data to the Enterprise.

Businesses live on the uninterrupted flow of context-specific data.

Data	Value
Accounts Receivable/Payable	Standing of customers; company revenue projections
Business Intelligence	Assessment of business compositeness, based on information on the competition and the overall market
Decision Support Systems	Assessment of business decisions, based on data and statistical and AI tools
Employee Benefits	Identification of employees with time saved for sick leave, retirement plans; government reporting
Hours Worked	Verification of employee compensation; federal and state reporting
Intellectual Property	Management of trade secrets, trademarks, patents, white papers, and other corporate assets; defend patents
Inventory	Cost; supply of equipment and parts
Personnel Files	Complaints; contributions; training
Process Control	Complex assembly; chemistry; definitions
Product/Service Data	Maintenance of core competencies, including process technologies
Project Management	Delivery timelines; archives of past, similar projects that can serve as templates for new projects
R&D Support	Development of company core competency
Robotics Control	Manufacturing plant control; data in software
Scheduling	Fair distribution of call schedules; customer scheduling
Simulation	What-if analysis of business and product decisions
Supplier Data	Ranking of quality, cost, responsiveness, and payment options for suppliers
Training	Video; CD-ROM just-in-time training

really large transactional databases in the United States, namely, those of Visa, MasterCard, and American Express, contain huge amounts of data that can potentially provide insight into customer behavior. Searching for hidden relationships in huge stores of transactional data, referred to as data mining, is often more rewarding than mining for gold.

Data mining involves the mathematical analysis of large volumes of transactional data—whether from online sales, records of credit card charges, prescribing behavior of clinicians, or grocery purchase records keyed from discount cards—to identify patterns and trends that may have value. For example, data mined from charge card transactions are useful for generating targeted mailing lists of potential customers for specific products and services. American Express customers who charge more than $5,000 a year for airline tickets to extravagant resorts are probably more likely to respond to direct marketing advertisements from luxury car manufacturers than are MasterCard customers who spend less than $500 a year on airline tickets to any location.

Data mining is based on statistical summaries of large quantities of transactional data as well as rule-based systems that sift through data, searching for patterns. However, because data mining looks at high-level data patterns, it provides few clues about the behavior of specific individuals. It can, however, be used to classify and predict the behavior of groups. For example, data mining of charge card information might show that males between 35 and 45 who subscribe to *The Wall Street Journal* are more likely to respond positively to an offer to subscribe to *Fortune Magazine* than are males between 45 and 65 who subscribe to the *National Enquirer*.

In the insurance industry, data mining is used to predict classes of customers most likely to buy particular policies, to spot fraudulent claims, and to identify behavior patterns that increase insurance risk. In health care, a $1.2 trillion business, data mining is used to predict drug efficacy and to rank successful therapies for different illnesses. These types of data are especially valuable to third-party payers who are always looking for ways of minimizing health care costs. In transportation, data mining is used to optimize scheduling and vehicle use.

One of the more prominent areas in business that benefits directly from data mining is Customer Relationship Management, or CRM. Data mined from archives of customer data that have been cleaned, filtered, and combined with real-time data can be used to regulate the flow—and cost—of customer service. From a business perspective, providing profitable customers with customer service, at a national average cost of between $7 and $13 per call, may be more important than providing the same service to customers who are costing the company money and yet aren't significant sources of revenue.

Customer data that have been mined to categorize customers based on profitability can be used to direct the flow of customer support dollars to those responsible for the profitability of a company and to minimize the dollars wasted on those who represent a loss for the company. For example, many companies use a tiered customer service model in which the top two or three hundred clients may have a group of five or six highly trained customer service representatives who answer the phone within ten or fifteen seconds. The status of these VIP customers is derived from either caller-ID information linked to the corporate database or from the customer's ID, either keyed in or spoken into their telephone handsets. Similarly, the next tier of five or six customer service representatives is assigned to the next five or six thousand customers who are only marginally profitable for the company and therefore are not as influential as the top-tier customers. Finally, the tens of thousands of customers calling in for support who are not profitable for the company may be assigned two or three minimally trained customer service representatives. For these customers, who may be individuals, home businesses, or corporations, service is available on a first-come, first-served basis, and long holds of 15 minutes or more are the norm.

The approach of using mined customer data to regulate customer service is common in the banking industry, where the basis for customer categorization is a database of account balances and transaction records. Customers with low balances or low credit card activity, and therefore low profitability, are ranked below those who have large balances and who regularly invest funds in a variety of financial instruments. When a bank customer enters his account information through a telephone touch-tone pad, his name and profile show up on a computer monitor where customer service representatives can see who is on cue, in terms of their value to the bank.

Customers who produce a profit for the bank are handled promptly and may be given concessions, such as fee waivers, for their continued business. Customers who are ranked as marginally profitable are given relatively poor service and are always handled after the best customers have been served. Customers who are ranked as nonprofitable may actually be discouraged from doing business with the bank by being placed on extended hold. The categories are based on the availability data from customers' past year or more of activity, as well as their current balances, and different banks and other financial institutions use different rules to determine where a customer fits on the scale of desirability or undesirability.

Providing customer service as a function of profitability is nothing new. The airline industry allows customers to define their desired level of service by selecting first, business, or economy class. With phone-based CRM, however, the categorization isn't so obvious, nor is the logic behind the categorization generally advertised to customers.

Data mining and the other components of the digital data economy are inextricably linked to economic developments in the digital hardware market. As described in the next section, the current digital data economy is based on the tumultuous evolution of digital hardware systems.

The Digital Hardware Economy

The economic history of the computer, especially the microcomputer, is one of turbulence, a massive influx of venture capital, and the worldwide prominence of heretofore unknown companies like Microsoft, Compaq, Apple, and Dell. One of the reasons for this pattern has been the relative lack of consumer knowledge about the computers, peripherals, and software. Aside from hobbyists, most people regard the inner workings of the constantly evolving PC largely as a mystery. At the same time, the utility of the technology has been demonstrated in dozens of industries.

These are the conditions that marketers dream about—because they are able to mold the image of a PC or peripheral into something that a customer must have, even though he doesn't need it. In this respect, customers typically buy what they want, not simply what they need. Marketing professionals emphasize the magic of a product in order to associate an emotive state change with it.

For example, consider the Palm Pilot, the most successful personal digital assistant (PDA) in the history of the category. To a non-PDA user, successive versions of the Palm have changed little. All Palms provide a to-do list, address book, and calendar. However, to a PDA user, subtle changes in size and construction make the older versions seem outdated, compared to the sleek, new models. Many Palm users upgrade to the new versions as soon as they're announced. These PDA owners rarely need the latest model, but they want it, if only to have the most up-to-date hardware for appearance's sake. Similarly, the high-tech market is replete with products, from laptops, PDAs, wireless devices, and software, that are perceived as outdated as soon as the follow-up model is introduced. High-tech marketing has convinced most potential customers that smaller, thinner, and more powerful is always better, even if the functionality really hasn't changed.

The Alchemy Continuum

To understand the sudden appearance of new computer hardware and software and why some last for years while others seemingly disappear as soon as they're introduced, it helps to view the computer technology phenomenon in terms of the Alchemy Continuum, illustrated graphically in Figure 5-3 and referred to hereafter as the Continuum. The start of the Continuum is characterized by an overwhelming preponderance of magic with little or no real technology.

Magic is the power to create inexplicable results through the use of the product. In other words, the product is positioned as a substance that empowers the user to create an outcome that defies immediate logical explanation. Magic is the crux of marketing, which seeks to create an emotive state change in potential customers. Marketing professionals, like sales professionals, know that customers buy what they want, not only what they need, and that if a product can be associated with a state change—from sedate to happy or excited, for example—customers will be more likely to buy the product. Marketing knows that customers use logic to rationalize a pur-

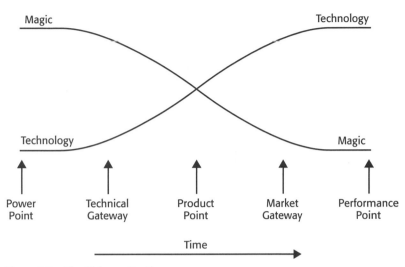

Figure 5-3 The Alchemy Continuum.
The Continuum is one way marketing seeks to control customer perceptions of a product.

chase, but the buy decision is an emotive one. Marketing is successful when it uses magic to impart an "I want some of that" attitude in the minds of potential customers.

In terms of product life cycle, the start of the Continuum corresponds to the inception stage, when the PDA, laptop, or other product may be little more than a scribbling on a paper napkin. At the other end of the spectrum, little or no magic is involved, and the product is a pure technology. In the Continuum, technology is a means of creating consistent results. Technology can be a process or a device that creates quantifiable results, typically measured in money, timesavings, or increased service.

Between the two extremes, magic is replaced with technology in a stereotypical way over time. The process of moving a product from a magical state to a technologic one is characterized by several key points along the way, which in turn define distinct phases.

The Power Point — A product may begin as a diagram sketched out on a napkin over lunch with a colleague. However, unlike the fate of most marked-up napkins, the ideas that make it to the Power Point of the Continuum are typically instantiated and clarified by a working document or PowerPoint presentation (hence the name).

The Power Point, the entry point into the Continuum, is characterized by a preponderance of magic.

The Technical Gateway — The second major point in the Continuum is the Technical Gateway, a decision point where product development and management determine whether or not the technology involved in the proposed product is worth pursuing. The Technical Gateway is usually characterized by the appearance of a prototype that demonstrates some version of the technology involved in the proposed final product. At this point, the company has typically invested significant resources, especially developer time, in achieving the prototype or demonstration stage. In doing so, the company, whether it's a startup with two people or a large corporation, typically has a good idea of what will be required, in terms of development resources, to productize the prototype.

Many companies announce their products at this stage in the Continuum to thwart competition. Once a company announces a product, it is usually difficult for other companies to raise capital to develop a similar product, especially if the first company to announce has particularly deep pockets. Microsoft Windows was announced years before its actual release, for example.

The Product Point — The third key point along the Continuum, the Product Point, marks a significant shift in the magic-technology mix from a preponderance of magic to an equal magic-technology mix. Although this determination is based on qualitative measures, the Product Point is also characterized by a product that can be tested and evaluated, even if only in a limited way and inside the company (alpha testing).

High-tech companies often release products at this point in the Continuum because of the imminent appearance of a competitor, the need for revenue to satisfy or attract investors, or simply to gauge market response. Customers who buy a product at this point in the Continuum become paying test subjects. Most often, these customers must have the newest "new thing" and are willing to pay for the privilege of owning the thinnest, lightest, fastest, or most powerful gizmo.

The Apple Newton is an example of a product that was introduced at the Product Point. Although the PDA was ahead of its time in many ways, it was too clunky and not really pocketable. Moreover, the user interface, which was based on a stylus and writing recognition, wasn't ready for prime time. Unlike the writing recognition used on the successful Palm PDA, the handwriting recognition introduced on the Newton was difficult to use and the poor accuracy frustrated many users.

The Market Gateway — The fourth point in the Continuum, the Market Gateway, is the point where the technology is advanced sufficiently for most customers to decide whether a product will satisfy their wants and at least some of their needs. From this point on, only minor advances in the core technology may be realized, and it's marketing's job to make these small differences seem significant. Success then depends primarily on gaining acceptance in the market and only minimally on furthering the technology.

The Performance Point — The final point in the Continuum, the Performance Point, marks the end point of technical development. The product performs as defined in the functional specification, and there are no dangling, "any time now" additions. The Performance Point is stable, but only to the extent that customer needs don't shift the desired performance point to satisfy some perceived or real customer need. The main variable remaining for those in marketing is the price, which can be manipulated to improve the product's price/performance point in response to competition.

The relevance of the Continuum to the discussion of data longevity is that it provides a model that explains the rapid introduction and withdrawal of products in the marketplace, including how a product introduced as a standard one week is suddenly displaced by a competing technology the next week. Examples of computer products at the Product Point include the $3\frac{1}{2}$-inch floppy disk, the standard video monitor, and the CD-ROM. These products are mere commodities; that is, they are completely devoid of magic. With a number of competitors in the market and production outsourced to overseas companies, prices and margins tend to be low. In contrast, the latest wireless device that has no direct competition and has nothing else to be compared to can be shaped by marketing to emphasize the perceived magic in the device, increasing customer demand.

COMPUTATION VERSUS COMMUNICATIONS

In addition to the marketing pressure on customers to want the latest gadgets that the microcomputer manufacturers and software developers offer, there are at least semblances of planned obsolescence. Instead of the approach taken by Detroit in the 1980s, Silicon Valley drives sales through a seemingly endless cycle of increased hardware power, operating system and application software upgrades that require more powerful hardware, and demand for more hardware power. However, the digital data market isn't always a simple matter of processor speed and computational power in the conventional sense. With the prominence of digital data in the digital economy, the relevance of the computer as a communications engine is becoming more important than raw computational ability, as suggested by the processor speed or size of the display.

As shown in Figure 5-4, from a data management perspective, computers are increasingly used as asynchronous communication devices. That is, unlike a telephone or other synchronous communication device, communications don't normally occur in real time and are independent of any clock. Instead, communications are event driven. For example, in the normal operation of a database server, data are sent to a computer where they may be stored for a few microseconds or for a decade before they are output to a printer or monitor.

Computers are often employed as communications devices (right) and less as numerical processors (left). For computations, the same user generally enters the data and receives the results, and the value of the system increases with decreasing response time. When the system is configured as a communication device, the users who generate the data tend to be different from the users who receive the results, and the response time may be hours or days.

DATA OWNERSHIP

Regardless of how valuable data are to an individual, enterprise, or government, there is often the issue of ownership. That is, data may be valuable to an individual and yet not really owned by the individ-

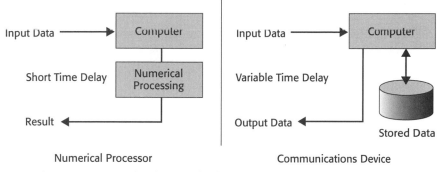

Figure 5-4 Supporting the Digital Value Chain.

ual. Just as charge cards are normally the property of the card issuer and only "loaned" to the holder, data are often not the property of the creator or holder. The purchaser of a software program, for example, isn't legally free to make an unlimited number of copies of the software and distribute copies to his friends. Software is rarely sold outright. A license to use the software is what is sold, and software use is restricted to owners of the license. The data, in the form of compiled software code, can be extremely valuable to the user, but it may never belong to the user, and the user's rights to archive the program to a corporate database for others to use, for example, may be prohibited by law.

Similarly, the creators of intellectual property, when working for an employer, generally assign all intellectual property rights, including copyright, to their employer. However, some rights, such as the right to be the designated inventor on a patent, may show the inventor's name, even if the commercial rights of the certificate belong to the employer. Intellectual property rights of early nondigital works often did not include digital rights, including Web publication, for example, which are increasingly important today. In the realm of commercial music, Napster and similar companies, while a boon to listeners, violated the copyright of music authors and the companies that promoted the music. Similarly, the copyright of CDs, videos, and other copyrighted content is not respected in countries such as China, where bootleg copies of computer software, computer games, and music often appear before they hit the shelves in the United States.

It's Academic

In academia, computer-based intellectual property developed with academic resources is usually divvied up in thirds—1/3 of profits to the inventor, 1/3 to the school, and 1/3 to the department. The exact distribution changes, depending on the institution and how it handles the up-front costs, such as patent attorney fees. With the institution of worldwide distribution of academic content on the Web, the traditional model of academic publishing is changing. For example, consider the controversial work underway at MIT, where all academic materials, from class handouts to lecture notes, will soon be made available on the Web, free of charge. The move is controversial because some professors feel that they are being cheated of their intellectual property.

In addition to giving data away, academic institutions frequently license data and technology. The first wave of successful biotech and eCommerce companies is often credited to academic institutions. For example, the ownership policy at Stanford University in the early 1980s, which encouraged entrepreneurship among faculty, is credited with the success in Silicon Valley. Today, the environment at many major institutions is less generous toward faculty, especially if faculty use university resources for research and development (R&D). Many faculty members discover that, after years of R&D, including what they consider personal time, their product is controlled by and the property of their employer.

Crime Pays

For some people and organizations, anything worth having—such as data—is worth stealing. Software is routinely copied and distributed in corporate America without the requisite number of software licenses. Copyrighted music is freely distributed on homebrew CD compilations and, even with the legal action against Napster, on the Web. Often, data theft is subtler, as when grade school students copy text directly from a Microsoft Encarta disk and include the text and images in a report—without a reference to the original source—with no idea they are plagiarizing.

On the more serious side of data theft, stolen identities, charge card numbers, and personal data are bought and sold on the Internet. The Web and CD-ROM make it easy for employees and consultants to steal ideas, data, and even software from employers and manufacturers. Computer games are cracked and the software patches that remove copy protection appear on the Web within weeks of the games' publication. Similarly, trial versions of business software are extended to full versions by patches that revoke the date-based termination of the software. Given the data analysis tools available today, it's easy to generate a database full of falsified study results to gain promotion in a university or large corporation. Also given that most academic institutions don't impose standards for reporting actual results and that all that generally appear in publications are summary data, there is significant potential for fraud. Even though an academic institution may own the data and the government may have funded the research, it's commonly left to the investigator to manage and archive the data.

Some research results, such as data from the analysis of a military weapons system, are obvious exceptions. Similarly, privately funded drug trial information is kept for possible auditing by the FDA. However, there are no formats, media, operating system, or application software standards established by most agencies.

THE DIGITAL ECONOMY

As the discussion above suggests, the worldwide digital economy is a strong, pervasive force that has no indications of abating. In developed countries, data, especially in digital form, hold the position that steel and lumber held in the 19th century. Similarly, from a personal perspective, more of what we normally consider to be possessions are becoming ephemeral and less tangible. More often now, personal data are more valuable to individuals than their tangible belongings. Such data include personal finance records in Quicken or another database, tax data, email, activity plans and records, to-do lists, car repair records, credit card, social security, and membership numbers, as well as data generated and manipulated at work. Given the choice between a PDA with the only copy of their address book or their favorite shirt or sweater, most people would prefer to keep their PDA.

Despite the prominence of data in a service economy, there are, and will continue to be, inevitable ripples in the economy as companies and countries jostle for dominance. This thread is continued in the following chapter, which explores the economics of data loss and illustrates how interlocking economic relationships can place everyone at risk.

6

Spin Control

 s a literary form, science fiction has a number of characteristics that make it an ideal vehicle for exploring new worlds— worlds that are free of society's normal customs and laws. Sci-fi writers invent nonhuman life forms and explore mankind's creativity and technology's social, economic, and cultural implications. The sci-fi genre trains our attention on technologies that are usually invisible and makes us evaluate their ultimate effect on humanity. When it comes to science fiction that has a basis in reality, it's sometimes difficult to differentiate what is real, what is imagination, and whether fact or fiction came first. Jules Verne successfully transported thousands of readers to the moon in his *From the Earth to the Moon* long before science caught up with his imagination. While scientists were still working on how to get a rocket to break free of earth's gravity, Arthur C. Clarke, author of *2001, A Space Odyssey,* examined what life would be like in a shrinking world linked by communications satellites. In *The Martian Chronicles*, Ray Bradbury explored the societal implications surrounding the rapacious human conquest of the Martian homeland long before the first probe from NASA landed on the planet. Isaac Asimov's *I, Robot* detailed how man and machine will co-evolve, with robots eventually taking on organic forms and characteristics. These and other authors obviously influenced the budding scientists and engineers of the time who internalized the authors' dreams and eventually made them a reality.

Today, Hollywood's ability to create virtual reality—a concept first introduced by William Gibson's *Neuromancer*—is almost incomprehensible. Thanks to the TV and motion picture industries, the characters in Gene Roddenberry's *Star Trek* series and George Lucas' *Star Wars* epics are part of the national culture. As these films illustrate, good science fiction is rarely limited to exploring the beneficial aspects of technology but also concerns itself with the potential of a dark side looming behind every technological advance. Every science fiction reader knows the conflict between humanity and aliens or between humanity and some form of evil or uncontrollable technology.

Most successful science fiction authors spin a tale in which humanity somehow wins out over evil technology or other challenges. As H. G. Wells demonstrated in his *War of the Worlds*, one recipe for a successful science fiction story is to have at least one character to whom readers can relate to and who triumphs over technology in the end.

In reality, as in science fiction, the frailty of complex systems is obvious everywhere. Accidents seem to occur continually, but with the exception of incidents that make the evening news, they're lost in the noise of everyday life. For example, although the error rate in the United States medical system results in fatalities comparable to a 747 crash every day, all of those deaths go unnoticed against a background of natural deaths, unavoidable deaths in hospitals, and traffic fatalities.

However, in science fiction the stark realities of technology and humanity, viewed out of everyday context, become crystal clear. Consider the infamous Mars Climate Orbiter and its partner in space, the Polar Lander. The $125 million Orbiter approached Mars at too low an altitude and was smashed to bits on the Martian surface because the engineers who programmed the onboard computer confused English and metric units of measurement. To make matters worse, the Mars Polar Lander crashed only ten weeks later, due to another software error that caused the engine to shut down prematurely.

In addition to tarnishing NASA's image, the errors cost United States taxpayers hundreds of millions of dollars. They also cost the contractor that built the Lander and Orbiter, Lockheed Martin. The company realized a 60 percent reduction in earning from 1998 to 2000, in part because of failure to secure additional satellite contracts from NASA following the Orbiter debacle. Lockheed has since cut its workforce in response to diminished demand for commercial satellite launches.

Today, NASA is attempting to redeem itself with the Mars Odyssey system, named in honor of Arthur C. Clarke's *2001, A Space Odyssey*. The $300 million Odyssey is intended to orbit Mars for $2\frac{1}{2}$ years, studying minerals in the rocks and looking for signs of water and, by extension, life. Unfortunately, the successful launch of the Odyssey satellite in early April of 2001 was overshadowed by a fiasco involving the 58-foot, billion dollar robotic arm aboard Space Station Alpha. Despite the years of planning and the cost of lifting the $1\frac{1}{2}$ ton arm into space, the time-bound American and Russian astronauts were stymied in their efforts to maneuver the arm because of glitches in the station's computer system.

All three of Alpha's command and control computers—one main computer and two backups—were unable to connect to the station's server. Furthermore, efforts to get one of the three computers working disrupted the main communications link between Alpha and Mission Control. As a workaround, communications with astronauts were relayed through the space shuttle that was parked at the station. Although there were person-to-person communications, Mission Control lost control of Alpha's steering system, postponing critical maneuvers intended to raise the space station's orbit by a few miles.

Back on earth, tens of thousands of networked computers daily fail to connect to servers, resulting in lost productivity and lost data. It's simply expected. After all, computers are complex systems, and most people have grown accustomed to occasional computer meltdowns, crashes, virus attacks, and vandalism. The cost, in terms of lost productivity, lost data, and repairs is millions of dollars a day across the United States. And yet, like the accidental deaths in hospitals and traffic fatalities, against the noise of everyday life, these events don't reach the public consciousness.

Even so, as the events aboard Alpha demonstrate, the economics of digital data—the production, distribution, and consumption of data—is at least as important to the overall economy as are the automobile, housing, and agricultural industries. This chapter highlights the economics of digital data. In particular, it looks at the investment required to manage the risk of data loss from a variety of threats. In addition, it explores the business of data recovery and the practical implications for organizations and individuals.

WHAT COULD POSSIBLY GO WRONG?

Millions of computers operate flawlessly for years without anyone ever noticing anything out of the ordinary. However, given the complexity and interconnectedness of modern society, when a computer system containing critical data fails, the repercussions ripple throughout the fabric of an organization. Knowing what can go wrong with computer systems, learning to recognize the relevant situations, and then preparing to deal with the most likely outcomes is a reasonable approach to managing the risk of digital data loss in a rapidly evolving technological environment.

As shown in Figure 6-1, a variety of events can put data at risk. The major events include accidents, corporate espionage, hardware failure, intentional data corruption, natural disaster, intentional destruction, network failure, operator error, power failure, software failure, theft, vandalism, and vendor failure.

Accidents

In spite of the efforts of the Occupational Safety and Health Administration (OSHA) and corporate training, accidents happen. Spilling coffee or cereal into a laptop, dropping a laptop or PDA onto a concrete floor, tripping on a power cord and destroying a PC's hard drive, and accidentally erasing important files happen every day. Although lack of familiarity with computers and computer hardware is becoming less of a problem, one of the favorite stories told by customer service representatives with Dell Computer is the call from an office worker complaining about the coffee cup holder on her PC. Apparently, the coffee cup holder had a tendency to suddenly retract, at often inopportune times, during the day. After consider-

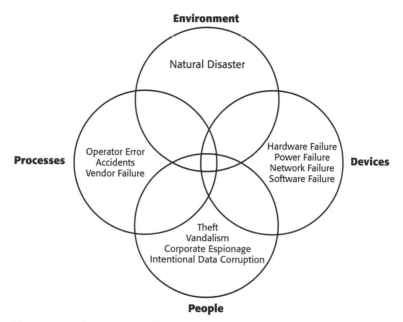

Figure 6-1 What Can Go Wrong.

able discussion, it became clear to the customer service representative that the woman was using the CD-ROM drive bay to hold her coffee cup and that her company didn't use CD-ROMs.

As shown in Table 6-1, minimizing the risk of data loss due to accidents involves maintaining a safe work environment by following OSHA and corporate guidelines, using common sense, exercising good judgment, and developing safe work habits. Making frequent backups of important data, regularly moving data from laptops and PDAs to desktop PCs, installing un-erase and data recovery utilities on PCs, and getting enough sleep are all examples of reasonable steps that can reduce the likelihood of accidents and minimize their effects when they occur.

Corporate Espionage

The intentional, surreptitious monitoring and copying of data is common in government, the military, and in corporate America. What's more, the problem is increasing in severity; according to the

Table 6-1   Data Loss Resolution.

Event	Example	Resolution
Accidents	Trip over power cord, spilt coffee, dropped laptop	Maintain a safe work environment, good work habits
Corporate Espionage	Remote monitoring of wireless networks	Use security precautions on wireless devices
Hardware Failure	Hard drive, memory, microprocessor, network connect failure	Add redundant hardware, back up frequently, have extended warranty, practice periodic disk maintenance
Intentional Data Corruption	Manipulated data by disgruntled employees	Use multiple security levels, monitoring software
Natural Disaster	Fire, flood, and rodents	Back up frequently and store backups offsite, insure business, establish disaster recovery center
Network Failure	Overloaded commercial service, third-party hardware failure	Add redundant network connections, such as a cable modem connection backed up by an analog modem
Operator Error	Miskeyed and misread data	Automate data entry by using alternative input devices
Power Failure	Catastrophic power failure, power spikes and surges	Use Uninterruptible Power Supply (UPS), surge suppressor
Software Failure	Software bugs, memory leaks, incompatibility with other programs or operating system	Recode and recompile software, test software before globally upgrading to new operating systems
Theft	Stolen laptops and PDAs, cracked games	Exercise diligence when traveling, provide copy protection
Vandalism	Viruses, eavesdropping, hardware and network destruction	Use antiviral utilities, employ security system to restrict physical and electronic access, encrypt messages
Vendor Failure	Failed ASP with your data in their control	Establish escrow account with vendors

FBI and the Computer Security Institute, the percentage of computer security managers who have experienced security crimes and reported them to law enforcement increased from 16 percent in 1999 to 36 percent in 2001. With a few software tools and a connection to the Internet, it's a trivial matter to eavesdrop on communications between a commercial Web site and its visitors.

Although snooping through the Internet is a popular and relatively easily accomplished trick, data on a Web site are rarely corporate or personal secrets. High-profile data normally reside on corporate servers and laptops or on stand-alone PCs. However, new technologies such as wireless LANs can put private data at risk. Just as a United States spy plane flying in international waters can monitor radio frequency communications, including wireless network activity and satellite communications going into and out of China, anyone who knows what to look for can use a laptop and a $300 wireless modem to monitor a company's wireless LAN and other computer activity from the company's parking lot. What's more, with a small handheld receiver, a directional antenna, and a palm-sized amplifier, a company's LAN can be monitored from a mile or more away.

Connecting to an unprotected wireless LAN is like walking into a company's main office and plugging into their wired intranet. Given enough time and an understanding of computer networks, someone with even modest skills can copy gigabytes of sensitive data and then either insert a virus into the system or delete data at will. The situation is akin to the use of older radio scanners to monitor cell phone use. Before laws were passed requiring scanner manufacturers to cripple their devices so that the frequencies used for cell phone communications could not be monitored, it was possible for anyone to listen in on conversations going into and out of any cell (combination of transmitter and receiver). For example, a minor scandal arose in London when a reporter taped cell phone conversations between the late princess Diana and her lover.

Even wired networks are susceptible to corporate espionage from more sophisticated spies. For example, with a handheld receiver, a laptop, and a directional antenna, it's possible for someone in a van adjacent to a building (or even sitting on a park bench) to read what's displayed on any computer monitor that isn't shielded for radio frequencies. Every computer display system transmits radio frequency signals corresponding to the images generated by the video display hardware in the computer. The monitor cable, monitor, and other peripheral cables act as transmitting antennas that radiate the signal into space. Even though the video signals are relatively weak and, like all other radio frequency signals, decrease in intensity with the square of the distance from the source, the typical computer display can be monitored from several hundred feet away. Greater distances and intervening materials that absorb radio frequency signals, such as steel-reinforced walls, make reception increasingly difficult. However, a glass window that isn't covered with a metal screen offers little attenuation to a video signal.

A laptop computer used in an open area presents an even easier target for a corporate spy or simply an amateur data voyeur. A receiver, flat antenna, and digital recorder that easily fit in a leather briefcase or backpack can surreptitiously monitor and record everything displayed on a laptop computer used by an executive sitting on a park bench, in a train, airplane, or even a board meeting. Multiple laptops in use in the same area present a problem because of potential interference, but a spy can overcome this challenge by using a directional antenna and by getting closer to the laptop (or PDA) user.

The temptation for employees to sell data to competitors or other interested parties can be significant. For example, insurance companies have been known to pay handsomely—on the order of $10K per floppy disk—for information on internal hospital cost figures for patient care. Knowing the internal cost structure—akin to customers knowing how much dealers pay for cars—allows an insurance company to negotiate from a point of power when setting insurance rates.

The most obvious security precaution against internal and external espionage is to institute a strong security procedure, minimally including username and password protection, for computers and network connections. For greater levels of security, secure ID cards, which generate passwords that are good for only 60 seconds, encrypting and decrypting software, and a variety of biometric devices can be used. One of the most mature biometric security technologies is based on fingerprint authentication, which digitizes a user's fingerprints and compares the image to a description of the print stored in the computer system to verify the user's identity.

Small fingerprint readers are available as stand-alone units and, less obtrusively, built into keyboards and mouses. Biometric devices aren't foolproof, however. With enough motivation, any biometric system can be defeated. For example, since the output of a fingerprint reader is simply a string of characters, a program that captures the string and then regenerates it later can be used to bypass the reader. The most difficult part of the operation is installing the program, which can be done by inserting a virus into an email message. Although people typically believe cybercrime involves computer systems directly (as the Microsoft antitrust case illustrated), competitors make use of any means at their disposal to learn more about their competition. In Microsoft's case, agents paid by the database giant and Microsoft's arch-rival Oracle rifled through Microsoft's trash bins, looking for evidence that could be used against Microsoft in the antitrust case. In addition to paper documents, many companies routinely discard old computer hardware, complete with hard drives, in their trash dumpsters. These discarded hard drives, working or not, can be picked up by competitors, and the data contained thereon can be transferred to fully operational desktop computer systems. Once the data are on a working computer system, they can reveal everything from the company's customer and supplier lists, employee contact information and titles, and budget information, to marketing plans and information on products not yet released.

Corporate espionage is almost impossible to stop completely, especially if someone inside the target organization is involved. However, steps can be taken to minimize exposure to all but the savviest corporate spies. The most important action is to institute a security policy. For example, many small businesses and corporations place special restrictions on consultants who work in-house. They are commonly given access to the corporate network only through a special PC designated for consultants. The PC is typically networked to printers and other resources, but not to sensitive data. The PC usually has the floppy drive disabled, and the external ports are disabled as well to prevent data from being downloaded onto a floppy or an external storage device that the consultant may bring in. This latter route of data theft is especially prevalent, given the fact that thumbnail-sized hard drives can hold 65 MB or more of data. These devices, so small that some are available with key rings, simply plug into a computer's USB port and appear under Windows as an additional hard drive volume. Flash memory cards can be used in the same way with corporate laptops loaned to consultants, circumventing precautions such as removing floppy and Zip drive bays from the laptops.

Often, circumstances dictate even greater data security. For example, many military contractors use specially shielded monitors and computer cables and don't allow the access or display of sensitive content in rooms with unshielded windows. These contractors may use software that monitors employee Web access and applications to look for suspicious activity as well.

Corporate and private firewalls—software and hardware that block hackers from entering a corporate or private network through a modem or DSL connection—can minimize security threats from the outside. This type of protection will eventually become standard, as operating systems, such as Windows XP, include firewall protection as a standard utility. Data encryption software can be used to store sensitive information on corporate servers in a form that employees without sufficient clearance and encryption codes can't access. Finally, taking obvious precautions, such as using a utility that wipes a hard drive clean of data or simply destroying all hard drives before a PC is disposed of can reduced dumpster-style theft. Wiping hard drives clean before decommissioned PCs are given or sold to employees for take-home machines can reduce data leaks. Once a digital data crime—a cybercrime—has been committed, forensic media analysts have a variety of software tools at their disposal to identify, preserve, and analyze evidence of data tampering. Although determining the source of data leaks may not repair the damage that has been done, it may help identify the responsible parties and prevent additional crimes.

Hardware Failure

As discussed in the previous chapters, sometimes the culprit in a theft of data is time. Hardware, including media, has a finite expected useful lifetime. Over time, hard drives crash, heat and voltage spikes ruin RAM and other solid-state memory, unventilated, overheated environments and blocked fans destroy microprocessors, and network adapter cards and modems fail. For aesthetic reasons, computers and computer monitors are often embedded in desks, placed behind or beneath panels of glass and in other enclosures that stress the hardware far beyond design specifications. This same phenomenon was common in the 1980s, when it became popular to place large-screen TVs in walls to reduce their dominance in contemporary living spaces. However, as TV owners soon discovered, the components failed at a very high rate, especially when lint blocked the ventilation fans. Today, flat panels, which are still much more expensive to produce than traditional CRT monitors, can be mounted on the wall—as opposed to inside a wall—to give a more modern look to an office or home setting.

Although not all hardware failures cause data loss, they can temporarily keep data bottled up in the hard drive of a PC or laptop, resulting in costly productivity losses or, minimally, inconvenience. One can address this source of risk by maintaining an inventory of redundant hardware, performing frequent backups, buying extended warranties from vendors, especially those with onsite service, and performing periodic disk maintenance, using, for example, the utilities within Microsoft Windows to check for and repair disk errors. Maintaining a good Information Services (IS) staff helps ensure that periodic routine maintenance gets done, as opposed to requiring busy employees to maintain their own systems. Another approach is to buy quality, name-brand computers and peripherals that come with onsite warranties.

Intentional Data Corruption

Intentional manipulation and corruption of data by disgruntled or mischievous employees is one of the most insidious forms of data loss, and also one of the most difficult to trace. For example, a telephone operator for a mail order company can easily "mis-key" the quantity of an item, the customer's mailing address, or charge card information, resulting in a loss (or false gain) to the company. In addition, an employee who gains access to the corporate computer system through the use of another person's ID can operate with relative impunity. The perpetrator isn't implicated if errors are tracked to another employee. There are obvious military applications of intentional data corruption, including viral infections broadcast to PCs from radio transmitters, but these tactics are rarely used against commercial and private computer systems.

Obvious policies, such as firing employees at the end of the day and canceling employees' passwords and access privileges just before their dismissal, can minimize one source of data corruption. A favorite technique in the Boston area is to wait until an employee is on vacation and then have his belongings boxed up and waiting for him when he returns from vacation. He never gets a chance to step into the building again, except at the loading dock, where he can pick up his belongings. Automatically requiring employees to create new passwords for their computer accounts monthly or quarterly combats computer identity theft. Assuming passwords are updated quarterly, even if an employee steals the username and password of another employee, he or she can only use that information for a maximum of three months.

Natural Disaster

Fire, flood, pestilence, earthquakes, lightning strikes, and storms, like unpleasant situations at work, are difficult to avoid completely. At best, businesses can minimize their chances of being involved in a disaster by avoiding locating a business or residence in a flood plain, in an earthquake zone, in a tornado belt, or on a coast frequented by hurricanes, and by searching for a location with a good fire department and good weather most of the time. However, this approach rules out most of the high-tech centers in the United States. A complicating factor is that businesses locate where skilled people are, and skilled people flock to where the businesses are located. If not the occurrence, at least the effects of natural disasters can be partially mitigated by frequent data backups and storage of the backup media offsite, insurance against data loss, and, for corporations with the appropriate resources, a data recovery process and center. An insurance policy can cover replacement of hardware, but not data. The best remedy for potential data loss in this case is to create backups regularly and maintain them offsite, preferably in some other state, even using an out-of-state, Internet-based Storage Service Provider (SSP). The SSP's backup and archive services protect against loss of locally archived data.

Intentional Destruction

Although natural disasters are a significant, ever-present threat to the survival of data, the most significant disasters tend to be man-made. It seems that when it comes to weapons of mass destruction, history is full of stories of countermeasures, counter-countermeasures, and the like. For example, there was the multibillion dollar early warning system, a string of over-the-horizon radar systems set up to detect intercontinental ballistic missiles (ICBMs) as they traveled over the North Pole, en route to the United States from Russia. As part of the effort, billions more were spent to develop and deploy the anti-ICBM missiles, intended to intercept the missiles, much as the Patriot missiles were used in the United States Gulf War with Iraq.

Whether or not the follow-up Star Wars system, a space-based, multibillion dollar, anti-ICBM initiative ever becomes reality, some of the remnants of the military buildup have resurfaced as useful civilian technologies. One of the most notable spinoffs of the military buildups is the Internet, originally known as the ARPANET. The Internet was originally designed as a nuclear-war-proof communications network to provide communications between military and research centers in the United States in the event that the main telephone network succumbed to attack. However, despite its heritage, the Internet, like all other Internets and intranets, fails on occasion. As the experience with Space Station Alpha's computer system illustrates, something as simple as being unable to access a server over a network can initiate a cascade of seemingly unrelated events that bring the operations of a system to a halt.

Network Failure

Internets and networks fail every day for a variety of reasons, ranging from a backhoe tearing through an optical backbone to a server overwhelmed by legal or fraudulent data. Whatever the cause, the effects of network failure can be minimized by redundant systems. For example, an analog modem that provides dial-in access to AOL or another Internet service provider can serve as a backup for a DSL connection to the Internet. Other viable options include running parallel fiber optic cables in high-risk areas (such as near a construction site), installing redundant networking hardware, and increasing capacity by upgrading to a higher bandwidth intranet or Internet connection, such as DSL or a cable modem.

Operator Error

When it comes to failure in a complex system, there's a tendency to automatically blame the system. However, the operator is usually integral to the system. Take pilot error, for example. There are reliable statistics that predict with good accuracy how pilot error varies with the type of pilot and his experience on different aircraft. For example, twin-engine prop planes are commonly referred to a "doctor killers." The stereotypical scenario is the busy doctor who flies on weekends—just enough time to become marginally familiar with a twin-engine aircraft over a period of many months. However, at around 250 hours of accrued flight time—about a year in total elapsed time—these doctor pilots are at the height of vulnerability, even though they typically feel confident in their flying abilities. They simply haven't had the time—at least 500 hours—behind the wheel required to really master their aircraft. As a result, equipment problems that typically are handled easily by a pilot with 500 or more hours of flight time, such as failure of one of the engines, are often fatal.

Similarly, when it comes to working with computers, operator errors are simply a fact of life. Errors of omission and commission are inevitable in filling out online forms or transcribing data from printed to electronic forms. Employees fail to follow protocols on backup procedures for a variety of reasons. Sometimes, they are inadequately trained and unfamiliar with the equipment, or the equipment designers don't adequately consider the typical use of their product in the design stage. Other times, employees may fail to follow protocol when they are sleepy or careless, or under inordinate stress on the job or at home. Whatever the reason behind operator error, one remedy is to pay attention to human factors. Providing breaks from mind-numbing repetitive jobs can help ensure better performance, as can job training. Automating and simplifying the data gathering process, such as using pictures of products on cash registers instead of requiring operators to memorize and enter prices, is used successfully by McDonald's and other fast-food chains.

Sometimes extra diligence is warranted on a regular basis. For example, night shift workers are known to have more accidents than day shift workers. Nuclear power plant accidents and other mishaps are more frequent at night, when attention spans are shorter and decision making may be impaired. One form of extra diligence is to pay particular attention to data entered or manipulated at night— the time when most IS departments back up data on their servers.

Another approach to minimizing operator error is to use indirect data acquisition tools, such as bar code scanners, which can reduce mistakes that occur in dual entry of data. Integrated systems can also reduce dual data entry errors in hospitals and other businesses that have multiple, independent systems sharing data. For example, a patient admitted to a hospital with an integrated information system has his or her demographic information entered once into the admission system at the time of admission. By the time the patient arrives at one of the clinical areas, address, insurance information, allergies, and other relevant data are already in the clinic's computer system.

Transaction monitors can also be used to reduce the likelihood of operator error. For example, when a customer service representative submits an order for a product into the computer system, the system can check the transaction to determine not only that all of the necessary data have been entered but that the data are reasonable. For example, a mail order company that sells shoes may use a form that has a field for shoe size. A value out of the range of, say, 2 to 16, would be flagged by the monitor as potentially invalid. Similar systems are used in medicine to alert physicians of laboratory values and medication orders that are outside of the normal ranges.

Power Failure

Whether or not data are medically related, they are the lifeblood of our communications-based society, and electrical power is the heart that keeps it going. Power surges, brownouts, spikes, and surges all affect the reliability of computer systems, networks, and all of the peripheral and related electronics. Similarly, power failure can be secondary, such as voltage spikes coming in through an Internet connection, the telephone line to an analog or digital modem, cable modem, or wireless antenna. Even the discharge of static electricity generated by an office worker walking across a carpet on a dry day can ruin a flash memory card or other data-containing media. Power failures can also be indirect. For example, even though the power to a PC may be sustained, if the power to the air-conditioning system fails, then the computer system and network electronics may shut down because of overheating.

One solution to fluctuating and unreliable power, as practiced by an increasing number of companies in Silicon Valley, is to maintain a private power-generation facility. However, even with private power generation, there is dependence on external energy supplies, such as the fossil fuels used to power private electric generators. Other, less costly solutions to power fluctuations include the use of surge suppressors on modem lines, DSL lines, and all other peripheral connections. In addition, an uninterruptible power supply (UPS) can be used on the primary computer equipment. A UPS typically provides power conditioning—spike protection, for example—between ten minutes and an hour of continued operation after the main power fails, depending on the capacity of its battery.

Software Failure

Even if all forms of hardware failure could be circumvented, there would still be significant data loss. For one thing, no software is perfect, and when programs contain hundreds of thousands of lines of code, the chances of an error or two occurring somewhere in the code are significant. Bugs or program flaws due to programming errors can become significant if they affect the critical functionality of an application. Sometimes failures occur insidiously because of software flaws and perhaps only after a significant amount of time has been spent entering data into a system.

For example, all database management systems scale—to a point. The question is where that point is, in terms of data volume. The challenge is that a database that works with one volume of data on one system may scale differently on different hardware. That is, it may provide results within one second on a PC with 256 MB of RAM and within twenty seconds on a PC with only 128 MB of RAM. Another type of software flaw is a memory leak, in which the memory required by an application increases with use. For example, a database application that initially requires 50 MB of free RAM to operate may eventually require 60 to 80 MB of RAM after several hours or days of operation. If the RAM and other computer resources are insufficient to allow for this expansion in requirements, then the database application will fail. Similarly, if other applications are running just within their resource limits and if the database application consumes additional resources, then the other applications may fail as well. These are the most time-consuming failures to troubleshoot.

One solution to defective software is to switch to a new application. If the software was developed in-house, then utilities can be used to pinpoint the source of problems, such as memory leaks, and the code can be rewritten and compiled. Of course, this approach often requires considerable time and money.

Theft

When it comes to money, a thin, fast laptop is often worth its weight in silver. The deliberate theft of laptops and PDAs, either for the purpose of gaining corporate information or simply for sale of the hardware, is especially prevalent with the new, compact, lighter, and easier-to-steal personal devices. A CEO's entire to-do list, contact list, and calendar can be had for the stealing of a device no larger than a pack of cards. Similarly, a laptop containing corporate memoranda or simply a family's digital photo album can be stolen in the airport on the way to grandpa's for the holidays.

Another form of theft is piracy. Although not normally considered a "hard" theft by most users, software piracy, especially game software, costs software developers millions of dollars annually. Hackers circumvent the copy protection schemes of software on disk through a variety of means and then post patches or special routines that modify a game and render it copyable. Another form of data piracy is unscrambling satellite TV signals. Hackers defeat the protection software stored on a smart card—a form of flash RAM that contains authentication codes for different levels of TV service. This protection software provides legitimate users access for a monthly fee.

The obvious solutions to hardware theft are to exercise diligence when traveling, including keeping an eye on luggage containing laptops, disks, and PDAs. Given the popularity of laptop cases, swapping a case containing a dictionary for one with a $3,000 laptop doesn't take much effort.

In the game software industry, resolving the software piracy issue is typically one of keeping hackers at bay long enough for a game to sell unimpeded for the first few months after release. All software protection schemes eventually fall to hackers, but keeping patches off the Web for only a month or two is usually sufficient for the initial high volume of legal sales.

Vandalism

Often, the mechanism of payback for theft of data is indirect. For example, although it doesn't pay well, the intentional, targeted disruption of services, whether from computer virus attacks, hardware destruction, denial-of-service attacks on Web sites, or the use of explosives and other means to destroy communications devices and cables is a multibillion dollar problem. Denial-of-service attacks, where vandals inundate a Web server with traffic to the point that legitimate users are denied service and can't get through, has been deployed successfully against companies such as Yahoo and Amazon.com, as well as software security firms advertising their ability to protect against such activity.

Similarly, software viruses are a constant source of aggravation and data loss in the PC community, as well as a source of profit for companies that create antiviral utilities. The variety of viruses is as endless as their modes of action, with common classifications such as boot sector viruses, file infectors, macro viruses, Trojan horses, worms, and Trojan worms.

Regardless of their classification, viruses make their way into a computer system by the Internet, commercial media, intranets, and other networks. For example, Internet-based email is a popular mode of infection, and viruses sometimes make it to commercial programs or other seemingly controlled services. Even companies with obvious access to antiviral tools and expertise are not immune to spreading viruses. According to reports from Microsoft, in April of 2001, two of its Web sites designed for customer support were infected with a virus that was downloaded by Microsoft clients.

Security systems that restrict both physical and electronic access to mission-critical computer systems and message encryption to diminish the odds of eavesdropping can minimize the threat of vandalism. Another safeguard lies in installing and routinely upgrading antiviral utilities. Banks routinely have remote computing facilities that mirror computer activity locally because of the threat of real physical damage. If one of the data centers is destroyed with explosives, for example, then the other facility can take over immediately. Because it's much cheaper for a company with a sizable loan from a bank to spend a few hundred thousand dollars to blow up a building full of computers and data archives rather than pay off a multimillion dollar loan, these remote sites are typically constructed with bunkers and other deterrents to physical access.

Vendor Failure

Sometimes data loss isn't the result of a plot, espionage, operator error, or anything in the user's control. As in the natural environment, some organisms succeed and other fail. Similarly, as the dot-Com failure so adeptly illustrated, many high-tech businesses are evolutionary dead ends. In addition, like the infinite progression of little fish being eaten by larger fish behind them, businesses are frequently acquired by other businesses that take the intellectual property and discard the acquired company's customer base. Whatever the reason, the result is the same—the clients of these failed businesses are left without support for the software that controls the data in their organization or, worse yet, they are left without their data. This latter case is increasingly prevalent with the failure of Application Service Providers (ASPs) that provide applications through generic Web browsers and maintain control of the application and the clients' data.

Consider the effect ASP failure would have on a small business that is heavily dependent on data. A small clinical practice that uses an ASP for office management and clinical records can't operate if the data are unavailable, for example. Patient diagnoses, test results, drug allergies, and other data must be available during or immediately before a patient's visit. If the ASP fails, the data may be trapped in legal proceedings for weeks or even months.

The workaround for a company or an individual that relies on an ASP or other software or service vendor is to work with a legal firm to establish a software and data escrow account—an archive maintained by an independent third party. In this way, the software—with up-to-date documentation—and data become immediately accessible to the customer if the vendor can no longer support the service.

MANAGING RISK

Managing risk is part of life. For example, the mere act of crossing the street has a certain risk, normally outweighed by the desire for whatever lies on the other side. A man dares to cross a street, frequented by fast-moving cars and trucks, risking the potential of being hit and maimed or killed, in order to deposit a letter in a mailbox. However, the risk exposure, or the likelihood of being hit, multiplied by the loss of life, as measured in pain or lost income to the man's family, is obviously acceptable to him. The man's hesitance in crossing the street, if any, is typically minimized if a traffic light is present and reduced even further if a police officer in the intersection is directing traffic.

The probability or likelihood of the man being hit is still finite—the driver of a speeding car might be drunk or in a police chase or traveling in the wrong direction. In the latter case, the man can take a proactive role in minimizing his risk of being killed by looking both ways before he crosses. He can also wait a moment after the light changes, signaling cars to stop, to verify that the drivers are aware of the light and are actually stopping, for example.

Humans are very poor at estimating probabilities, much less probabilities multiplied by potential loss. For example, clinicians are notorious for not being able to intuitively resolve statistical probabilities in determining the best treatment options for patients, even though they may understand and work with statistical formulas and measures. For instance, if the probability of polio is very low in the general population, but a clinician sees five cases of polio in his office in a week, he's much more likely to think that his next patient may have polio as well. That is, his perception of the probability of a disease is influenced by recent events, even when the published statistical data are available. This characteristic isn't limited to clinicians; it's a general human trait. Most people are sensitized by recent events, and that sensitivity affects their perceptions from that point on.

Given the appropriate tools, however, most people can develop an appreciation for risk assessment and management. The theory of risk management involves fundamentals ranging from Bayes' theorem, chaos theory, and game theory, to probability and utility theory. For example, utility theory deals with individual differences in risk avoidance. Some people are simply more risk averse than others. They tend not to take chances, and when they do, they minimize their risk exposure by buying insurance, for example. Others are much less risk averse and may even gain pleasure from gambling and potentially beating the odds.

Although the formal approach to risk management has its place, when it comes to digital data loss, a common sense approach to managing risk seems at least equally applicable. In this regard, a reasonable risk management strategy is to first determine what data are at risk, what they're worth, and then use that information to determine what resources should be expended to reduce the risk to an acceptable level.

At one extreme, the data at risk may consist of one megabyte of downloads from a government Web site containing information that isn't likely to change in the next decade. Given that printed versions are available free for the asking, the data are worth whatever time it took to locate and download. Threats to the data include a hard drive crash, a viral infection, and theft. In this scenario, dedicating a 30-cent floppy backup for the data, labeled and stored in a shoebox in an office desk drawer with other archives, seems reasonable. Devoting a $10 Zip disk or taking the time to burn a CD-ROM of the data seems a little unreasonable.

In contrast, consider that the one-megabyte file has the only version of Jane's Ph.D. thesis, and it exists only on her laptop's hard drive. What's more, the laptop is about a decade old, there are no replacement parts or even batteries for the unit, and it's been acting up lately. In addition, as in the scenario above, there is a chance that the hard drive could crash, a virus could infect the system and her file, and her laptop, a portable device that she carries everywhere, could be stolen. Given these facts, the data deserve at least to be archived to several floppies, one stored at her home, one at her office, and another sent to a friend or relative. Assuming that the data could not be replaced, the cost and time involved in making several CD-ROMs seems very reasonable. What's more, at least one good quality printout on acid-free paper should be made as well. In a worst-case scenario in which all of the digital data perish, Jane will be able either to rekey the thesis into her computer or, more reasonably, feed the printed manuscript into a flat bed scanner equipped with optical character recognition (OCR) software to recreate the digital file.

These two scenarios illustrate a practical approach to managing risk, as illustrated in the process shown in Figure 6-2 and further described below.

1. *Identify and quantify the data at risk.* The first step in managing the risk of digital data loss is to identify and quantify the data at risk and to specify the application used in writing the data. Record its identifiers: storage location or path, file size, file and folder names, date of last save, and data type such as text, image, sound, video, or animation. Here's an example: Data consists of a 1.02-MB text file, "JanesThesis.doc," saved on March 13 of 2001 as a Microsoft Word 2000 document, residing on the hard drive in Jane's laptop. Note that the data identifiers become valuable data that should be archived for future use.

   In larger organizations, there may be tens of thousands of text documents, hundreds of electronic presentations, project management files, thousands of images, and hundreds of thousands of email messages at risk. In these situations, it often makes sense to perform regular data audits, patterned after periodic financial audits, to keep track of the data of an organization. Since data are assets, they should be subject to traditional accounting practices. Not only should the origin and current location of data be known, but also, like other assets, data should be categorized and organized in a way that supports the auditing process. That is, someone

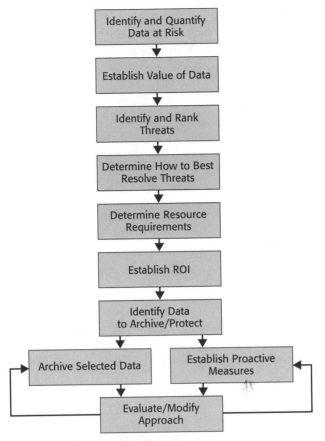

Figure 6-2 Managing Risk of Data Loss.

with the appropriate authority should be able to retrieve any particular data in the organization within minutes.

2. *Establish the value of the data.* Some data have more value than others. The value of data includes not only the production costs (time and materials) involved in data creation, but also replacement costs. Data may have sentimental value as well, based on emotional factors. For example, an image of a little boy on a beach captured with a digital camera may have very little inherent value. Perhaps the boy is unknown and the beach one of dozens of similar beaches in southern California. However, if the photographer is world-famous for his work, the image may be priceless.

Conversely, if the photograph is of a little boy who was recently killed in a hit-and-run accident, then the photo may have immense sentimental—but by no means priceless—value to his parents and grandparents. That is, his parents would not likely sell their home and car to buy the photograph. Finally, if the photograph was taken by a novice art student as part of a homework assignment and is one of dozens of similar photographs taken of the boy, then the value is relatively low—unless the student eventually becomes a great photographer, or the boy a celebrity. In each case, the value of the data is a judgment call. Collectors and private citizens routinely gamble on keeping objects that may appreciate in value and attain the status of antiques.

In the commercial arena, the value of data is often less fuzzy. A 1,000-image digital library may be worth $350,000 to a marketing firm, based on annual sales, cost of acquiring the images, and other easily quantified data.

The value of data is often highly time dependent. For example, if the photograph is needed for the cover of a major news magazine, then it may be worth tens of thousands of dollars to the publisher—as long as the photo makes it to press by the deadline. After the deadline has passed, the digital photograph may be worthless to the magazine. Similarly, if the photograph was taken by a true master, then the value of the data may increase sharply after the master's death, a common pattern in the art world.

3. *Identify and rank the threats.* Assuming that the data in question have some value, consider the possibilities of data loss, including those shown in Figure 6-1, and rank the threats according to the data type involved and why and how the data are maintained. For example, Jane probably ranks hardware failure, theft, accident, and operator error higher on her thesis threats list than software failure, corporate espionage, or network failure. Note that threats, like value, are time dependent. For example, the likelihood of Jane's laptop failing increases with time. At some point, her laptop will fail, even if she stores it in a safe, simply because the battery will eventually break down and corrode.

4. *Determine how to best resolve each threat.* At this stage, the techniques and processes best suited to resolving each threat are determined, within the constraints of available technologies. For example, referring to Table 6-1, the threat of natural disasters can be mitigated by creating frequent backups that are stored offsite, by establishing a disaster recovery center, and by taking out insurance on the hardware, network wiring, and other information infrastructure.

A reasonable backup scheme for a large organization might entail making a nightly tape backup that is stored offsite in the safe of a trusted and bonded employee. Similarly, a data recovery center should include backup servers and devices capable of reading backups, located a reasonable distance from the main site. What constitutes a reasonable distance depends on the natural threats to the primary center. For example, if the business is located on the bank of a river that has a history of flooding its banks every few years, then the offsite disaster recovery center should be located outside the river's flood plain.

Another approach is to resolve threats by outsourcing, as in using an external Storage Service Provider (SSP). However, outsourcing involves other work, such as performing a background check on the SSP. The vendor's market share, critical reviews of its products, financial status, and word-of-mouth reputation should be researched since they are critical to determining the long-term viability of the company. The assumptions made on outsourced service should be backed up with a service guarantee regarding the speed and reliability of their service. Any agreement with an SSP vendor should include an escrow account for the data and documentation on how the data can be restored to another SSP or other service provider. An insurance policy from a third-party insurer is a traditional way of managing risk as well.

5. *Determine resource requirements.* Once data have been identified, their value established, and the risks of loss identified and ranked, the next step is to determine what resources are required to protect the data. The goal at this stage is to identify the cost and time issues involved in archiving data, based on assumptions of how data will actually be preserved. For

example, properly archiving 1,000 digital images to CD-ROM, including creating a stand-alone database indexed to image number with two keywords per image, might take $4 per image for digitizing, CD-ROM blanks, database software, and about 10 minutes per image for indexing. Thus, the project would entail $4,000 and four 40-hour weeks from someone who is familiar enough with the content to index it properly.

6. *Establish return on investment (ROI).* The next step in determining whether or not it's worth the time and money to archive data is to determine the return on investment, or ROI, for each piece of data or library. The formula for return on investment, usually expressed as a percentage, is:

$$\text{ROI (\%)} = [\text{Value} \div \text{Investment}] \times 100$$

In calculating the ROI, the ratio of the cost savings over the money invested, all values should be converted to monetary figures. For example, four 40-hour weeks might be equivalent to $5,000, including overhead. Referring to the example mentioned in #5, the 1,000 digital images, if the value of the image library is $350,000 and the total investment is $9,000 ($4,000 for digitizing and media supplies plus $5,000 for 160 hours of work), then the ROI is:

$$\text{ROI} = [\$350,000 \div \$9,000] \times 100 = 38.9 \times 100 \text{ or } 3,890\%$$

That is, the investment returns almost 39 times the amount of money invested. However, not all returns are this significant, or the decision to archive the data so obvious. Consider that if the value of the library is $10 per slide or $10,000, then the ROI is:

$$\text{ROI} = [\$10,000 \div \$9,000] \times 100 = 1.1 \times 100 \text{ or } 110\%$$

That is, the ROI is only 110 percent. At this level of return, it isn't obvious whether or not to archive the data. If the decision maker is highly risk averse, he may decide to invest the $9,000 with the hopes of saving $1,000 later. However, he would also incur a certain cost of $9,000. A more risk tolerant person might simply decide to save the $9,000 and invest it elsewhere, instead of incurring a fixed lost opportunity. Similarly, if the data have no sentimental value, but only economic worth, then it may be cheaper to simply insure the data through a commercial agency, assuming that the policy cost is significantly less than the value of the data.

7. *Identify data to archive or protect.* Given the ROI figures for each file or data collection, the next step is to rank the data by ROI and then define the ROI cutoff for the archiving process. The cutoff value is in part determined by personal preference (remember, some people are more risk averse than others). The decision should also be based on simple economics. For example, if the budget will only support $5,000 worth of archiving activity, then data with the greatest ROI should be archived first, walking down the ROI ranking, until the budget is exhausted.

8. *Archive the selected data.* Once the data destined for archiving have been identified, the next step is to do the work. If an external SSP is involved, then this stage primarily involves moving data to their database through the Internet. If the archiving is done internally, then the appropriate backup procedures should be followed, with backup tapes or CD-ROMs moved offsite.

9. *Establish proactive measures.* A critical step in managing risk of data loss is to take a proactive stance in working with data. That is, instead of thinking of data only after it has been processed, formatted in final form, and is ready for archiving, it should be considered at all stages as part of an ongoing process. Proactive measures call for purchasing name-brand hardware, making frequent backups, using antiviral software to scan documents before they are loaded onto a hard drive, and saving files frequently as they're being processed to protect them from a software glitch or hardware failure (see threats, Figure 6-1). Something as simple as setting the *autosave* feature within Microsoft Word to save a file every five minutes can guard against massive data loss in the event that the operating system freezes or the power is suddenly disrupted. Similarly, obvious safety precautions, such as not loading software and files from unknown sources before scanning them for viruses, have few up-front resource requirements. Such sources include email attachments and files transferred on floppy or zip disks.

10. *Evaluate and modify the approach.* Feedback from periodic evaluations is key to the success of any management project. Too often, the only feedback in a data loss management project comes too late, when it's determined that the backup procedure doesn't actually work. There are accounts of actual cases where backups made by companies over periods of years contain nothing at all. For example, recall Ed's experience, detailed in Chapter 3, when he discovered that the backup tapes were unreadable because the heads on the tape drives were skewed.

Obvious questions to ask—and answer—during the evaluation stage include:

- Do the backups work?

- How well do the media tolerate storage?

- Are the storage conditions optimal for the media?

- Can the system be restored to normal from the backup tapes or CDs alone?

- How long does it take to fully restore the system?

- What resources, in terms of people and time, are required?

- If the system isn't perfect, what is the success rate and how can it be improved?

- What is the cost of the program, and what is the cost of a restoration, in terms of lost productivity and computer system downtime?

Unfortunately, surprisingly few companies—and even fewer individuals—have a data loss management plan. That is, they may have an inkling of what should be done and perform backups relatively regularly because everyone knows that backups are important. However, unless there's a written plan that can be read, examined, scrutinized, and followed, one or more of the above stages will be skipped or shortchanged. In particular, without a written plan in place, there is a much greater likelihood that there will be an actual data loss incident. As described here, there are ways to control and understand the economic ramifications of data loss and reduce the chances of it recurring in the future.

Managing Data Recovery

Whereas managing the risk of data loss can be considered a fire drill, being confronted with a real disk crash is akin to being faced with a real fire. Not only are there time pressures, heightened emotions, and reputations on the line, but normal business operations may be temporarily suspended. In addition to accruing fixed costs, loss of income while the system is inoperable can be significant, to the point that a company or individual may never fully recover from the disaster. However, just as a fire drill prepares everyone to act appropriately in the event of a real crisis, the often arduous challenge of data recovery can be managed as well.

Figure 6-3 illustrates the steps involved in managing data recovery; the steps are detailed below.

1. *Identify and quantify data loss.* Faced with a disk crash, stolen laptop, or server crash, one's first step in managing data loss is to determine, as accurately as possible, what has been lost. Often, this determination is expressed in terms of a certainty factor. For example, an IS manager may be 90 percent certain that all of the text files for a new presentation were lost when he dropped his laptop. Since it's practically impossible to read the crashed media to tell what it contains by mere visual inspection, the suspected and desired file may actually reside on another disk or other laptop. The only way to know for certain is to attempt to recover the data.

2. *Establish value of data.* As in managing data loss, establishing the value of lost data is key to moving forward. To determine the value of lost data, estimate its replacement value. If the replacement cost is trivial, as when the data on a drive or other media can be downloaded from the Web in a few minutes, then proceeding with a recovery procedure may not make business sense. Conversely, if the staff expect their files immediately and customers are clamoring for their data, the value of lost data may be high.

   Personal data, such as bank account numbers, checkbook balances, and pictures of relatives, have known values. At a minimum, each loss can be equated to the amount of time

Figure 6-3 Managing Data Recovery.

involved in rekeying. For example, reentering checkbook balances is simply a time-limited activity, especially when the original checkbook is available. When users realize the time involved in reentering nine months of bank statements, last year's tax return information, and redigitizing family photos, the replacement value of data becomes very obvious. Of course, establishing the value of lost data is facilitated if a company or the individual participates in a periodic data audit that identifies and categorizes all of the digital data holdings. If the data available to be recovered are predefined, the time pressure that builds up in data recovery situations can be controlled.

3. *Identify potentially recoverable data.* Identifying potentially recoverable data is really about identifying the media and hardware that may be recoverable. That is, it's rare that a single file can be identified and recovered on a crashed laptop disk. Rather, an attempt is made to recover an entire disk, in the hope that the desired files will be recovered in the process.

4. *Determine how best to recover data.* The avenues available for data recovery range from shareware recovery utilities to onsite consultant services and commercial data recovery services. The issues to consider in the selection process include the cost of the service, security of sensitive data, turnaround time, the nature of the data, and the likelihood of success. For example, if the data consist mainly of bank account numbers, hospital patient data, including names of VIPs who tested positive for the HIV virus, and other highly sensitive data, then an in-house approach may be best. An in-house IS staff member may be able to rescue a crashed disk drive, for example, by using a few utilities. However, if cost and security are secondary issues and the probability of recovery must be as large as possible, then a commercial service that specializes in data recovery is usually the best option. Even commercial services, which have a higher success rate than the typical internal service, boast best-case success rates of only 85 to 90 percent.

5. *Determine resource requirements.* The economics of data recovery are such that time is usually the limiting factor. Commercial services have a turnaround time of between 24 and 48 hours, returning the recovered data on CDs, Zip disks, or other media by overnight courier. Some commercial services offer do-it-yourself utilities, which are much more affordable than the onsite technicians.

As a point of reference, the best known commercial recovery houses typically have a minimum charge for looking at media, on the order of $100–$200, whether or not they can recover data from it. Asking one of the commercial houses to recover a 1.4-MB floppy disk for $200 may seem high or a bargain, depending on the data. If it contains the only full copy of Jane's thesis and her thesis defense is less than a week away, then Jane may be happy to pay \$200—or \$2,000 for that matter.

6. *Establish likely ROI and probability of success.* Determining the likely ROI should take into account the fixed cost of the system, which may be down or unusable until the data are restored. The probability of success must also be considered. For example, if Jane's thesis is worth \$5,000 to her and the cost of recovery is \$200, then the ROI is computed as:

$$ROI = [\$5,000 \div \$200] \times 100 = 25 \times 100 = 2,500\%$$

However, assuming the best self-reported service scores are correct, then Jane can only reasonably expect to recover up to 85 percent of her manuscript. Stated another way, there is an 85 percent chance that her thesis will be recovered. Expressed in ROI terms, the likely ROI becomes:

$$Likely\ ROI = [\$5,000 \div \$200] \times 100 \times 0.85 =$$
$$25 \times 100 \times 0.85 = 2,125\%$$

The \$200 represents a gamble, with fairly good odds, but it is a gamble nonetheless.

7. *Identify data to recover.* Given the ROI and probability figures, the next step is to identify exactly which hard drives, tapes, and other media to process for data recovery. If two dozen PCs were involved in a fire, then it may not make sense, given that a business in that situation may be financially extended, to recover data from all two dozen hard drives. In this case, it usually makes more sense to identify who was assigned to each PC and determine who in each workgroup was likely to have most complete, relevant, and up-to-date data.

8. *Attempt to recover selected data.* The result of the data recovery process is rarely a single file, but rather a partially recovered volume—a hard drive, for example—that may bear no resemblance to the original file structure on the volume. That is, there may be one long list of 3,000 files, devoid of folders or other directory information. With luck, the most important data will be recovered from the volume as well as the other, unnecessary files.

9. *Establish and modify data risk management.* If a data risk management process were in place and recovery went smoothly, then there may be no need to modify the process.

However, if some data could not be saved or there was significant damage to the media, such as broken tapes, then the management process should be modified. For example, simple changes like using new media every month would solve the media failure problem and greatly simplify the data recovery process next time. Similarly, if no data risk management program was in place, then this would be the perfect time to implement one. With the thought of the data loss fresh on everyone's mind, acquiring funding for the activity and establishing the political momentum behind the thrust is much easier than when everything is running smoothly.

THE DATA RECOVERY BUSINESS

Even with policies and procedures in place, odds are that sooner or later, chaos happens, and most companies and individual computer users will be faced with media and hardware failure. Most of the corporate computer failures will be handled by commercial utilities and in-house IS staff. However, for the high-profile, critical-data recovery projects, specialized data recovery services are available. The top recovery companies, such as Ontrack and DriveSavers, each handle over 5,000 recovery cases a year, primarily from commercial clients but also from educational, government, and private users. Prices vary depending on the operating system, the size of the hard drive or other damaged media, the nature of the work, and the cost of the media—typically CD or tape—that the recovered data will be delivered on. The top companies can provide a variety of services including rebuilding hard drives. When comparing the two dozen or so national recovery services, it may be difficult to determine whether or not their work will violate the drive manufacturer's warranty. In addition, many recovery services will not work on disks that use compression or other nonstandard formatting. Most services discourage users from attempting to run repair utilities because they may overwrite data and make it virtually impossible for the service to recover the data.

An obvious issue in evaluating these commercial service options is deciding whether they are reasonable for individuals. Most individual users will try a $50 commercial disk recovery utility as a first attempt at recovering data. However, as noted above, this adversely affects the odds that a commercial service could recover the data. If the data are important enough, it makes sense to go for the highest rate of return possible first. The most economical solution is to proactively initiate a data loss management program before the loss occurs.

Regarding the assessment of commercial recovery services, the most important factor is to perform the assessment before the service is required. That is, the determination of the best vendor for data recovery should be made before time pressure demands that it be done instantly. For larger businesses, part of the vendor evaluation should include the submission of a crashed hard disk to assess the responsiveness, success rate, and overall service level of each vendor.

· ·

TAKING A PROACTIVE STANCE

This chapter ends the section on Economics. Whereas the previous chapter explored the value of digital data in today's technologic society, this chapter examined the steps that can and should be taken to safeguard data deemed valuable. As illustrated here, it's usually more economical to have a process in place for managing the risk of data loss than to handle data loss as an afterthought.

However, human nature, limited time and money, and a higher personal tolerance for risk sometimes lead to situations where precautions against data loss are minimal. In those cases, there are sound processes for managing the data recovery process so that it occurs as effectively and economically as possible. There are also established businesses to aid individuals and corporations in the recovery process.

FOUR

Society

7

Pervasive Data

A veritable United Nations team of suppliers, engineers, and laborers builds today's computers. Skilled assemblers in Ireland may use microprocessors designed and manufactured in the United States, combined with RAM from Japan, disk drives manufactured in Mexico, and circuit boards designed and manufactured in Taiwan to create desktop and laptop computers sold primarily in the United States. With the exception of the United States, the penetration of microcomputers in the countries involved in the manufacture of PCs has been relatively minor. Scarce living space and office space, lack of a wired infrastructure, and the cultural bias of business professionals against devices viewed as secretarial tools have contributed to the lack of demand. In addition, U.S. marketing efforts in the 1980s and 1990s focused on the domestic market. As a result, the early computerization that occurred in most of the countries outside of the United States filled a real need, not a synthetic demand generated by a Madison Avenue advertising campaign.

When a new information technology comes along in the United States, vendors and those interested in technology for technology's sake typically attempt to apply the technology as a cure-all for society's woes. An initial period of hype, where interested parties promote the technology as a means of transforming society, gives way first to disappointment and then to a period of realism where the technology is applied to logically appropriate niches. This marketing tactic, while not limited to the United States, is extremely apparent when domestic companies attempt to apply information technologies to every possible problem in order to increase computer sales. Often the problems don't warrant the use of a PC, which may actually disrupt the existing workflow.

For example, despite clinician resistance, computer vendors often attempt to sell PC-based clinical information systems that interrupt the normal flow of information between clinician, patient, and nurse. Forcing health care professionals to communicate indirectly through a desktop PC that takes up valuable desktop space and that requires everyone to queue up in order to interact with the keyboard is rarely viewed as progress. It's only recently, with more compact computers, portable devices, and software that supports the existing work flow, that clinical computing is gaining some degree of acceptance among the general medical community in the United States. This experience highlights how technologies are most influential and least disruptive when they are selectively applied in a manner that supports existing workflow. This belief in the universal problem-solving ability of computers—that computers could cure all problems—dominated U.S. R&D in the last two decades of the 20th century and has led to the idea of pervasive computing: the anytime, anywhere ability to create, store, and retrieve data.

Many countries, like most of those in the Pacific Rim, didn't make the investment in wired networks and desktop PCs. Instead, free of the constraints of legacy systems, they have been able to go directly to pervasive computing, leapfrogging—but also learning from—the expensive, invasive computing experience of businesses in the United States. For example, whereas very few Japanese business professionals or general consumers have ever interacted with the Web through a desktop PC, millions of Japanese access the Web every day through miniature, wireless NTT DoCoMo handsets. Similarly, in many African countries, where there have been insufficient resources to run copper cables from one village to the next, relatively inexpensive cell phones provide reliable communications.

This chapter explores the social phenomenon of pervasive computing—the explosive increase in the creation of digital data in all areas of life—from the perspective of technological, cultural, and economic change agents. It identifies and examines the nature of the key change agents, from developments in virtual reality to international regulations and rising consumer expectations. It also explores the implications of the data explosion for digital data management.

A Visit to the Rim

After Roger's harrowing experience with his flooded laboratory (detailed in Chapter 4), he decided to accept an open invitation to visit an old friend in Singapore. Once there, Roger noted that virtually everyone carries a cell phone and that even the hotel rooms have high-speed Internet connectivity. However, what he found most remarkable was how the country managed to seamlessly incorporate information technology into its social fabric without adversely changing the culture. High technology coexists with and supports conventional and even unusual methods of data communications.

For example, many of the mall-based restaurants display menus in the form of photographs paired with graphic symbols posted above the order window. As patrons line up in front of the order window, they take from a row of containers car-key-sized pieces of plastic that correspond to their menu selection and place the plastic pieces on their food trays. The color of the plastic piece is significant, as is the shape. Color indicates, for example, the type of meat in the dish—red for pork, green for chicken, yellow for fish.

The plastic pieces have multiple uses. To the cashier operating the modern electronic cash register, the symbols are a quick way to enter prices, since the cash register keys correspond to the shape and color of plastic pieces. To the frontline cook, symbols represent a way to evaluate upcoming demand. With a glance at the trays in the queue, he knows what to throw in the wok or on the grill and when to use his cell phone to send a short text message to his supplier a block away for more ingredients.

Roger's friend in Singapore, Sam, a part owner of one of the mall-based restaurants, explained to Roger that the icon-based language provides a simple, common language between customers and the cashier, between the customer and the frontline cook, and between the counter help and the cooks in the back. The cell phone, like the electronic cash register that tracks sales for the government auditors, fits seamlessly into the workflow.

As part of the tour, Sam took Roger into the kitchen to meet his staff. Sam, who was all thumbs around anything other than a keyboard, couldn't resist showing off his prowess with the meat cleaver—and split his thumb in the process. Sam quickly wrapped his thumb with a clean cloth and the two jogged to Roger's car. By the time the two made it to the emergency room entrance, they were greeted by a health care professional dressed in the universal white coat. However, there were no insurance forms to fill out and no lengthy interview about health care provider. Sam was whisked away, and Roger was told that he could leave his cell phone number and that someone from the hospital would call when Sam was ready.

Before Roger left the hospital, he investigated the hospital information system, which was more advanced than anything he had seen in the states. A nurse showed how the surgical team would verify the availability of a surgical suite for Sam and a view of the recovery room, where data from Sam, such as his temperature or pulse, would be available to the surgical staff via computer from anywhere in the hospital. When Sam was discharged two hours later, his entire electronic medical record had been updated to reflect the procedure. Sam's data could be combined with national databases, allowing hospital administrators to make comparisons of use patterns of certain drugs by hospital, region, or nation.

Back Home

After Roger's brief two-week stay in Singapore, he was eager to continue with his training for an upcoming Marine Corps marathon. On his way home from work, he stopped by a mall, in search of a sports drink for his longer runs. Roger noted the chip delivery person who used a handheld laser barcode reader to count and categorize stock in the store. When Roger brought his selection to the checkout counter, he also noted how the results of the UPC scan showed up on an LCD monitor mounted on the register, all indexed to his special shopping card ID number. He knew that his shopping pattern, from brand selections to the time of day he tended to shop, was being stored in a database somewhere that would eventually be mined to determine, for example, his likelihood of buying a new brand of exercise drink.

The next morning, during his run, Roger felt a twinge in his left knee as he came down from a curb and soon made an appointment with his primary care physician. A week later, Roger was in his physician's office. Unfortunately, his physician hadn't had time to locate—much less read—

Roger's paper-based medical record. What's more, Roger had to spend a half-hour filling out insurance forms. When Roger was finally granted the short five minutes of physician time that Roger was allotted, he wasn't convinced that his physician had any clue about the severity of his knee problem. Frustrated, Roger stopped by his corner health food store and bought some herbal supplements.

About a month later, stretching a few hundred yards behind the starting line, Roger's knee felt better than ever. He verified that his radio frequency tracking medallion, which was coded with his running number, was securely attached to his shoes. Roger's medallion allowed anyone on the Web to track his progress along the race course. As he passed each checkpoint, his medallion was detected and the time and place were fed into a database. After crossing the finish line, Roger, exhausted, but happy with his accomplishment, retrieved his bag of belongings, including his cell phone. Unfortunately, he had to wait until he returned to his hotel room to contact his family—his cell phone didn't work in the Washington, D.C. area. A week after the race, fully recovered, Roger was excited to receive mail from the marathon organizers. The mail contained a personalized printout of his split times, average time, and other information that would be useful in his training next year.

In the same batch of mail, Roger found a bill for unpaid medical fees from his physician's office for the knee checkup, as well as a notice that the office visit fee for insured patients had jumped from $5 to $10, effective immediately. There were no details on the bill, other than "office visit," and no information that would help Roger avoid knee problems later or even no hint whether his complaints and concerns would ever find their way into his medical record.

· ·

· ·

CHANGE AGENTS

Roger's experiences in the United States and Singapore highlight cultural differences in how different data are valued. In the United States, the handling of medical data is abysmal, despite the amount of money devoted to medicine. Paradoxically, the systems established to automate the purchase and stocking of chips and even the system to track the progress of marathon runners have not been successfully applied to medicine.

Only a handful of hospitals in the United States can track the whereabouts of a patient in his path through a surgical procedure, for example. In comparison, the radio frequency ID tag system used by the U.S. military can track the location of a pallet of ammunition anywhere in the world. The military maintains a database that provides a history of the movement of any piece of equipment from the time it leaves the factory. In addition, the radio frequency ID tag on a pallet of ammunition or on the carrier of a cruise missile can be queried directly by a soldier in the field, using a handheld device.

In contrast, although the restaurants and stores in Singapore do most things the old-fashioned way, their medical system, especially their electronic medical system, is superior to most systems in the United States. Similarly, although the cell phone system in Singapore is relatively new, it's far more reliable and provides better coverage than any system in the United States. Whereas Roger couldn't use his cell phone because of incompatibilities of his hardware or because his service provider didn't cover the D.C. area, cell phone users in Singapore can choose a handset that not only works throughout their country but throughout the Pacific Rim as well. The same holds true for cell phone users in the European Union. Because of international standards and better coverage, a cell phone user in Denmark can travel to Spain and use the same phone.

The differences in how computer and communications technologies are applied in different countries obviously reflect more than the availability of technology. The particular application of technologies and, by extension, the type of data generated and stored by a society, is a function of interdependent cultural, economic, and technologic factors or change agents.

For example, the use of plastic tokens in the food malls of Singapore illustrates how the ready availability of digital communications and computation devices and services is necessary but not sufficient in and of itself to transform every business transaction or personal encounter into bits and bytes. The fit of a particular technology in a given area is a complex function of availability, cost, return on investment, training requirements, personal and cultural biases, and, most importantly, the changes required to integrate the technology into established ways of doing things.

For example, the electronic cash registers in the food malls create transactional data records that can be analyzed for trends—which meals are popular on what days, for example—that can help the restaurant owner estimate her needs for the following day. Similarly, the cell phone network, already in place, allows a restaurant manager to quickly send email to all of her suppliers and get the best price on ingredients as they're needed. The cell phone allows the owner and the supplier to continue in a dialogue that may have started decades earlier, one based on personal trust and familiarity, as well as prompt payment on the restaurant owner's part for quality products from the suppliers.

However, not too long ago, the cell phones weren't used by managers to call for supplies, and the cash register consisted of merely a little wooden box. Something about the *technology*, the *economics* of the situation, and the *culture* was enough to encourage restaurant owners to purchase cash registers and cell phones. That is, there were specific, interrelated environmental, technical, social, accelerants, or change agents that contributed to the move toward pervasive computing, and, by extension, the pervasive data phenomenon (see Figure 7-1).

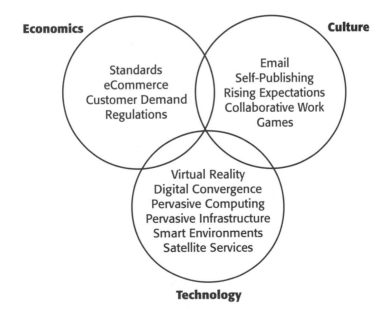

Figure 7-1   Pervasive Data Change Agents.

Technology

From a technologic perspective, the exponential rise in the amount of data—in particular, digital data—that is being generated, manipulated, and eventually archived is due to a myriad of technologic advances. Even though the contemporary technologies that contribute most prominently to pervasive data are built on the shoulders of giants from the past, the key technologic developments include new forms of virtual reality, the digital convergence of entertainment, education, and communications, pervasive computing and infrastructures, smart environments, and increasingly affordable and available satellite services.

Although the holodeck in *Star Trek: The Next Generation* probably represents the ultimate in a virtual reality technology, authors of good books have been transporting readers to places and placing them in heart-stopping situations for centuries. What's different today is the new data modalities and higher bandwidth computer systems to help create more realistic illusions of reality. For example, avatars and bots, which are simulations of human actors, are being used to provide interfaces to applications and information. Bots or software robots, when combined with text-to-speech (TTS) and an intelligent text interpretation front end, can carry on conversations with users in a manner that often seems real. Haptic or force-feedback systems, which are used in flight simulators for the military, in clinical simulators for medical students, and in commercial and home-based computer games, provide an added sense of realism.

New data modalities are also affecting everyday interaction with data. For example, digital wallets, based on wireless technologies, allow customers to make charge purchases without ever taking their charge cards out of their wallets. Wearable exercise monitors track fitness levels by monitoring heart rate in response to exercise. Personal, digital simulations allow patients to explore what-if scenarios, from predicting the effects of plastic surgery or exercise to diet and drug therapy for diabetes. EBooks, digital movie theaters, invoices and receipts posted on the Web, online banking, and music CDs are replacing their analog and nonelectronic equivalents. In addition, many of the new data modalities facilitate other technologies. For example, the satellite-based global positioning service (GPS) devices that allow hikers to find their way home enable tactical bombers to locate their targets with pinpoint accuracies.

The digital convergence of TV, movies, music, computer games, voice communications, the Web, and other data into a standard digital representation capable of being transported, manipulated, and reproduced on common hardware is increasing the creation of digital data. For example, digital handheld devices can now display video images, handle two-way email and voice communications, play computer games—either solo or with other networked players—play an MP3 music file, and help students manage their studies and their time.

With convergence to a digital standard, the amount of digital data that must be cataloged or at least temporarily archived is increasing exponentially. Consider, for example, how quickly the CD supplanted vinyl records and how recordable CDs and MP3 music systems are replacing cassette tapes. The same phenomenon is occurring with DVDs and analog video tapes. To increase the pressure on consumers to move to the more expensive—but cheaper to produce—DVD format, the studios that produce the content are inflating the price of video tapes and limiting their production.

Gateway, Radio Shack, and others have tried to combine their computer systems with TV and interactive computer games, but the content wasn't there and the hardware wasn't yet up to the task. That has changed today with the introduction of powerful game consoles that pack more power and provide better Internet connectivity than most desktop PCs. As noted, the computer game industry is growing faster than the general computing industry. Digital technologies, such as personalized avatars and higher-performance game consoles, are increasing the realism and entertainment value of computer games. Game consoles are rapidly approaching the performance and resolution required to support photorealistic scenes and actions. Similarly, the software developed for modern game systems takes advantage of the power of the digital microcomputer at a rate higher than software development in the general computing industry.

Web radio, just-in-time multimedia learning, virtual reality systems for education and entertainment, and other forms of Web- and media-based entertainment and education are increasingly popular alternatives and supplements to traditional media. In addition, the proliferation of desktop PCs, PDAs, cell phones, and other pocketable and wearable digital data devices are obvious contributors to the proliferation of digital data. However, less obvious and potentially more significant contributors to the pervasive data movement are the smart environments that surround us. For example, the typical modern luxury car has over a dozen microprocessors distributed throughout its system. The computer-controlled antilock braking system, the digital radio receiver, environmental control system, automatic transmission, fuel injection system, and onboard GPS-based navigation system may be supplemented with a cell phone system as well. On some models, an onboard microcomputer tracks mileage, speed, and other parameters that can be downloaded in the dealer's repair shop, suggesting what should be repaired or replaced before a problem actually develops.

Similarly, homes, which are increasingly microprocessor dependent, are the sources of torrents of digital data. Computer-controlled environmental control systems regulate temperatures throughout the day, saving energy at night by lowering the temperature during the winter, for example. Microprocessors control hot water heaters, the various cycles available in washing machines and dryers, the stitching patterns available on electronic sewing machines, the timing and power of microwave ovens, the messages stored in digital cordless phones and answering systems, security systems, and the timing of lights going on and off when no one is home. These and other systems are increasingly compatible with home computer systems, allowing everything to be networked and controlled and monitored by a PC.

Satellites compete with cable and terrestrial services for customers in the United States and provide the only means of access to digital data in many countries. In addition, the increasing number of digital satellite-based services is creating even more data that must be tracked and archived. Consider the automatic accident notification system available on some luxury cars. If one of these cars is involved in an accident, an onboard GPS collision detection system automatically notifies the nearest police and ambulance services.

As more people gain access to the Internet, whether by dial-up modem, slow-speed wireless modem, or high-speed fiber network, more and more digital data are being generated, accessed, and stored. Similarly, wireless companies are fighting over federal licenses for space in the radio frequency spectrum, cable companies are digging up city streets to lay copper and fiber optic cables, and microwave repeater stations dot the skyscrapers with their dish antennas—all in an effort to provide more bandwidth for digital data and voice communications. Pervasive hardware is adding to the digital data load as well. Smart phones, wireless personal information managers, and other palm-sized devices support time- and place-independent connectivity. Hardware is becoming ever present, more portable, easier to use, and, with the introduction of prepaid, disposable cell phones, even more affordable.

Economics

To an entrepreneur, the economics of technology are often as important as the original creative concept. For new devices and more efficient processes to become more than scribblings on a dinner napkin, the economics of the technology, in light of the overall economic environment, have to be considered. One of the key differences between a visionary and an entrepreneur is that the former can often spin fantastic tales of life and technologies in the future, but the latter can take dreams and turn them into reality.

Consider how a supportive economic environment helped boost the use of computers in K-12 schools by offering tax relief to computer companies that donated the computers. Similarly, co-marketing campaigns helped introduce computers into graduate schools throughout the country. These campaigns not only offered computer companies tax write-offs for their gifts but allowed the companies to be associated with a prestigious university. For example, Palm has made arrangements with several universities, such as Southwestern University and the University of South Dakota, to provide Palm Pilots to students and technical support for faculty.

As a result of donations and special discount programs, schools at all levels throughout the United States operate in a digital computing and communications environment. Parents contact their children's grade school teachers by email. Medical students review class notes posted to the Web. Professors post class readings and other notices to the Internet. Students increasingly exchange information and post questions through Internet bulletin boards and Web sites and take their exams on a computer, often from the comfort of their dorm rooms. Similarly, college students preparing for entrance into business, law, or medical school take their exams on a computer and receive their results within minutes instead of weeks.

The economic environment is defined in part by standards and regulations, especially those related to eCommerce, and in part by the simple demand for particular products and services, such as mass customization. The growth in mass customization, from companies that create custom-fitted designer jeans from body scans to user-designed cereals that are formulated to the customer's tastes, is increasing the storage requirements for customer-specific digital data. For example, the Levi's outlet in San Francisco creates a digital scan of the customer's silhouette and uses the digital data to create a pair of custom jeans. The fitting data, once generated, are archived for use in future purchases.

Standards for digital data transfer and storage enable disparate and remote devices to communicate and share data, whether because of symbiotic relationships or because of legal regulations. For example, several handheld digital devices are compatible with the infrared communications protocol supported by the Palm line of PDAs. By supporting the standard, these other devices, including optical character recognition (OCR) pens, can quickly and easily transfer data between devices. As a result, the data generated by a variety of means is available in a common format that can be managed and archived.

In many cases, the transfer of data between devices and systems is dictated by local, state, or federal regulations, and standards allow these communications to take place digitally. For example, the computer systems used by hospitals in the Veterans Administration Hospital System use a standard format for clinical and administrative data so that the information for a particular patient can be accessed, regardless of which hospital this patient was admitted to. Similarly, financial institutions abide by standards established by their industry to facilitate transfer of data between local branches and the federal banking system.

Where the government is involved, investment in the computerization of paper-based processes is often justified either by increased tax revenues or decreased spending. For example, in the United States, the IRS maintains a large taxpayer database—much larger and more complete than any domestic electronic medical record system—to help ensure reporting accuracy. The IRS takes an adversarial approach to maintaining taxpayer records, akin to the FBI's

Carnivore system that scans virtually every email document on the Internet. In contrast, approaches to computerization of records in other countries have resulted in monetary savings, but as a side effect, and not from design.

For example, in Holland, a parallel to the U.S. social security system was established shortly after World War II. As in the United States, the service had to be promoted at first because normally self-sufficient citizens felt embarrassed taking money from the government. However, the prevailing attitude quickly changed to one of entitlement. By the mid-1960s, five agencies operating in Holland were providing monetary support of the citizenry: through the general social assistance act, the unemployment act, the sickness benefit act, the disablement benefits act, and a general old-age benefit.

Through the 1980s and early 1990s these programs, which were run at local, regional, and national levels, were slowly computerized. However, as most of the early invasive computer projects were established, the agencies used their own standard for computer hardware, networking, and data format. In a move to streamline administration of the system, a major integration project was undertaken, resulting in a fully integrated system by 1995.

One of the first accidental discoveries made when the integrated system came online was that some citizens were double- or even triple-dipping. For example, the sickness benefit act covers the first year of an illness, after which time the disablement benefit act takes over. However, some citizens applied for and were receiving funds from both accounts. There were other, similar discoveries as well, resulting in a significant cost savings for the government.

One of the most significant economic factors behind the pervasive data phenomenon is the popularity of eCommerce. Doing business electronically over the Internet in the United States now accounts for about one percent of the multibillion dollar retail industry. Thousands of other retail and wholesale businesses regularly transact business over the Web. These businesses, from financial institutions to toy stores, capture and store transaction data that promote the use of data mining, customer profiling, and customer service.

Culture

Just as the cultural resistance to receiving government assistance had to be overcome for the U.S. social support services to survive, cultural perceptions and mores are affecting the rate at which digital data technologies are being embraced by the society as a whole. As a culture, we are now producing more digital data than ever before. For example, consider email, the "killer application" of the Internet, which is responsible for the generation of huge amounts of digital data, especially in corporate America. Email now overshadows all types of personal communications over the traditional mails. Because of the rapid decrease in the volume of traditional mail, the U.S. Postal Service is continually raising postage rates and curtailing traditional services. In addition, because the switch to digital communications is happening at such a rapid rate, the Postal Service is exploring ways to tap into the email market, such as by offering the electronic equivalent of certified mail.

Also contributing to the flood of data is the self-publishing movement, where anyone with access to a word processor and a laser printer can generate a book. Similarly, anyone with access to the Internet can create a Web site and post ideas to an electronic bulletin board. The quantity of digital data on the Web is growing rapidly, in part because of the ease with which writers can upload their work on the Web. Although there are issues of questionable data quality and the lack of peer review, the use of the Web as a vehicle for self-publishing continues to rise rapidly, with something on the order of a million new Web pages posted to the Internet every day.

The cultural trend of increased data production is visible in the eBook arena, where publishers accept electronic manuscripts for posting to the Web. There they can be downloaded, for a fee, and read on a laptop, PDA, or dedicated electronic book reader. However, the eBook phenomenon, while adding to society's store of digital data, doesn't necessarily fit the trend of rising customer expectations with products and services. Although there are exceptions, many of the eBook publishers impose little in the way of standards and allow any manuscript to be uploaded to the eBook publisher's Web site.

In the realm of rising customer expectations, museums and libraries are under increasing pressure to digitize their collections and put them on the Web, simply because it's possible and because it's been done by some institutions. Similarly, there is pressure on state and federal governments to continue to list their services on the Web. As a result, many state and federal notices, such as the availability of funds for special projects, are now available on the Web.

On the lighter side of reality, one of the more pervasive trends in the U.S. "plugged in" culture is an increasing appetite for continuous stimulation. On any given day in any major U.S. city, the sidewalks, parks, and shopping malls are filled with people toting portable radios; MP3 and CD players and cell phones adorn the ears of the young and old. Virtual chat rooms are more likely to be frequented than is the local pub, and virtual actors and environments are appreciated in movies as much as in reality. In addition to these sources of digital data, there is also a renewed interest in computer games as a pastime. As noted, game console sales are skyrocketing as games offer more power, flexibility, and capabilities to work with content on the Internet. Fortunately, game developers are more than happy to author the bits and bytes that transport gamers into interactive fictional virtual environments where they can take on roles from conquering new worlds to spelunking in search of treasure.

IMPLICATIONS FOR DIGITAL DATA MANAGEMENT

As this chapter illustrates, the start of the 21st century marks a time of explosive data growth. At issue is the type of data being created and archived, which is a function of the culture, economics, and available technologies. For example, it's easier to track a bag of potato chips on its two-week journey from a factory, through the domestic transportation system, to a warehouse, and finally to store shelves than it is to track a patient for six hours in a typical U.S. hospital. Experience from different societies suggests that, as an information technology is introduced into a culture, the quantity of digital data generated, manipulated, and archived will increase, but that the area of increase is a reflection of what the society values.

That is, the volume of data generated and ultimately archived in a given area is related to the value of the data only to the degree that the data reflect local preferences. For example, a potato chip company charged with maintaining a profitable distribution matrix will be concerned with historical trends in chip consumption, time to market, and other data. Conversely, a country that focuses on the health, welfare, and education of its population may use the same technology to create an electronic medical system that can communicate and archive patient data efficiently and effectively.

The issue of who decides what data are valuable and should be saved and what data should be disposed of seems critical in larger social systems, such as health care. In the United States, short-term economics often dictates many corporate practices, with little or no regard for time horizons past, say, five years. However, except for stockholders and those who like potato chips, it seems that the chip companies should decide the fate of their data. To allow other companies, such as large health care enterprises, to decide on their own how to handle patient data seems less appropriate. It may be more appropriate for federal legislation to decree the value of universal health care data.

The next chapter, The Socio-Technologic Future, continues the exploration of the social aspects of potential digital data loss, focusing on the new relationship modern society is developing with data.

The Socio-Technologic Future

As data become increasingly significant in our technologic, service-oriented society, our relationship with data will necessarily evolve, incorporating new behaviors, new rules, and a new set of values. The following vignette suggests that as data become less ephemeral and more real, future generations will have to grapple with complex social, legal, and economic issues that we can only anticipate today.

There was a click.

Still half-asleep, Ben Riley grimaced as he dislodged his blood-starved appendage from underneath the unfamiliar woman sleeping beside him. As he sat up in bed, his eyes tracked the extent of the bedroom and then fell on his companion. Oh, the avatar was exquisite—and much better than advertised. She had the tanned, taut skin of youth, infinitely deep brown eyes, cherry-red lips that bordered chalk-white teeth, and a voluptuous figure any man would die for. Her shoulder-length blond hair, laid out on the blue satin bedsheet, looked like a sunrise on a smog-free day. He should be pleased, he thought to himself; for in this world, where appearance was everything, she was his.

As promised, Miss May of 2027—a digital veneer of skin, hair, sound, and scent—transformed the physical presence of his girlfriend into a virtual object of utter sensual pleasure. For a split second, he became conscious of the ephemeral quality of Miss May and thought of Debbie, his roommate and physical companion, and the physical presence that gave Miss May tactile substance. With her long, shiny black hair and a trim figure, Debbie was attractive. However, when she was experienced as Miss May through Ben's sensory implants, she was a sexual fantasy come true.

The implants, inserted surgically when Ben was sixteen, were tuned to the frequency of his channel of the entertainment system, allowing him to see, hear, and smell—but not feel—whatever program was beamed into the apartment. When he was younger, he made use of his implants to listen to spiders walk across the floor by setting his entertainment system to amplify all sounds by a factor of a thousand. His thoughts were interrupted by another click. Whatever its origin, Ben was certain that it didn't belong in his environment. Ignoring the receding tingle in his right arm, Ben again surveyed Debbie's apartment. In the dimly lit bedroom, he experienced Debbie's idea of ultimate living as he saw the golden tassels drooping out of sanguine velvet borders of antique French tapestries reflecting off of the mirrorlike parquet floor. The massive teak table held a sterling silver candelabra and glittering place settings for two. Off to one corner, a set of chest-high mesquite bookcases displayed two leather-bound books with gilt trim, as well as dozens of delicate baubles. Ivory and green wallpaper, spotted every few feet with lush, green air plants, provided an appropriate backdrop for the Renoir. An antique armoire guarded the far corner of the room, and a crystal vase of magnolia blossoms graced the room with a sweet scent that was wafted about by the lazy ceiling fan. Outside, he could just make out a jazz band a block down the street, and in the corner in its litter box, was Tabs, the kitten avatar he bought for Debbie last week, fast asleep.

From his perch on the brass bed, he could see the pearly blue LEDs of the entertainment system embedded in the far wall. The bank of lights on the left—his channel, which he used to play his programs, superimposed on the general environment—blinked with a rhythm that seemed to match his heartbeat. Debbie's channel, which also broadcast the general living environment—the air plants, kitten, and table—wasn't executing any personal programs.

There was another click, much clearer now. Disentangling himself from Debbie's unconscious hug, Ben rolled out of bed. He walked over to the entertainment console and terminated the Miss May avatar with a full five minutes of life remaining on the pay-per-experience channel.

With a sigh, Ben keyed in the code to pause his channel on the entertainment system. There was a blinding flash of darkness as Ben's optical implants switched from the entertainment signal to signals from his own retinas. Simultaneously, the sudden, nearly tactile din of the street traffic shook Ben as the noise cancellation feeding his auditory implant went offline. The cacophony of traffic in the streets below, the hollow beat of footsteps from the apartment above, and the rolling of an empty trash barrel, kicked down the street by the scorching summer wind, clawed their way into his mind. Ben unconsciously curled his upper lip in disgust as the smell of decay, ozone, and sweat filled his nostrils.

Ben turned to face the living space. There was something strangely comforting in the aseptic white walls, interrupted by darker patches of spackling and the torn jazz poster that served as a placeholder for the Renoir. A recessed lighting unit with two burned-out bulbs; a one-piece, molded plastic table and chairs; and a plastic serving set for two constituted their physical possessions. The cracked gray linoleum floor was patched and worn in several places, and the gray particleboard bookcase held two plastic-covered tan volumes of virgin paper.

Confident that the apartment wasn't being burglarized, Ben restarted the general environmental program. Tabs was back, sleeping in her box, her chest rhythmically expanding and contracting in virtual life. The air plants again graced the walls, and the magnolia blossoms again filled the air with the sweet smell of life. Back in bed and in the serenity of Debbie's custom virtual world, he curled up to Debbie and began to fade into yet another world of his own making.

"Hi sweetie."

Ben blinked, temporarily trapped in the haze between sleep and consciousness.

"How are you, sweetie?" repeated the voice.

The voice was unmistakable. It was Sarah, the tour guide from San Francisco whom he net-dated over a year ago. Now she stood at the foot of the bed, her tall, slender silhouette rising from behind the curves and folds of Debbie's sheet-wrapped torso. Ben rolled out of bed again and stood to meet her. He tentatively pushed his hand forward and was relieved that his hand disappeared into the center of her chest.

Ignoring his response, she asked, "Don't you miss me? "

Ben took a moment to take in Sarah's hourglass figure, only partially obscured by a semi-transparent, silky black cloth.

Ben backed away from the bed and asked, "How did you get in?"

Sarah moved closer to Ben, her stiletto heels menacing the floor. She draped her weightless forearm on his shoulders, letting her hands dangle from her wrists, and whispered, "I thought it was time to pay you a visit."

He could smell her hair and almost feel the electricity of her body, even though he knew that the real Sarah was thousands of miles away, immersed in a virtual reality chamber where she could experience everything in the apartment.

"Are you still with *her*?" she retorted.

"You hacked the e-system. You know exactly who's here."

"Don't you miss me?" she queried, her eyes melting directly into his. Motioning to Debbie behind her, Sarah said, "I know you're not happy with *her*. If you were, you wouldn't be wasting your money on those brainless skin downloads."

"It's time you left."

Sarah continued, "All I want is to be with you again. Is that so bad?"

"Look. I have a life, a *real* life. Leave me alone."

"But don't you love me?" she repeated.

He distanced himself from her and turned toward the entertainment system.

"Ben, don't do it. If you do, you'll never see me again. Do you understand?"

Ben began working the controls.

Then there was a scream. He spun around to see Debbie sitting up in bed, clutching her chest, as waves of blood poured onto the sheets. He looked down at his splattered feet and the blood-streaked, military-style knife in his right hand.

When he realized what was happening, he dropped the knife, spun back around and keyed in the command to erase everything in memory. He pulled the archive crystal out of its container on the wall and, within seconds, reloaded Debbie's environment. He rushed over to Debbie, sweat trickling down his arms as he neared her.

"What's the matter, honey? You okay?"

"I had a terrible nightmare," she started. "You were with another woman—she held me down while you stabbed me with a knife. It was terrible."

Ben put his hand gently on her shoulder, "What a terrible dream. Can I get you something?"

"No. Just hold me."

And he did. Within a few minutes, she was fast asleep in his arms, even though his heart was still racing as he listened for the sound of a virtual intruder, disrupting the tranquility of the world he shared with her. It could have been worse, he thought. Besides his sleep, his only real loss was the week of training he invested in the kitten. Another day of work and he'd have enough eMoney to buy another kitten, or maybe even a miniature dachshund.

Finally, exhausted, confident that his new password was unbreakable, even by someone as determined as Sarah, he fell asleep.

Minutes or hours later—he couldn't tell—Ben suddenly found himself awake. Was there another click that woke him, or was it a dream?
. . . .

The vignette, an extrapolation of the contemporary computer game market—of which 50 percent of sales are to adult males—a few decades into the future, highlights many of the issues related to the increasing relevance of digital data in everyday life. In the pervasive data culture, the streams of 0's and 1's are becoming more than descriptors of what exists in reality; data are becoming reality. Today, data are increasingly valued as art, entertainment, a form of money, and a means to behavior modification. For example, Bill Gates doesn't hang expensive oils on the walls of his multimillion dollar house but displays whatever art suits his mood on wall-mounted LCD panels, from a library of digitized images. Similarly, companies spend millions of dollars on commercials designed to create desire where none existed before.

Unknowns

At the start of any relationship there are usually more questions than answers, and the relationship between Ben and Debbie—and their environment—provides the seed for a multitude of questions. For example, what will happen to the natural environment if the inhabitants of a city can see and smell green trees and grass-covered medians even if they're breathing carbon monoxide in an overpopulated, concrete-and-steel matrix that is devoid of anything resembling vegetation?

Who controls access to and pricing of data, such as the Miss May program? Are there privacy issues here? Is there a special tax on what some might consider pornography? Should the government be able to regulate what types of data Ben or Debbie download from the "OmniNet"? Should Ben be restricted in the age, sex, or species of the body downloaded? For example, what if the download is of a computer-generated, 12-year-old girl—or boy—or an 80-year-old man or woman? What if Ben prefers sex with a virtual seal or sheep? Should those concerned about animal rights be allowed to influence what Ben or Debbie do in the confines of their apartment? Furthermore, if some data are monitored, then how could Ben be certain that all data aren't monitored?

From a legal perspective, if Ben and Debbie Riley had been married for five years, would Ben's virtual relationship with Sarah have been legal grounds for divorce? What if the person controlling Sarah turned out to be a man instead of a woman? What if Sarah is actually run by an artificial intelligence program developed by a 12-year-old? What about the moral implications of the virtual affair, from either a social or a religious perspective? If the data from Ben's previous encounters with Sarah were archived in some FBI cybercrime database, could Debbie subpoena them in a real or virtual court hearing?

How do laws and rights developed for a physical world—such as protection against stalking—translate to virtual worlds? What penalties should be applied to cybercrime, such as virtual stalking, mugging, or, as explored in the sci-fi movie *The 13th Floor*, virtual murder? On a related issue, how will the increasing popularity of online mediation change the dynamics of the legal system? Can the original developer of a program that learns through experience be held liable for the end result of that learning, as parents are responsible for their children? Should there be a level of machine intelligence, like a human age of majority, above which the original developer is no longer held responsible for the actions of a program?

Although not up to the level displayed by Sarah, today's software robots or bots can be programmed to simulate personal encounters, including voice and facial expressions. Moreover, the voice as well as the face used by an avatar can be "borrowed" from anyone. For example, companies like LifeF/X and Haptek can take front and side headshots of anyone and turn them into realistic 3D "talking heads" that smile, wink, and lip sync to prerecorded words or to text-to-speech (TTS) engines from IBM and other vendors. As such, the likeness of anyone who has been photographed can be made to look real and its speech to say anything that the designer wishes. However, what of the intellectual property rights of the person photographed? As the use of photographs to create 3D avatars increases in popularity, will lawsuits be brought forth by the original models or even political figures and celebrities, limiting the use of their likenesses in the new medium? Will the current turmoil between traditional book authors and the publishing houses, who want to bring many of the book titles to eBooks without consulting with the authors, be repeated in the semivirtual world of avatars?

How will intellectual property rights of avatars and bots evolve? For example, if an avatar or a computer program creates computer art, to whom does the artwork belong—the author of the virtual environment or the person who manipulated the virtual environment to create the artwork? Similarly, in terms of authors receiving their just rewards, what is the relationship between money and eMoney?

How will a virtual veneer affect morality and, by extension, religion? How will unrestricted virtual realities alter social institutions, such as marriage? In a 24×7 plugged-in world, when does entertainment end and reality begin? When do data move from a personal record to a societal asset? How do our Constitutional rights affect freedom of data access?

Extrapolating to more complex data relationships, in a virtual world what constitutes a standard psychological makeup or normalcy in sexuality and gender preferences? Just as people can become addicted to the Internet experience, what are the psychological implications of online addictions? That is, if an online user engages in gender-inappropriate behavior, such as impersonating someone of the opposite sex online, or spends her time in games with explicit violence, is this a cause for concern? Should addictions or behaviors online be treated as psychological imbalances? In other words, at what point should human interactions with a virtual reality be treated as real?

Given the inevitable fluctuations in the political, economic, and natural environments, and in human nature itself, what data can and should be trusted? What will be the psychological significance of authoring nontangible works for ephemeral media instead of creating tangible documents, such as music CDs, books, and movies on DVD?

What of those who are frustrated with the data saturation and want to return to the pre-data days? What will be the fate of those who shun the digital world when eLearning, eBanking, and all of the higher-paying, nonlaborer jobs involve working with data in virtual worlds? How will life change for today's professional knowledge workers as they are transformed into professional knowledge brokers who are paid for their store of easily transferred data, and not for their ability to fill an office chair?

A Matter of Perception

Perhaps the greatest challenges in the evolution toward whatever the socio-technologic future has in store are related to perception and expectation. In our capitalistic society, consumers are accustomed to trading money for *things*. Even though the U.S. economy has shifted from a manufacturing to a service-oriented one, consumers—especially older consumers—are used to exchanging money, even if in plastic form, in exchange for something real. For example, many people don't use credit cards but prefer to use checks (to the consternation of everyone standing in line behind them) or cash. Bank ATMs are doing more business than ever, and subways, buses, telephones, newspaper machines, street-side doughnut vendors, and most of the services that commuters or pedestrians are likely to encounter still require cash. Similarly, despite the popularity of digital music downloaded to MP3 players and laptops, many listeners find it comforting to hold a CD in their hands and know that they can play the music at any time.

Despite our continued dependence on physical money and our need to receive physical goods in exchange, times are changing. Many consumers are increasingly accustomed to paying for ephemeral data—cable and satellite TV, for example—with nothing to show for their money after the experience is gone from memory.

Consider how the increasing relevance of digital data in everyday life is affecting the institution of the library. The availability of data over the Web is changing the evolving role of many libraries from an archive of books to an access point to digital data. For many potential library patrons, deciding whether or not to visit a library—in person or online—becomes a cost and time issue, in that many of the Web-based resources are available at home or at work through a PC, and there may be little motivation to visit a library in person. Most recent books, for example, are available at corner bookstores, and shopping at a bookstore is a social event, usually involving a coffee bar, bakery, and good conversation.

For those without the income to afford in-home or in-the-office access to the Web, the library remains a reliable resource. With these patrons in mind, many librarians are questioning the wisdom of paying database companies' relatively large monthly access fees but having nothing to show for their money when the subscription ends. However, as the demographics of library users change, the support for traditional library practices will likely diminish. One of the endangered practices is having a reference librarian on staff, even though many people, Internet equipped or not, don't know how to look up what they need to know.

The Duality of Data

There are two sides to most technologies and to most data. For example, atomic energy can power a satellite reliably for decades or destroy a city in a millisecond. The same technology used to provide patients with interactive alerts reminding them to take their medications or to remind a car owner that it's time to change the oil can be used to invade the privacy of consumers. Similarly, the automatic systems that allow drivers to pass through toll booths without having to stop, but instead have the toll automatically charged to their VISA account, also empower the police to track the average speed of a car from toll booth to toll booth and issue automatic tickets to speeding motorists. The core issue related to the duality of data is that of trust. Most educated people don't believe everything they see on TV or read in print and are extremely skeptical of what they read or see on the Web. This isn't to say that print generated with a word processor and then output to a laser printer is any more believable than bits displayed on a screen, but established processes and institutions have been developed to verify the accuracy of traditionally printed materials, such as books and academic journals. Even so, there are often economic or other motives to use data to imply one thing and deliver on another.

The issue of accountability is especially relevant on the Web, where the authors of content are unknown and generally unknowable. Because of the inexpensive Web authoring tools and clip art, it's possible for anyone with a modicum of experience with a word processor to create a Web site that has the look of a site developed by a $100 million corporation. Unfortunately, unsuspecting consumers of data on the Web may believe information generated by a mentally deranged, unemployed programmer on topics ranging from how to treat a life-threatening cancer to investing in the stock market.

The Broken Link

The relationship between man and data changed when the intermediary evolved from a simple intellectual fulcrum, such as a magnifying glass or an abacus, to a complex translation mechanism, such as an electron microscope or computer chip. That is, the direct link between man and data was broken when data moved from the directly observable to something that must go through multiple levels of translation before it can be interpreted or understood. This disconnect is most obvious in virtual reality applications, but it's also apparent when one uses cell phones or views a program on a TV.

Although the concept of virtual reality is often taken to mean full immersion in some other experience, the technology is actually pervasive today in everyday life. People carry on virtual conversations through cell phones. That is, each person is talking to a handheld device—an inanimate object—that creates a virtual link to another person. In effect, the two people are conversing with each other, almost with the fidelity and effect of meeting in person. At another level, the TV sets in most homes are a form of virtual reality, bringing a football game or a newscaster into the home. Because virtual reality technology is constantly improving, the definition of virtual reality keeps being pushed further ahead into the future, encompassing even more functionality.

TV has evolved from a simple virtual reality device—a small round tube with black-and-white images that could transport a boxing match into a bar for patrons to experience in real time—to widescreen, full-color, high-resolution home theater systems with surround sound. Similarly, the virtual reality of the music industry has evolved from early, wired stereo telephone systems that were used by patrons to listen to plays and music from the comfort of their homes, to MTV-type experiences, where musicians can be appreciated for their physical presence as well as their music. Similarly, the musicians are increasingly shown in fantastic situations through the wizardry of special effects.

The concept of accuracy, precision, and other statistical terms typically applied to data only makes sense when the data are compared to the physical world. In an MTV-type world composed of data—a virtual reality—accuracy, precision, and even concepts such as linear time that are normally taken for granted are meaningless. For example, what is the accuracy of a sound produced by a synthesizer that has no parallel in the physical world? Just as there are international weight and time standards for length, mass, and time, will there eventually need to be international standards for data as well? For example, with the time distortion possible with virtual reality, will a second of virtual time necessarily equal a second of real time? Should there be standard limits on ambient noise level, as there are in reality, even though extreme sound levels may not damage virtual hearing? Similarly, should there be standards for the intensity of smells and aromas, like those used in the perfume industry?

. . . .

REALITY CHECK

When considering the future of data in a socio-technologic culture, it's possible to overlook those in society who work with real objects—the janitors, repair staff, and other hands-on employees who make certain that power is available and that the computer hardware is functioning properly. At home, someone has to maintain the household, do the shopping, cooking, and cleaning. Even if most physical work is outsourced, until robots are as ubiquitous as they are in Steven Spielberg's *A.I.: Artificial Intelligence*, someone has to do the physical work.

When it comes to digital data, it isn't a question of "if we build it, they will come." Every successful relationship, even between data and society, requires work. Fortunately, with a shared vision of what the future holds, society can tolerate most bumps along the way. Assuming that data and the technologies that create them will continue to become increasingly pervasive and significant in our society, several issues and challenges will have to be resolved sooner or later. Some of these issues are relatively insignificant and are readily addressed by the natural evolution of technology. Others, especially the issues that require social changes and modified perceptions, will likely require a significant investment in time, effort, and political cooperation.

Consider some of the more immediate, practical issues that need to be addressed. Although cell phones and wireless PDAs are proliferating like mushrooms throughout society, most users are discontent with the high cost of connectivity, especially when they have multiple devices to carry. A businesswoman might have a cell phone, a pager, a wireless PDA, and a laptop with her at all times. In addition to the hassle of carrying something like a Batman Utility Belt, in the United States she has to contend with spotty, slow-speed wireless service. What's more, because of multiple, evolving standards and the practice of companies offering thinner, faster models every six months, her company's return on investment for her wearable computing devices will be limited.

Uppermost in the minds of most users of digital devices is the provision for security and privacy. For this reason, hardware and software vendors are keen to add features to their products that help maintain secure and private transactions. As noted in previous chapters, threats to security and privacy come from the hacker community, which is ostensibly poised to either break into a system or unleash a virus that may destroy valuable data.

It's not unreasonable that many computer users view the government as a significant threat to their privacy, given the federal legislation aimed at enhancing the FBI's ability to locate and tap in to any wireless transaction in the United States. For example, the E-911 federal legislation mandates that the location of an active cell phone user must be identifiable within 125 meters. Another threat to the privacy of computer users is the FBI's Carnivore, which can locate email anywhere on the Internet addressed to a particular person.

Not all federal activity is focused on monitoring the activity of private citizens. Some legislation is actually designed to enhance privacy. For example, the Health Insurance Portability and Accountability Act (HIPPA) requires that patients be notified as to how their medical records will be used, kept, and disclosed. Patients have a chance to see and amend records and must be asked for their consent before their data are disclosed. Although this legislation bodes well for patients, especially those interested in electronic access to their medical records, the immediate hurdle is the investment in the tools and processes hospitals and clinics will need in order to follow the guidelines.

Some new sources of data present challenges of balancing personal rights to privacy and the right of others to know a computer user's whereabouts. For example, many online merchants are now using HTML-based email as a tracking device—allowing the merchants to track the behavior of specific users on their site. What's more, the user's email address and purchasing profile can be sold to another company without the user's permission. These systems work by planting Web bugs—invisible, 1×1 pixel images—that supply the online merchant with the user's IP address when it is downloaded by a Web-enabled email program such as Outlook or Eudora that is connected to the Web through a constant IP address. Online merchants match up the IP address with the user's email address through a database supplied by companies such as DoubleClick.

Email systems that assign a new IP address with each session, such as AOL used with a dial-in connection, aren't susceptible to HTML-based tracking. However, users who shop from the comfort of their office cubicles, using PCs with high-speed, constant IP address connectivity to the Internet, can be tracked. Similarly, users with email programs such as Microsoft Outlook who use DSL—which has a constant IP address—at home are susceptible to HTML-based tracking.

Location-based services, made possible by the upcoming wave of mobile or m-commerce, threaten privacy as well. There is at least one wristwatch-styled wireless locator that can be used to track the location of the wearer. For example, Wherify's Wireless Locator GPS watch can receive pager messages, automatically dial 911, and be locked or unlocked remotely. The watch also sends an alert if someone tries to tamper with it. Although the technology may be a boon to parents who want to keep tabs on their children, their parents with Alzheimer's, or their pets, the technology also provides law enforcement officials and the government with a tool that could be used in ways not acceptable to most citizens.

In addition to issues of privacy and security, technical, legal, and logistical concerns may impede the rate of progress toward a digital future. For example, in the wireless world, there are numerous, often confusing, international, national, regional, and even local standards organizations to contend with, and there is serious contention for the increasingly limited radio frequency spectrum. The U.S. legal environment is especially egregious in this regard, in that movement into wireless communications is thwarted because of contention for bandwidth.

There are numerous intellectual property issues regarding voice and data communications over networks. As the Napster case has demonstrated, the creators of intellectual property and their representatives can control how and whether their work can be accessed through the Web. For example, even though Napster didn't store copyrighted music on its computers, its services facilitated the sharing of copyrighted music between users—and this facilitation was deemed unlawful.

Less clear are the issues associated with fraud and licensing. For example, since an Internet phone doubles as an electronic wallet, the phone has value beyond that of a communications device. Since there are no laws against treating cell phones as charge cards, the implications of a lost or stolen corporate cell phone or wireless PDA, in terms of liability for unauthorized charges made by a third party, are not yet clear.

Other legal issues that have the potential to slow progress toward a data-pervasive future include public safety concerns of accessing, manipulating, or creating data while driving. For example, a number of automobile accidents have been linked directly to cell phone use, even though more accidents are attributed to drivers changing radio stations, reading newspapers, and eating fast food. Several companies have gone as far as requiring employees who want to use their company cell phones while on the road to pull over and stop before dialing. A growing number of city and state governments have enacted cell phone use laws as well. For example, there is a cell phone ban on New York City taxi drivers and a statewide ban in Massachusetts on cell phone use by school bus drivers.

Legal issues also extend from copyright and encryption to freedom of speech. For example, the Digital Millennium Copyright Act, which makes any program that removes copyright protection illegal, is fueling the debate over DVD encryption. The code that defeats the DVD encryption, DeCSS, is viewed by some as defiance of the Act, and by others as free speech. Some have gone as far as creating poems, images, games, and blueprints that contain the instructions. DeCSS makes it possible for users to treat a DVD as another digital file and send it over the Internet, for example.

From a technical perspective, ubiquitous computing is limited by engineers' ability to create devices that are small, unobtrusive, powerful, and not overly complex for ordinary day-to-day use. Lack of equipment and too many standards have been the downfall of many data-related products. For example, when the first DVD recordable units hit the market, they were crippled by an inability to create DVDs that could be read by other systems.

From a social perspective, the potential challenges associated with advancing into the pervasive data future include dealing with the new technologic elite and reality distortion on one hand and, on the other hand, with tech burnout and the global high-tech worker shortage. For example, the typical CEO working in Silicon Valley has a distorted perception of how pervasive wireless communications and computer technology is in most of America. The penetration of wireless PDAs, Web-enabled cell phones, and MP3 players is still very limited in the United States.

The last, and perhaps most important, caveat is that of tech burnout, where users can no longer tolerate their ever-present electronic tethers. A small but growing population are electing to opt out of the move toward a socio-technology future. There are CEOs and employees who simply refuse to be connected to their office on a 24 × 7 basis. Similarly, many employees refuse to use wireless devices that allow their employer or the government to track their whereabouts every minute of the day. Having an ex-lover visit unexpectedly is one thing, but having a virtual supervisor appear in the middle of a lunch break is another.

THE SOCIETY PAGE

The concept of pervasive data and a future world in which bits and bytes are manufactured, packaged, transported, traded, bought, and sold is more a reality than it is science fiction. The number of knowledge workers who commute through teleconferencing or an intranet is growing. PCs are now commodity items, almost as common as the telephone in corporations and small businesses throughout the United States and, increasingly, Europe and Asia.

The reliance on written language and an increasing amount of graphs, animations, and video are redefining literacy and what it means to be educated. Being able to work a Palm Pilot or other PDA and synchronize the data to a corporate database may soon be more important than being able to balance a checkbook by hand—a skill still taught to many high-school students in the United States. Today, college and graduate students from the University of South Dakota to Harvard Medical School use PDAs to access class notes, communicate with their peers and professors, and prepare for exams.

From an intellectual property perspective, the use of wireless PDAs in higher education, which allows sharing of data—including answers during an exam—raises questions of how to best ensure the integrity of data generated by each student. What constitutes plagiarism in a wired, collaborative environment? After all, isn't collaborative computing and generation of data rewarded in business? On a related note, with the popularity of eBooks expected to rise to about 10 percent of total book sales within a few years, how will an author's intellectual property rights be maintained? When a digital book can be shared at the press of a button, why would cash-strapped students want to pay their campus bookstore for an eBook?

In addition to issues of security, privacy, and the business of managing the production and distribution of digital data, there is the implied societal effect of globalization. Although, as the Web has demonstrated, markets are regionalized because of differences in language and established money handling infrastructures, as these issues are dealt with there will be increasing pressure to offer more data at better prices. The market for software, including music, video, video games, formatted and filtered data, and so-called news, is such that the inherent natural resources of a nation will eventually be measured in the number of highly intelligent, adaptable brains, not the acres of timber, number of iron mines, or wealth of mineral deposits. Given that the national brain trust will eventually be the most important determinant of a society's worth, developing reliable, affordable means of storing and accessing the product of the brain trust becomes imperative.

For now, in the hybrid society of the early 21st century, when digital data are still fairly tightly associated with physical reality, the imperative for preserving data is clearer in some areas than in others. On a personal level, digital records of some events and people are more significant than others—a video of the birth of a child or a wedding photograph, for example. On a corporate or governmental level, the society dictates whether it's more imperative to track potato chips en route to a store or patients on their way to surgery. In either case, as described in the next chapter, methods at the disposal of everyone and for every budget can ensure that data survive the ravages of time for as long as possible.

FIVE

··

Solutions

Ensuring the Survival
of Digital Data

. . . .

The excellent is new forever.

– Ralph Waldo Emerson

The National Library of Medicine's Lister Hill building in Washington, D.C. was completed in 1980 with a massive, circular concrete roof supported by special columns. In the event of an atomic explosion, the roof is designed to collapse down upon the subterranean holdings of the library, hermetically sealing the knowledge of Western medicine for some future civilization.

The millions of men and women in the United States who came of age during the time of the Cold War—the baby boomers—caught the virus of doubt about their future survival, and developed either a sense of urgency or a sense of resignation in response. The news of intercontinental ballistic missiles, the stories of suicide cobalt bombs in the mountains of the western desert, the frequent tests of the Emergency Broadcast System on TV and radio were signs of the times impossible to ignore. Movies, such as *Planet of the Apes*, foretold a postnuclear population, more Neanderthal than human.

Even the comic book heroes of the era—the Fantastic Four, The Hulk, Spider Man, and others—were transmogrified humans who not only survived exposure to deadly gamma radiation but were endowed with special powers as a result of their ordeal. Whether intentional or not, these heroes eased the minds of their fans by showing that nuclear war was survivable, even enabling for those made powerful by exposure to nuclear radiation. Given the spirit of the times, it's not surprising that there was a national preoccupation with ensuring that something of our culture survived into the future. Fallout shelters, civil defense drills, and time capsules of all forms—from cryogenics and bomb-proof architectures to satellites carrying the equivalent of a message in a bottle—were in vogue. Dozens of moribund people arranged to be frozen in liquid nitrogen until some future, unspecified date when the world would be at peace and whatever had caused their demise could be cured.

The federal government did its share to leave an indelible mark on history when it commissioned the Lister Hill building. Local governments got into the act as well. Thousands of public time-capsule-burial ceremonies were held in cities throughout the country, in which civic memorabilia were buried deep below the town square. Many grade schools participated in a similar morbid activity: students were required to contribute a page to the future and then watch as the bundles of paper were encased in plastic ice chests or other makeshift caskets and then lowered into the ground.

Against this backdrop of impending doom, the severity of which I either didn't fully appreciate at the time or have since pushed out of my consciousness, my father decided to create a family time capsule. Ceremoniously, every family member produced a small treasure that would somehow be transported, unscathed, into the distant future. As a precocious eight-year-old, my contribution to the family time capsule was my favorite ink pen and, inside the pen, wrapped around the ink cartridge, a sheet of paper listing what I considered to be the most important information to pass on to the future—the Pythagorean theorem, the value of pi, and Einstein's equation relating energy and mass. The magical time machine—a Mason jar that was sealed in wax, foil, and plastic—was entombed in concrete and, within a few months, forgotten.

Everyone and every society want to leave something behind; it's human nature. What's intriguing is the difference between what we leave behind as an artifact of our normal, daily activity, and what we consciously choose to leave behind. To a young schoolboy presented with a plastic casket for his sheet of paper, a drawing of a favorite pet may sum up his world. Scientists at NASA preparing to send the first Voyager spacecraft on its galactic voyage summed up our world with a twelve-inch, gold-plated copper disk containing images, sounds, and greetings. Interestingly, the data were encoded in analog form, after the vinyl phonograph record, the most popular entertainment media of the late 1960s.

What would a person of normal intelligence do upon finding a replica of the Voyager disk today, much less twenty or thirty years from now? Consider, for example, if a Voyager craft were sent from a parallel universe through a black hole, and a college student found the disk in a small crater on her way to class? As a student of the class of 2030, she might have no experience listening to analog music on cassette or playing vinyl records or CDs, but only have experience with the evolutionary descendent of the memory chips used in today's solid-state MP3 players. That is, even if the media survived the hazards of time and space travel unscathed and was eventually discovered by an intelligent life form, it isn't clear that the data would ever be recovered because of the lack of experience with the media and no equipment to extract the data. Perhaps analog data and media in the shape of platters would be so foreign to the student's way of thinking that she'd interpret the disk as a form of art and end up using the disk as the centerpiece of a hanging mobile.

Whether or not the Voyager disk is ever read and properly interpreted by intelligent life somewhere in the universe, the experiment illustrates how rapidly media change and how even indestructible media are of no value as a carrier of data without the appropriate technology to extract the data. The Voyager disk also illustrates how quickly a media format can be displaced by a new technology, rendering the data useless in the hands of someone without the necessary training and equipment. This chapter continues exploring the question of how best to ensure the survival of digital data. It offers practical advice for creating and maintaining personal archives, based on current best practices in business and government. It also looks at the most elegant data archiving medium on the planet—DNA.

BEST PRACTICES

The ideal process, like a good recipe, is repeatable, infinitely scalable, works in a variety of settings, has modest resource requirements, and is compatible with a variety of other technologies. A family recipe that has been perfected over generations usually provides better and more consistent results than something derived by trial and error over the course of a weekend. The same can be said of someone looking for a way to manage and archive data. It's one thing to look at a few marketing brochures for hardware and software solutions, but it's much better to get a recommendation from someone who's actually used the technology. It's also helpful to see how those with unlimited resources go about archiving their data and then translating the technique to something more practical—like watching Martha Stewart demonstrate a cooking technique in her $200,000 kitchen with home-grown vegetables and then preparing a similar meal with a $40 wok and vegetables from the corner store.

Storing the medium in a constant, low-humidity, and low-temperature environment, away from direct sunlight, can extend the longevity of data on paper, photographic film, magnetic tape, and CD-ROM. When money is no object, the ideal location for an archive can suddenly become available. For example, the Bettmann archive, the collection of 17 million photographs that catalogs the 20th century, belongs to Bill Gates's private company, Corbis. The collection is destined to be archived 220 feet down in a limestone mine 60 miles northeast of Pittsburgh, where, during the next few decades, many of the images will be digitized and made available to historians. In the long term, the 10,000-square-foot archive area should protect the collection from the effects of weather, bleaching from the sun, and nuclear war. Only time will tell if the limestone mine, like the contents of the Egyptian pyramids, will survive the ravages of time or succumb to vandals.

This chapter discusses large-scale data and media management and then explores processes for managing personal data.

Data and Media Management

When it comes to best practices for data and media management, the National Archives and Records Administration (NARA) is the gold standard. NARA is home to nearly 3 billion text documents, 4 million maps, charts, and drawings, over 9 million still photographs, and another 9 million aerial photographs, almost a half-million videotapes, reels of motion picture film, and sound recordings, and at least 30 thousand computer files, all housed in 33 facilities. Paper documents in the archives date back to the Declaration of Independence; most of the electronic records have been created since the 1960s. The Archives offer free publications in print and on the Web (see the contact information in "Resources"), including information on how its Center for Electronic Records manages digital data. For example, according to NARA guidelines, data on CD-ROM are stored in standard ISO 9660 format, without compression, in plain ASCII or EBCDIC form. Similarly, data files and databases are stored as simple text arrays, lists, or tables. As a result, any data on CD-ROM can be read by a simple text editor, including any version of any current word processing program, or database, or other proprietary program.

NARA's medium of choice for long-term archiving is microfilm—the first newspaper to be microfilmed was the *London Evening News*, filmed in 1853 to demonstrate the viability of the technique. However, before 1940, the life expectancy of film was only a few decades. In contrast, modern microfilming technology is inexpensive and easy to work with, the viewing equipment is straightforward and easy to maintain, and the format is stable.

To facilitate the distribution of frequently requested data, NARA selectively digitizes text, photographs, maps, and drawings, following a uniform digitizing specification. For example, photographs are digitized and saved as uncompressed TIFF (Tagged Image File Format) files that are compatible with the IBM PC (though not the Macintosh). These high-resolution (on the order of $1,000 \times 1,000$ pixels) TIFF master files are then reformatted and compressed into smaller GIF (Graphics Interchange Format) and JPEG (Joint Photographic Expert Group) files that are made available to patrons of the Archives. The original files are available in an uncompressed form for future uses. In comparison, the space-saving JPEG and GIF images, which have less data than the original images, can be more easily viewed and manipulated by patrons of the Archives.

NARA's proactive stance against potential disasters is also worth noting. Its disaster prevention process includes the monitoring of temperature and humidity control equipment, guidelines for storing media, fire prevention, exact methods for storing media to prevent fire, and ways to monitor for water leaks. For example, NARA maintains a constant temperature of 70 ±5 degrees and a relative humidity of 50 ±5 percent in the archives, as verified by hygrothermographs that are checked and maintained weekly. Records must be stored at least 6 inches from the ceiling or suspended lights and at least 18 inches from sprinkler heads. Eating and drinking in the stack areas and research rooms is prohibited, and each building is inspected quarterly for pests.

In the event of a disaster, such as a fire, flood, storm, or earthquake, NARA guidelines specify the appropriate response and designate the responsible parties. For example, in the event of a power outage of more than a day, power generators maintain air circulation. Because rapid changes in temperature and humidity can cloud microfilm, promote the growth of mold and mildew on organic surfaces, and in general promote the deterioration process, the most valuable and fragile materials are moved to locations that can be maintained at standard temperature and humidity.

NARA also issues guidelines that are specific to electronic records management, addressing topics like these:

- Creation and use of data files
- Security of electronic records
- Selection and maintenance of storage media
- Destruction of electronic records

The guidelines take cost, compatibility, and storage capacity into account and specifically warn against relying on floppy disks as a long-term storage medium. NARA mandates periodic transfer of data to new storage media formats to avoid data loss because of changing technology or deterioration. Backups are dictated on a regular schedule, with the backup media stored in a location separate from the originals. The backup media are tested and certified error free before they are used. NARA suggests that electronic media be maintained in an environment with a constant temperature of 65 ±3 degrees and constant relative humidity of 40 ±5 percent, with no smoking or eating allowed in the storage areas.

The long-term care and treatment of storage media, especially magnetic tape, is dictated as well. For example, magnetic tape is rewound every $3\frac{1}{2}$ years, copied onto new tape before 10 years, and statistically sampled for errors. Tapes with over a specified number of errors are replaced. The labels used to identify magnetic tapes and removable media contain or refer to the information listed in Table 9-1.

Table 9-1 NARA Labeling Requirements.

Tapes and Removable Media	Temporary Storage Media
Organization responsible for the records	Organization responsible for the records
Title of contents	Title of contents
Dates of creation	Dates of creation
Security classification	Security classification
File titles	Software used to create the data
Dates of coverage	Hardware platform
Recording density	
Type of internal labels	
Number of tracks	
Record formats and lengths	

NARA is also involved in the controlled destruction of data. However, records, including email, can only be destroyed after a specified review process, and when data are destroyed, sensitive information is protected. For example, media previously used to store sensitive or proprietary data cannot be reused if the previously recorded data can be retrieved in any way.

Computer Hardware

When it comes to hardware, large commercial organizations that manage huge amounts of critical data on mainframe computer systems set the standards for best practices. For example, large computer installations generally follow vendor-specific standards for power and environmental control. Computer rooms for large mainframes are generally built around the vendor-specified requirements—from the raised floors to the air- and power-conditioning equipment. A typical mainframe isn't connected to the power mains, but the power is conditioned—fluctuations in voltage, voltage spikes, and high-frequency signals traveling on the power lines are filtered out by massive power-conditioning devices that weigh several tons. The ambient temperature and humidity are controlled to within a narrow range, and the air flow on the computer equipment is maintained above a minimum number of cubic feet per minute. Day-to-day data management relies on large, high-speed disk drives that fill refrigerator-sized racks, and long-term archiving is typically on 12-inch optical platters that are loaded and unloaded with a robotic mechanism. The optical disks created by these juke boxes are stored offsite, several miles from the computer center, in fire-resistant safes that are environmentally controlled.

In comparison to mainframe systems with full-time staff that are trained on specific hardware, there is much more variability—and room for error—in installations that rely on microcomputer hardware. The best of these installations use name-brand servers from companies such as Dell, IBM, or Hewlett Packard, with separate servers for testing and deployment. In addition, the disks are usually configured as redundant arrays that minimize the chances of data loss, even in the event of a disk crash, and a hot backup server is ready in the event that the first server fails. The hot backup server contains all of the information communicated to the first server up until the time of failure.

The best installations also use UPS hardware for filtering the power mains as well as for providing several minutes to several hours of backup power in the event of power outage. Companies located in areas with frequent or prolonged power outages have backup generators to take over when the batteries in the UPS systems are exhausted. The best systems also rely on automatic tape backup systems that perform incremental or full backups at a particular time of night or whenever the system load is lowest.

From a process perspective, the best small computer shops have trained technicians that religiously verify that each tape archive has data on it before it is labeled and stored offsite. The better small computer facilities use optical jukeboxes that automatically save data to optical disks. These shops also simulate disasters and document their ability to recover data, including measuring the amount of time involved to return a system to its fully operational state. The top banking institutions, health care facilities, and legal practices maintain an in-house IS staff that is on call on a 24×7 basis.

Personal Process Practices

With the increasing number of telecommuters and work-at-home consultants, best practices at the personal level are becoming increasingly important. For the most part, these are scaled-down versions of the best practices used in the government and in private industry. For example, a UPS power conditioner can provide 15 to 20 minutes of emergency power, allowing the consultant to shut everything down without losing data. Software firewalls can provide protection against hackers. Automatic tape backups can perform nightly incremental backups and weekly or monthly full backups, depending on the quantity, quality, and value of the data to be archived. Software utilities, available both within the operating system and as add-ons, can be used to check disks for errors and repair damaged sectors.

When it comes to best practices at the personal level, the issue is less whether hardware or media management can be scaled down, but whether the processes can be replicated. For example, it doesn't do much good if a work-at-home graphics designer religiously backs up her work on a 20-GB tape drive, only to leave the tape in her PC. If the PC is stolen, the backup media and data will be lost.

When the storage location farthest from the original data residing on a PC is another room in a two-room apartment, it's best to give data away, and the more copies the better, assuming there are no security or proprietary data concerns. Giving data away is like having more children to increase the odds that progeny will survive into the next generation. Following Roger's example from the New Year's flood, sending a tape or CD to a relative in another state is one way to minimize the risk that all data would be destroyed in a house fire or other disaster.

TAKE-AWAY HEURISTICS

The best practices described above, Roger's experience with the flood, and Ed's unfortunate encounter with a malfunctioning tape backup unit relate to particular circumstances. However, all of these scenarios have in common several principles that apply across systems ranging from a PDA to a supercomputer, and from a few text files to thousands of hours of digital video. These heuristics or rules of thumb are described below.

Keep It Simple

When Intel first introduced the microprocessor, it faced an uphill battle of getting engineers to take notice of its new digital technology. To increase awareness of the new digital device at a time when most electrical engineers and engineering students worked with and studied analog devices, Intel held a contest that was open to electrical engineering students in the United States. The task was to create an electronic mouse that could navigate a maze. A $10,000 first prize awaited the team that created—using the Intel chip—a mouse that made it out of the maze in the shortest time.

Physically, the mouse was limited to about the size of a shoe, and there were some practical constraints, such as the size of the electric motors used to drive the wheels, the size of the battery, and the amount of RAM on board. However, for the most part, the inner workings of the mouse were up to the student's imagination and ingenuity. As in today's robots, the real challenge was creating the software that could direct the robot to traverse the maze.

As a result of the contest, students throughout the United States tried a variety of approaches, from using IR light sensors and switches on all sides of the mouse body, to whiskers that detected contact with the walls of the maze. Most of the designs attempted to create a map of the maze in the mouse's onboard RAM. However, the mouse design that won the contest took a much simpler and more elegant approach. The designers of the winning mouse took the time to study the habits of real mice and how they managed to survive in the mazes in the walls of buildings in every major city on the planet.

Real mice come in two basic varieties: left-handed and right-handed. Left-handed mice, when faced with a choice of turning left or right at the end of a tunnel, favor the left. Right-handed mice, in contrast, favor taking the right when presented with the same choice. It turns out that the strategy of consistently taking the right or left turn when presented with a left-right choice always brings a mouse out of a maze, regardless of the size or complexity of the maze—assuming the mouse has adequate food and water for the journey. Although there may be quicker strategies, the mice don't risk being stuck in a dead end or running around in circles until they die.

The winning team used the strategy of real mice and made a right-handed robot mouse. The development team didn't need the powerful microprocessor or the RAM to build the robot, but incorporated it into the design in order to satisfy the contest rules. The designers used the microprocessor to monitor contact with the right-hand wall of the maze, as indicated by a switch activated by pressure on a plastic whisker attached to the nose of the mouse. When the whisker lost contact with the right wall, the robot turned right until it regained contact with the wall. In this way, it hugged the right-hand wall and eventually made its way out of the maze. The other mouse robots, some using very complex machine-learning algorithms, either became lost in the maze or found their way out—but in significantly more time than the right-handed mouse took to traverse the maze.

The point is that the best methodology for solving a particular problem—minimizing the loss of digital data, for example—is usually the simplest. However, given the preponderance of technology surrounding the creation and application of digital data, it's easy to lose sight of the obvious and things that worked in the past with other data. The most obvious solutions to ensuring the survival of digital data borrow techniques used with media throughout the ages.

Watch the Big Guys

Many financial institutions, health care enterprises, and major corporations are working frantically to create workable data archiving and access technologies, ranging from huge disk farms to network storage systems, to support future business models. Of the institutions heavily invested in generating, acquiring, and managing data—the government, military, hospitals, legal firms, and financial institutions—the last-named are probably the most accomplished. Their task is simplified in that the data are understandable without external contextual queues. That is, tables of payment schedules and account balances are self-evident even to a casual reader. More challenging are complex areas, such as medicine and law, that have layers of contextual cues associated with data. Laboratory values recorded in an electronic medical record, for example, have meaning when associated with a given patient, his or her diagnosis, previous laboratory test results, and even the time of day the laboratory test was performed.

Don't Always Buy in Bulk

Buying a case of light bulbs at one of the bulk outlets has an obvious cost benefit. However, if the bulbs are all installed at the same time, as ceiling lights in a warehouse, for example, and assuming the bulbs are all from the same batch, they'll all fail around the same time, leaving the warehouse in near or total darkness.

Similarly, disk drives manufactured in the same batch tend to fail after the same number of hours of operation. Like the massive light bulb outage in the warehouse, widespread failure in disk drive hardware is much more disruptive to normal business operation than if a single drive fails. It's far better to order disk drives from different manufacturers or at least in different batches.

Use the Right Technology

Archiving data on a case of Zip disks in a fireproof safe makes sense if the safe is stored in a cool, dry place, not in the trunk of a car. Similarly, when it comes to archiving, it pays to know something about the media, especially the packaging and the hazards facing it.

Of the catastrophic data loss events most commonly insured against—fire, theft, and water damage—fire is consistently the most lethal hazard. For example, a CD-ROM stored in a paper or windowless Tyvek (a material made with plastic and paper) sleeve might last an hour in a fireproof safe, but only 10 minutes in the same safe if the CD is stored in a jewel case, which melts at a much lower temperature than the CD. Similarly, a Zip disk stored in a clear plastic case might last 15 minutes in the same safe before the case melts or ignites. Stored without the dust case (which isn't very useful in a closed safe anyway), the Zip disk's plastic shell might last over an hour in the same safe before it melts. The physical characteristics of media are available from the National Media Laboratory (see "Resources"), and safe manufacturers often list survival times for media, with and without cases, at various temperatures.

Use Common Sense

Be wary of vendor claims. For example, media vendors often provide lifetime guarantees for their media. However, the fine print on the media packing typically limits the liability of the manufacturer to replacement media, less postage and handling. That is, if a CD-ROM containing the equivalent of 1,000 person-hours of work should fail, the manufacturer's lifetime guarantee may entitle the holder of the CD-ROM to an 85-cent replacement CD-ROM blank—less postage and handling.

Define the Data Horizon

It's common practice for corporate America to establish milestones measured in quarters and occasionally years, even before the concept of Internet time—when business events that normally took years appeared to occur in months or weeks—came into vogue. As such, the perceived value of data rarely extends beyond five years in service-oriented corporate America. The economics of computer technology, orchestrated by manufacturers, includes the planned obsolescence of computer hardware, operating systems, and application software. Even videotapes, CDs, and electronic components are manufactured with a tradeoff between cost and expected lifetimes. In addition, customer data are valuable to brick-and-mortar businesses only in the short term, in part because of the mobile population.

In traditional brick-and-mortar businesses, there is often no immediate financial incentive to create data archives, and the lost opportunity cost is too great if new information is ignored in order to archive the old. The obvious exception is the wildly popular entertainment programming available on DVD or, increasingly less commonly, on videotape. However, the hoards of smaller budget films, including foreign films, may be lost to the potential viewer forever because there may be no short-term financial gain associated with creating archives.

Keep the Good Stuff

From an economic perspective, it's difficult to rationalize the practice of archiving data when there is an oversupply of new data. The solution is to be objective and systematic in evaluating the worth of data before it is archived. Refer to Chapter 6 to review the value of data.

Allow for Human Error

We live and work with increasingly complex systems that leave little room for inevitable human error. Consider the original Space Shuttle design. Because there simply wasn't room for computer error, the main onboard computer system was based on a relatively simple computer that has been used for decades in manufacturing plants. An antiquated system that uses core memory (a matrix of miniature iron doughnuts wired by hand) is used in the shuttle because of the central processor unit's long history of error-free performance. The goal is to minimize the chances of a mishap from a surprise computational error like the one that turned up in the original Intel Pentium chip. An advantage of using a computer system in space based on core memory is that, unlike the case with most types of solid-state RAM, a stray gamma particle can't easily erase or change a data bit in memory. However, despite all of these provisions, the Challenger disaster highlights the difficulty in foreseeing all eventualities, especially those related to human error, in complex systems.

The point is that mistakes are inevitable, and given the increasing density of storage media, never before has it been so easy for one person to destroy so much data so easily in so short a time. This reality is reflected in the fact that hospitals, financial institutions, and the government routinely lose massive quantities of data because of human error. Of course, these disasters aren't advertised to the general public, for the same reason that financial institutions don't advertise failed investments and hospitals don't advertise the number of failed medical procedures. Ed's mishap with the defective tape drive, for example, was never reported to an insurance agency, administration outside of the department, and, with the exception of this book, the account never appeared in print.

Keep Up with the Joneses

Because of competing architectures, rapidly evolving hardware, and the lack of enduring standards, it's difficult to share data among contemporary systems, much less work with media from a decade ago. The rapid evolution of the microcomputer, from the Altair to the modern PC, and of media, from paper and cassette tape to floppy disks to flash RAM, illustrates how media, operating systems, and data formats have yet to stabilize. If the world changes to a new microcomputer platform—a descendent of Linux, for example— then prudent computer users will migrate their data to the new system as soon as it's stable.

Don't Forget the People

A company holding a case full of tape archives and a PC may physically have all of its data, but without the trained staff that designed the database and the backup procedure, the company may never get all of the data back. As a nation, we're forward looking and time conscious, almost to a fault. Most Americans have been conditioned to expect and want the next new thing, the next job, and the next life. Because of this attitude, companies increasingly depend on short-term workers and consultants. As a result, the core competency of most companies or divisions is kept in the heads of a very select few, and when these few migrate to other jobs, their expertise leaves with them.

Trust, but Verify

As in the former United States arms policy with the Soviet Union of "trust but verify," when it comes to backups, it's critical to verify that the technology is working as advertised. Ed's predicament with the tape drive wouldn't have happened if he had implemented a verification component in his data backup routine. This means not only checking a tape or other media to determine that data have been written to it, but also verifying that the data can be fully restored to a test computer.

Know When to Call for Help

Some things are best left to the professionals. For example, if a computer boots up and starts making loud grinding sounds indicative of a disk crash, the safest procedure is to shut the system down and call a professional. Depending on the environment, this means either contacting someone in the corporate IS department or calling a commercial recovery service. Don't try to run a repair utility. That will likely only make matters worse.

Do the Documentation

Even if the original system designers have disappeared, if the archiving process has been meticulously documented, it's possible for an intelligent technician to reconstitute any database. Similarly, a personal archive, properly documented, can be accessed and properly interpreted much more easily if documentation accompanies the archive. Typical documentation includes the hardware platform, the version of the operating system, the name of the application software used to create the files, and other information listed in Table 9-1.

Don't Wear Real Jewelry in Public

Duplicate files, like costume jewelry, travel much better than the real thing. In other words, it's dangerous to travel with the only copy of a file. Information on a PDA or laptop should be synchronized to a desktop PC or otherwise backed up before the portable unit is packed away for a flight—potentially never to return because of theft or accidental loss.

Beware of Changing Roles

The roles of public institutions are constantly being challenged by information technology. Consider the diminishing role of the library as a source of information. A businesswoman pressed for time is more likely to search for information online than visit a library. A less harried college student is more likely to stop by his local bookstore-coffee shop than stop by the sterile library when he's looking for a "new" book to read. In the former case, the gatekeepers of what is considered important data may be largely unknown, since virtually anyone can establish an online presence and publish his version of the truth on any subject. In the latter case, unseen publishers decide which books to promote, based on what the market will bear.

Publishers of newspapers and tabloids, for example, increasingly focus on what can be delivered and easily digested in sound bytes. Coverage of global issues may therefore be displaced by details of the latest scandal. An awareness of the changing roles of the media can help in assessing the value of data from a variety of sources.

Think Storage First, Speed Second

When it comes to archiving data, storage, not speed, is the primary concern. The emphasis on computer processor speeds and the bandwidth of Internet access is akin to building racecars and superhighways without thinking about parking spaces. Given that marketing has historically emphasized processor speed, it's not difficult to imagine how computers were not valued primarily for their capacity to store and retrieve data, but for their ability to compute, that is, to perform a large number of mathematical calculations quickly.

Today, however, unless a computer user is working with video or computer graphics, there is surplus computing power at the hands of people who have no use for it. Conversely, the provision for archiving and data backup are typically barely adequate. For example, duplicating a CD on a single CD-ROM drive system is possible, but time consuming. A far better approach is to equip a PC with a standard CD-Reader, a CD-ROM writer, and a Zip drive.

Manage Metadata

Metadata isn't an afterthought, but is often the key to the underlying data. It doesn't matter how well data are stored on a disk if they can't be located in less than a half hour. Their exact name and disk location must be identifiable. Keeping metadata synchronized with the corresponding data is especially important, given that the data can have a very different meaning, depending on the metadata description. For example, let's say that before October 7, 1958, all values for ambient temperature at a weather station are stored in degrees Fahrenheit, and after that time, in degrees Centigrade. Without the metadata, performing statistical analysis on weather trends will be meaningless at best, and, at worst, result in disaster, as illustrated by the Mars Orbiter fiasco.

Be an Educated Consumer

Media companies, hardware manufacturers, and other companies commonly put their product descriptions on their corporate Web sites for the benefit of their potential customers. For example, many of the magnetic media companies list detailed specifications of their products, including archival and nonarchival environmental limitations, warranty, and physical characteristics. These specifications should define how the media are treated.

Establish Rules

When it comes to archiving, randomly saving data that appeal to a particular person or a seemingly prominent project can result in important data falling through the cracks. It's important to establish rules and to understand their implications. For example, if data are discarded after their use level drops below a threshold set for storage needs, then long-term accessibility is compromised for short-term savings of storage costs. Depending on the data, the cost savings may be significant, and the value of the data in the future minimal—or the opposite could be true. This sort of challenge is most easily resolved by establishment of rules for archiving that can be followed regardless of the particular data qualities.

Make It Personal

There is no one best way to manage and archive data. Every situation, every budget, and everyone is different. Often the best solution is to combine the heuristics provided above with personal experience. For example, the suggestions of a $5,000-a-day database consultant won't work if the proposed solution to archiving doesn't fit the politics and culture of the people involved. It's far better to implement a less complete system that will be followed 99 percent of the time than to try and enforce a more stringent system that looks great on paper but that won't be followed.

Similarly, data management technologies are constantly evolving, and what's in vogue one day may be out of favor the next. It makes sense, therefore, to examine every technology from the perspective of how well it fits with the particular data management needs and strategies of an individual or of an organization. For example, although a central data warehouse design may be in vogue, keeping all data in one place represents both power of access and vulnerability to loss. As illustrated by the library at Alexandria, catastrophic data loss is more likely with a geographically centralized data archive design.

. . . .

SPECIFIC RECOMMENDATIONS

Heuristics are good for long-term planning and evaluating new data management technologies as they become available, but for practical applications, heuristics need to be incorporated into data management strategy. From the perspective of personal archiving—that is, archiving a single person's or a small group's work—the planning process outlined in Figure 9-1 is a good place to start. As outlined in the figure and described here, the key steps in archive planning are qualifying the data; selecting the media, hardware, and software tools; defining an archiving process; and, most importantly, following through on the plan.

Qualify the data. The first step in planning a personal archive is to qualify the nature of the data to be archived, in terms of the data format, quantity of data to be archived, the time value of data, likely

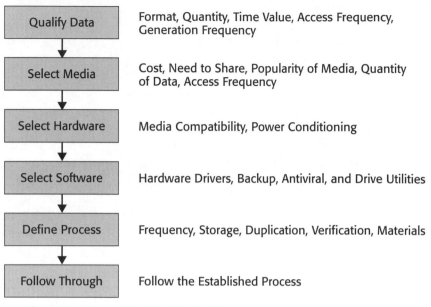

Qualify Data	Format, Quantity, Time Value, Access Frequency, Generation Frequency
Select Media	Cost, Need to Share, Popularity of Media, Quantity of Data, Access Frequency
Select Hardware	Media Compatibility, Power Conditioning
Select Software	Hardware Drivers, Backup, Antiviral, and Drive Utilities
Define Process	Frequency, Storage, Duplication, Verification, Materials
Follow Through	Follow the Established Process

Figure 9-1 Personal Archive Planning Steps.

frequency of access to the archived data, and frequency of new data generation for inclusion in the archive. All of these factors affect media selection, hardware, and the other steps in the planning stage.

Examples of format include plain text, Microsoft Word documents, Adobe Photoshop images, digital video, TIFF, GIF, JPEG, and MPEG-3 encoded images, WAV sound files, Endnote bibliographic database files, Microsoft Access, PowerPoint, Excel files, and other proprietary file formats. Format also includes operating-system-specific files. For example, TIFF image files for Windows are stored differently from TIFF image files for the Apple Macintosh operating system. The quantity of data that must be archived might vary from a few hundred kilobytes to several gigabytes per week. Of course, an underlying assumption in the planning process is that the time value of data is significant; otherwise, there is no point in archiving the data.

Select the media. Media selection should reflect the cost of archiving, the need to share the media with others, the popularity of the media in the general marketplace, the quantity of data that must be archived at one time, the access frequency, as well as the other characteristics of the data described above. Figure 9-2 shows a media

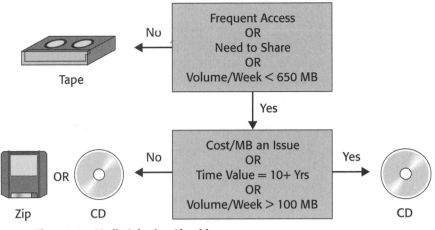

Figure 9-2   Media Selection Algorithm.

selection algorithm that one can use to decide between the three most popular media used in personal archiving today: tape, removable magnetic media (Zip disks), and recordable CDs.

As represented in Figure 9-2, if there will be frequent access to the data, need to share the media with others, or if the volume of data to store every week is less than 650 MB (the capacity of a CD-ROM), then removable magnetic media (like Zip disks with a capacity of 100 MB) or recordable CDs are a good option—otherwise, tape is a reasonable choice for archiving media. That is, if an archive is intended to be shared among users in a single office or across the country, it's more likely that most of those users will have a CD-ROM drive in their desktop or laptop PC than a specific model of tape drive. Similarly, if archives are shared across the country, it's much easier and cheaper to duplicate a CD or a Zip disk and drop it in a mailer than to duplicate a tape and put it in a box for mailing.

In deciding between removable magnetic media and recordable CD technology (lower box, Figure 9-2), the main issues are the time value of data and the volume of data created per week. For the greatest cost savings and longevity, with data volumes greater than 100 MB a week (assuming the now-standard 100-MB Zip disks are the most popular removable magnetic media), the recordable CD is the medium of choice. For smaller volumes of data and more focus on short-term archiving and if media cost isn't a factor (several dollars for a 100-MB Zip disk versus less than a dollar for a 650-MB CD-

ROM blank), then either 100-MB Zip disks or recordable CD-ROM will do.

In differentiating between the Zip and CD-ROM formats, compatibility may be an issue, especially when laptop computers are involved. Although many desktop computers come with both Zip and CD-ROM drives, most laptop designs offer a Zip drive as optional equipment. Conversely, when time is an issue, the Zip disk is best for quick, frequent backups. A recordable CD-ROM drive is generally significantly slower than a Zip disk in creating archives because recordable CD-ROMs must be processed—a two- to five-minute operation—before they can be shared with users who have CD-ROM readers.

Of course, in addition to the appropriate digital media, a good quality, all-cotton, acid-free paper should be selected for creating a parallel printed archive of the data. A printed archive, while not very space efficient, can provide insurance against catastrophic loss of data in the event that the means of accessing digital data on electronic media are unavailable.

Select the hardware. Hardware selection is a natural extension of the media selected. For example, if CD-ROM media are selected, then a CD-writer is required. Regardless of the microcomputer hardware configuration, a power conditioner, preferably incorporated in an uninterruptible power supply (UPS), should be used to minimize the chances of data loss due to power outages and disturbances.

Select the software. The software tools required for an archiving project follow from the hardware selection and include appropriate drivers for the tape, CD, or Zip drives, backup utilities that streamline the task of creating incremental backups, and standard antiviral and drive utility software. It's critical to archive the software drivers for all storage devices. If the drivers are part of the current operating system, then a CD of the operating system should be archived with the data.

Define the process. The archiving process description must explicitly define every step of the process, from frequency of storage, the storage medium, hardware, duplication, verification, and the materials used. Recall that the materials used in the archiving process can significantly affect the survivability of data. As previously mentioned, CDs stored in plastic jewel cases in a fireproof safe will typically last one-fifth or one-sixth of the time as CDs stored in paper sleeves because the jewel cases melt at a relatively low temperature.

Follow through. The archiving process is only useful if it's implemented. Following through may entail training family members, business partners, or employees. Following up on the plan is also easier if blank media, labels, and software utilities are on hand.

To illustrate the practical application of the heuristics offered above and the end product of the archive planning process, three archiving plans are offered, designed for three different kinds of data creators: a graphic artist working at home, a small company with a Web site, and a retiring CEO. You should be able to apply one or all of these scenarios to your archiving project.

Archiving Plan, Scenario 1.
A Graphic Artist Working at Home

This scenario involves a graphic artist working at home on a Macintosh computer system. She works with typical tools of the graphics art trade, including Adobe Photoshop, Adobe Illustrator, and Microsoft Word—all Macintosh format.

The main concern is the long-term Macintosh-Windows cross-compatibility issue, which is related to the long-term viability of the Macintosh operating system. For example, although the Macintosh and Windows versions of the Adobe and Microsoft products can be converted to work with either platform, data are often lost in the process because features supported by the Windows version of a program (for example, embedded fonts) may not be supported in the Macintosh version of the program.

Because of long-term archiving issues, it may make sense for the artist to translate all Macintosh-format images and text files to operating-system-independent equivalents by using batch process utilities designed for that purpose. For example, all Microsoft Word documents can be exported as plain text files written to an ISO 9096-compatible recordable CD-ROM.

Plan 1:
    Data:
        Format—Adobe Photoshop and Illustrator Images, Microsoft Word documents, all for the Macintosh

Quantity—100 MB/week

Time Value—10+ years

Access Frequency—Once a month

Generation Frequency—Daily

Media:

CD-ROM

Hardware:

Dual CD-ROM drives (one reader and one reader/writer)

UPS with power conditioning

Software:

CD-writer software that supports ISO 9096 format

File conversion utilities (batch conversion from Macintosh to operating-system-independent file formats)

Antiviral utility

Disk utility

Process (nonsequential):

- Verify CD blanks are error free.
- Write data to CD at the end of every day, and remove the CD from the PC and store it in another room in the house.
- Burn an archive CD (and start a new CD) every month.
- Verify that the CD contains data.
- Label each CD with data, project name, and description and date.
- Put the CD in a fireproof safe, located as far as possible from the work room, in an air-conditioned room, using paper envelopes to protect the CD.
- For critical data, consider making a second CD and sending it to a friend or relative, in a paper envelope, to put in a second safe.
- Verify that CDs are readable on second CD drive every 6 months, including reading it on a Windows machine.
- Never delete files from the hard drive without making a CD of the most important files—if there is only one copy on CD, then there is no backup of the CD.
- Duplicate (copy) archived CDs every 5 years, and consider converting to the dominant microcomputer platform.

- Print the work on high-quality, acid-free paper.
- Store paper documents away from digital data, in a stable, low-humidity environment.

As noted in the "Best Practices" section, this plan should be modified to reflect the most current media, operating system, and hardware standards, as well as cost and other practical constraints.

Archiving Plan, Scenario 2.
A Small Company with a Web Site

The second scenario is that of a small company with an active Web site that must be frequently updated and archived. The issues in this scenario are the large number of data types and applications used and the need to archive a complete copy of a complex, interconnected system of files. That is, in the course of a day, a word might be changed here, an icon there, and a sound added to a page. In addition, the content used on the Web site, such as images, needs to be archived as well, in the event that an image or other content needs to be reworked and repurposed for another location in the Web site or for a printed publication.

Because of the nature of the Web, the perceived archival requirements are only out to five years, given the constant change in content. Most Web sites undergo complete graphical and textual makeovers every two years or less. Note that, unlike the first scenario, where everything took place on one machine, this scenario involves the use of an NT server and a PC running Windows 2000.

Plan 2:

Data:

Format—Web content: Microsoft Word, FrontPage, and Access, Adobe Photoshop, WAV sound files, Dreamweaver files, and Flash animations, all under Microsoft NT and Windows 2000

Quantity—1 MB/week, distributed throughout a 50-MB Web site, as well as support files

Time Value—5 years

Access Frequency—Infrequent; only when required to recover from server crashes

Generation Frequency—Daily

Media:

20-GB tape

Hardware:

Internal tape drive

UPS for power conditioning

Software:

Tape-writer software

Antiviral utility

Disk utility

Process:

- Create an incremental backup tape (one that contains only changes since the last incremental backup) nightly, and remove the tape from the machine at the end of every backup.
- Rotate incremental backup tapes weekly (after two weeks, a tape is reused to back up the latest version of the Web site).
- Create a full backup tape weekly.
- Verify that backups contain data.
- Label tapes appropriately.
- Store full backup tapes in an offsite, fireproof safe in a secure, air-conditioned room.
- Verify that full backup tapes are readable on a second drive every 3 months.
- Perform a full install from tape every 6 months.
- Rewind full backup tapes every 2 years.
- Annually, consider exporting all content to agnostic file formats, such as from Adobe Photoshop to TIFF for Windows.

Note that this plan can also be applied to personal use, especially if there regularly is a large amount of data to archive. However, working with tapes tends to be more labor intensive for small amounts of data, and nightly tape backups often require that the computer equipment remain on overnight.

Archiving Plan, Scenario 3. A Retiring CEO

The final scenario, that of a retiring CEO, illustrates the challenge of archiving someone's life work, whether the person is a retiring president, CEO, author, college professor, or simply someone with a lot of "stuff" collected throughout a lifetime. "Stuff" can include traditional content such as newspaper clippings, handouts, brochures, articles torn out from journals, 35mm slides, color and black-and-white photographs, cassette audio recordings, and VHS video tapes of presentations and events. The collection can also include digital content, including email, PowerPoint presentations, Microsoft Word documents, digital images, and digital video tapes of more recent presentations and events. This scenario illustrates how few people have a digital-only past but have a collection of old photographs, handwritten documents, newspaper articles, journals, perhaps a book or two, hand-drawn graphs, and legal documents, as well as more recent, computer-generated content.

One way to preserve nondigital data is to transfer it to new media that are at least as durable as the original. For example, microfilm is a common storage medium for the transfer of newspaper clippings, journal articles, legal documents, and photographs. Although generally suitable for plain text documents, microfilming of color prints and drawings often doesn't capture the more subtle qualities of the original—the interplay of colors, the sense of artistry, and the more ephemeral qualities of artwork.

The most common issue when dealing with traditional legacy data is determining whether or not to bring it into the digital realm. As discussed earlier, digitization is useful as a means of distribution and providing access to data, but not as an archival method. A black-and-white photo or a book printed on acid-free paper, properly stored, will most likely outlast any digital facsimile. Similarly, simply photocopying newspaper clippings, journal articles, legal documents, and other printed materials onto acid-free 100 percent cotton (archival) paper can extend the life of data printed on newsprint and other nonarchival paper.

When the original data are stored on audiocassettes and analog video formats, it is a good idea to digitize the data as well. In either case, digitization, rather than simply making an analog copy, will at least halt the generational noise gain—the noise introduced in each copy. For the conversion of analog audio and video to digital audio and video, a wide variety of digital video and analog capture hardware is available. In addition, special filters are available to remove the hissing and pops from old audio tapes and to allow the user to adjust the contrast and color balance of digitized video. Once analog tapes have been transformed into digital files, they can be stored on CD-ROM or tape, depending on the volume of data involved.

In any project of this size and complexity, documenting and indexing the digital and traditional data will be critical in retrieving the data later. Depending on the nature of the data and the plans for future uses, the data can be organized by year, alphabetically, by publication, company, or project. The other size-related issue is knowing when to call in the professionals. Properly archiving one box of photos, cassette tapes, and old papers is one thing, but archiving the life's work of a prolific author or inventor is another. The matter of cost should also be considered. For example, the cost of digitizing and indexing each of the 17 million images in the Bettmann Archives in 2001 is estimated to be about $20 per image.

Now consider how the digital data can be handled.

Plan 3:
    Data (Digital):
        Format—Microsoft PowerPoint, Microsoft Access, and Word files, Outlook email files, digital video
        Quantity—20 GB—a one-time archive
        Time Value—Indefinitely
        Access Frequency—Once a year or less
        Generation Frequency—Once
    Media:
        CD-ROM and tape
    Hardware:
        Dual CD-ROM drives (one reader, one reader/writer)
        Tape writer
        UPS for power conditioning
    Software:
        CD-writer software
        Tape-writer software
        Antiviral utility
        Disk utility

Process:

- Copy all files to a hard drive.
- Convert all files to nonproprietary formats, e.g., Word documents to ASCII text, all image files to TIFF files, and Access database tables to ASCII text tables.
- Organize all files according to project, time, or other index.
- Create several tapes, verifying that data are on the tapes after each copy.
- Distribute copies to several friends or associates.
- Maintain at least one copy in a fireproof safe, away from the original data.
- Create two sets of CD-ROMs, one for local use and one to be stored in a fireproof safe, away from both the originals and the tape archives.
- Consider copying the data to a second hard drive and archiving the drive, along with the associated driver software, as well, especially if the data are valuable.
- Duplicate the archived CDs every 5 years, to either CDs or the current media standard.
- Rewind tapes every 2 years.
- Duplicate tapes every 5 years, transferring to the most common tape standard at the time.
- Print the work on high-quality, acid-free paper.
- Store paper documents with the other printed materials, away from the digital data.

It's important to follow the progress of technology when dealing with a sizable archive that may not be accessed for several years. As the history of the PC has illustrated, within three or four years the operating system, applications, and underlying hardware can undergo a complete transformation. Furthermore, since conversion utilities may not extend past one generation, it's critical to translate data as the standards change—along the lines of the industrywide conversion from $5\frac{1}{4}$-inch disks to $3\frac{1}{2}$-inch disks and from the 45-MB SyQuest platter to the 100-MB Zip disk.

For example, Norsam Technologies is experimenting with an archiving method based on 2-inch micro-etched nickel disks. Data, which are written in traditional pages on the disk, can be read with a powerful light microscope. Like microfilm, the disks carry analog data, including line art and other monochrome images. However, unlike microfilm, the nickel disk is relatively impervious to water and high and low temperatures. Whether or not this or similar technology ever becomes commercially viable, there will most certainly be a follow-up technology to the current generation of media and machines.

SAVING THE FUTURE

Saving the past, whether through scratches on rocks, marks on paper, or microscopic pits on a thin metal disk, is about saving the future and fighting the ultimate silence of time. All cultures are characterized by a store of data that is passed from one generation to the next, and throughout most of history, this transfer of data has been based on written documents—a continuation of the much older oral tradition—as well as plays, music, paintings, and other artistic endeavors. Today, cyberspace is creating its own culture. However, based on the phenomenal loss of data—from programs and operating systems to database and application-specific files—after only a few generations of computer hardware, software, and Web content, there is little in the way of an enduring cultural heritage to build upon.

The rapidity with which old digital data are routinely discarded in favor of the new is problematic. Consider the implications of following this practice until it is disrupted by biological or nuclear warfare, which could effectively pull the plug on the national power grid for a year or two. In that time, not only would the discarded data be lost, all of the digital data on the Web, corporate intranets and PCs, and even most home PCs would be lost and at least partially forgotten. Can a culture this fragile be relied upon for critical information? More importantly, is it worthy of the time and energy invested in authoring content for the Web, eBooks, and other digital services?

In considering these issues, it may help to take the view that the past and the future, like the concept of Yin and Yang, are opposite and yet inextricably connected. The traditional approach to preserving data is confrontational, pitting the intellect and ingenuity of humanity against the invincible forces of time. In this regard, the result is inevitable; the only question is when time will win. For example, consider that time is the primary difference between an ice sculpture and one made of stone. Both will succumb to the effects of time eventually. The sculptor's investment in time is proportional to the life span of the product. That is, an ice sculpture can usually be created in much less time than it takes for it to melt away on a warm day. A stone sculptor may take a year to complete his work, but the statue may last for centuries, long after the sculptor himself dies.

Most of us intuitively value the ephemeral: the magic of a kiss, a chance encounter with a long-lost friend, the triumph on the face of a marathon runner as he crosses the finish line, the electricity of a live performance. In each case, there is the sense that the moment is special, never to be experienced again.

Returning to the concept of opposing but complementary forces, the ultimate answer to the question of how to pass on the knowledge of humanity to future generations most likely lies right in front of us. Like the team that studied mice to determine how to win the microprocessor contest, the answer undoubtedly lies in nature and involves working with nature, not against it. Although we often think that humanity is special—that we are somehow in charge of changing the world, creating enduring structures, bulldozing mountains, erecting monuments, and domesticating animals—from an evolutionary perspective, humanity is simply another variety of DNA expressing itself within the confines of the big blue planet Earth.

Virtually all life on earth passes on properties to the next generation by passing DNA to its offspring. Unlike confronting nature with cold metal inscribed with marks that will eventually succumb to the elements, DNA expresses itself in the nature of the current environment. In other words, a particular combination of DNA is successful if it manages to appear in the next generation. In this regard, humans are definitely not the most successful life form on the planet. Many viruses, for example, have managed to permanently pass on their DNA sequence to humans to be propagated in each generation of human offspring. In this regard, the human genome is the medium for the viral message that is being broadcast into the future.

As we experiment with the human genome, modifying it here and there to change hair color, athletic ability, and IQ—as in the case of Ben Riley from Chapter 8—we will eventually learn how to encode data in our DNA in a way that doesn't interfere with normal biological processes. The same contemporary biogenetics technology that is fully capable of adding components of pig DNA to tomato DNA to make a longer-lasting fruit can be used to modify sequences of human DNA. Less invasive technologies, perhaps through the use of designer drugs, will certainly be available in the near future. The question is, can the approximately 10 percent of the human genome that contains "garbage" sequences—sequences that don't code for any known proteins necessary for life—be used to pass a message on to our descendents? That is, if the human genome is fully deciphered by some future generation, wouldn't it be something if it sent them a message of some sort encoded into the DNA in the ultimate form of data preservation? And what should this message contain? A time capsule of sorts, with the family recipe for grandma's turkey stuffing? Quotations from a favorite author? Universal constants, such as the value of pi or the speed of light in a vacuum? The Ten Commandments?

What if the current "garbage" DNA isn't really garbage but is, in fact, messages encoded by our ancestors from a long-lost culture? Are we, like the student who discovered the Voyager disk, simply unable to recognize what has been in front of us all along? Will fully deciphering the human genome and proteome reveal the work of bioengineers from thousands of years ago? What would be the effect on the study of science, religion, and anthropology if future families in one area of Europe were found to have DNA with the message "You are descendents of the family of Argus, from Atlantis, sent out upon the land in 10102, the year of the great flood" encrypted in their "garbage" DNA?

Regarding the preservation of digital data, perhaps the best approach is to model the adaptive process that occurs in nature through technologies we are studying now in machine leaning and AI, such as genetic algorithms, self-modifying hardware, and adaptive software. Genetic algorithms are models of machine learning in which a population of simulated individuals are created and undergo a process of evolution in a simulated competitive environment. Self-modifying hardware can virtually rewire itself as needed.

For example, in response to damage to one part of a circuit—a burned-out component in a satellite, for example—self-modifying hardware can reroute signals to another, fully functioning part of the circuit. Adaptive software is similar to adaptive hardware in that it can reconfigure itself to suit the new operating conditions. However, instead of simply rerouting signals, adaptive software can actually rewrite itself, providing functionality that was not available before.

Whether or not some form of adaptive, silicon-based "life" can manage to propagate itself through mutation and adaptation, transporting data into the future, the issue will be who will read and interpret the data and how. How will some future generation, temporarily cast back into a pretechnology era because of war or natural disaster, know what to look for?

Finally, if human or perhaps mouse DNA holds the key to the ultimate digital data repository, what does this portend for the ethics of biology and life? Do racks of mouse or monkey neural tissues, grown in sheets to be spread on silicon wafers to create DNA-powered bio-chips, lie in our future? If life is a struggle for the right to exist in the future, will data eventually take on a life of its own, with expression in both silicon and organic entities?

For example, if, as some futurists theorize, machines someday surpass humans in intelligence, data will take on a new meaning. In the world of thinking machines, data won't be things lightly handled so that they could simply be lost by accident but will be treated more like the blood of a human, with equal gravity, appreciation of its value, and awareness of the dreadful consequences of loss.

Bibliography

Chapter 1

Appignanesi, R., P. Cobley, and L. Jansz, eds. *Introducing Semiotics.* 1998, New York: Totem Books.

Beckwith, H., *The Invisible Touch.* 2000, New York: Warner Books.

Bergeron, B., *The Eternal E-Customer: How Emotionally Intelligent Interfaces Can Create Long-Lasting Customer Relationships.* 2001, New York: McGraw-Hill.

Chomsky, N., *Knowledge of Language: Its Nature, Origin, and Use.* 1986, New York: Praeger.

Jones, J., and W. Wilson, *An Incomplete Education.* 1987, New York: Ballantine Books.

Lieberman, P., *Human Language and Our Reptilian Brain: The Subcortical Basis of Speech, Syntax, and Thought.* 2000, Cambridge: Harvard University Press.

Porter, D., *The Greatest Benefit to Mankind.* 1997, New York: W.W. Norton & Co.

Schopenhauer, A., *The World as Will and Representation.* Vol. 2. 1958, New York: Dover Publications, Inc.

Stalnaker, R., *Context and Content: Essays on Intentionality in Speech and Thought.* 1999, New York: Oxford University Press, Inc.

Steinhauer, J., So, the brain tumor's on the left, right? *The New York Times,* April 1, 2001:23–24.

Virilio, P., *Open Sky.* 1997, New York: Verso.

Virilio, P., *The Information Bomb.* 2000, New York: Verso.

Chapter 2

Bergeron, B. P., *Know Your Body.* 1984, New Orleans: Home Health Software.

Bergeron, B. P., *HeartLab.* 1988, Baltimore: Williams & Wilkins Publishers.

Bergeron, B. P., Surface acoustic wave devices. *Communications Quarterly* 4(2):83–93, 1994.

Catanzarite, V., and B. P. Bergeron, *FMTutor.* 1990, Baltimore: Williams & Wilkins Publishers.

Fairley, P., Power to the people. *Technology Review* 104(4):71–77, 2001.

Fink, D., and D. Christiansen, eds. *Electrical Engineering Handbook.* 1986, McGraw-Hill: New York.

Frauenfelder, M., Death match. *Wired* 9(5):150–153, 2001.

Long, L., and N. Long, *Computers: Brief Edition.* 2001, Upper Saddle River, NJ: Prentice Hall.

Messmer, H., *The Indispensable PC Hardware Book: Your Hardware Questions Answered.* 3rd ed. 1997, New York: Addison-Wesley.

Parsons, J., and D. Oja, *Computer Concepts.* 3rd ed. 2000, Cambridge: Course Technology.

Ranade, S., *Mass Storage Technology.* 1991, London: Meckler.

Satoh, S., Y. Tosaka, and S. Wender, Geometric effect of multiple-bit soft errors induced by cosmic ray neutrons on DRAMs. *IEEE Electron Device Letters* 21(6):310–312, 2000.

Silberman, S., The hot new medium: paper. *Wired* 9(4):184–191, 2001.

Taylor, D., *Object-Oriented Technology.* 1990, New York: Addison-Wesley Publishing Co., Inc.

Voss, D., Protein chips. *Technology Review* 104(4):35, 2001.

White, R., *How Computers Work, Millennium Edition.* 1999, Indianapolis: Que.

Williams, E., *The CD-ROM and Optical Disc Recording Systems.* 1994, Oxford: Oxford Science Publishers.

Yoshida, S., et al., Optical pickup employing a hologram-laser-photodiode unit. *Japanese Journal of Applied Physics, Part 1: Regular Papers and Short Notes and Review Papers* 39(2B):877–882, 2000.

Chapter 3

Barker, J., Video CD: the argument. *CD-ROM Professional* 8(6):44–50, 1995.

Bergeron, B. P., *The Alchemy-Technology Continuum.* 2001 (in press), New York: John Wiley & Sons.

Bhushan, B., *Tribology and Mechanics of Magnetic Storage Devices.* 1996, New York: Springer.

Casey, C., The cyber-archive: a look at the storage and preservation of web sites. *College and Research Libraries* 59(4):304–310, 1998.

Feder, B., IBM to show advanced chips for net use. *The New York Times,* Aprill 13, 2001:C4.

Hegel, R., Tribological comparisons of particulate magnetic tape coatings in destructive wear testing. *Tribology International* 31(8):407–412, 1998.

Hempstock, M., and J. Sullivan, Characterization of surface changes to metal evaporated and metal particle media following durability tests in helical scan Hi-8 recorders at ambient and high humidity conditions. *Tribology International* 31(8):419–424, 1998.

Johnson, M., Magnetoelectronic memories last and last. *IEEE Spectrum* 37(2):33–40, 2000.

Jon, E., Specifying reliability in the disk drive industry: no more MTBF's. In *Annual Reliability and Maintainability Symposium: Advancing the Technology—A Commitment to Lifelong Learning.* 2000, Los Angeles: Elsevier Engineering Information, Inc.

Longhurst, J., C. Brebbie, and H. Power, eds. *Air Pollution VIII.* 2000, Southampton: WIT Press.

Mansuripur, M., Rewritable optical disk technologies. In *Proceedings of SPIE—The International Society for Optical Engineering.* 2000, Amsterdam: Elsevier Engineering Information, Inc.

Martin, M., and J. Hyon. Evaluation of DVD-R for archival purposes. In *Proceedings of the 1999 Joint International Symposium on Optical Memory and Optical Data Storage.* 1999, Loloa, HI: Elsevier Engineering Information, Inc.

Mee, C., and E. Daniel, *Magnetic Recording Technology.* 1996, New York: McGraw-Hill.

National Research Council, *Preserving Scientific Data on Our Physical Universe.* 1995, Washington, D.C.: National Academy Press.

Patton, S., and B. Bhushan, Origins of friction and wear of the thin metallic layer of metal evaporated magnetic tape. *Wear* 224(1):126–140, 1999.

Ramesh, R., ed. *Thin Film Ferroelectric Materials and Devices.* 1997, Boston: Kluwer Academic Publishers.

Richharia, M., *Satellite Communication Systems: Design Principles.* 2nd ed. 1999, New York: McGraw-Hill.

Rothenberg, J., Ensuring the longevity of digital documents. *Scientific American* 272(1):24–29, 1995.

Sardar, Z., and I. Abrams, *Introducing Chaos.* 1999, Cambridge: Icon.

Chapter 4

Bergeron, B., Data Repositories, Data Marts, and Data Warehouses. In *Electronic Medical Records: A Guide for Clinicians and Administrators,* J. Carter, ed. 2001, Philadelphia: American College of Physicians, pp. 73–102.

Celko, J., *Data & Databases: Concepts in Practice.* 1999, San Francisco: Morgan Kaufmann Publishers.

Humphries, M., M. Hawkins, and M. Dy, *Data Warehousing Architecture and Implementation.* 1999, Upper Saddle River, NJ: Prentice Hall.

Simon, A., *Data Warehousing for Dummies.* 1997, Foster City, CA: IDG Books Worldwide, Inc.

Taylor, D., *Object-Oriented Technology.* 1990, New York: Addison-Wesley Publishing Co., Inc.

Chapter 5

Brackett, M., *Data Resource Quality: Turning Bad Habits into Good Practices.* 2000, Boston: Addison-Wesley.

Cabena, P., et al., *Discovering Datamining: From Concept to Implementation.* 1998, Upper Saddle River, NJ: Prentice Hall.

Daley, S., In Europe, some fear national languages are endangered. *The New York Times,* April 16, 2001:1–10.

Deutsch, D., One tool, many functions: words and pictures are combined to form a new industry. *The New York Times,* April 17, 2001:1.

Loshin, D., *Enterprise Knowledge Management: The Data Quality Approach.* 2001, New York: Morgan Kaufmann.

Sanders, G., *Data Modeling.* 1995, New York: Boyd & Fraser Publishing Company.

Tapscott, D., D. Ticoll, and A. Lowy, *Digital Capital: Harnessing the Power of Business Webs.* 2000, Boston: Harvard Business School Press.

Chapter 6

Armstrong, I., Computer forensics: tracking down the clues. *SC Magazine* April:24–30, 2001.

Betz, F., *Managing Technological Innovation: Competitive Advantage from Change.* 1998, New York: John Wiley and Sons.

Bitta, M., Stealing satellite. *PC Magazine* 20(9):69–70, 2001.

Darkins, A., and M. Cary, *Telemedicine and Telehealth: Principles, Policies, Performance, and Pitfalls.* 2000, New York: Springer Publishing Company.

Dodd, G., Keeping the pirates at bay. *Game Developer* 8(5):44–49, 2001.

Glass, B., Know your enemy. *PC Magazine* 20(9):90–98, 2001.

Gomes, L., Silicon Valley's open secrets. *The Wall Street Journal,* April 27, 2001:B1.

Hall, E., *Managing Risk: Methods for Software Systems Development.* 1998, Reading, MA: Addison-Wesley.

Kerstetter, J., Software shakeout. *BusinessWeek,* March 5, 2001:72–80.

Lam, J., Secure your web applications. *PC Magazine* 20(9):IP01–4, 2001.

Chapter 7

Bergeron, B., *The Eternal E-Customer: How Emotionally Intelligent Interfaces Can Create Long-Lasting Customer Relationships.* 2001, New York: McGraw-Hill.

Davenport, G., Your own virtual storyworld. *Scientific American* 283(11): 79–82, 2000.

Delsol, M., Under house awrist. *Fortune,* April 30, 2001:196.

Fisher, A., The first time ever I shot your face. *Wired* 9(2):76, 2001.

Hamilton, D., Banned code lives in poetry and song. *The Wall Street Journal,* April 12, 2001:B4.

Kahaner, L., Hungry for your e-mail. *Information Week* April 23:59–64, 2001.

McCook, A., Hack job. *Scientific American* 284(5):24, 2001.

Poe, R., Location disorder. *Business 2.0* April 3:46–49, 2001.

Rich, L., And now, our digital presentation. *The Industry Standard* Feb. 12: 64–66, 2001.

Sandberg, J., People who love gadgets can't get enough of them. *The Wall Street Journal,* May 2, 2001:1.

Talagala, N., et al., Art of massive storage: a Web image archive. *Computer* 33(11):22–28, 2000.

Tulsi, B., and P. Zera, 2001, a satellite odyssey. *Technology Investor* Jan.: 50–55, 2001.

Weber, T., To librarians in Queens, "fair use," "first sale" are keys to knowledge. *The Wall Street Journal,* April 9, 2001:B1.

Wildstrom, S., DVDs aren't ready for home movies yet. *BusinessWeek* May 7:28, 2001.

Chapter 8

Brand, S., Founding father. *Wired* 9(3):145–153, 2001.

Bruk, D., Copyrightable functions and patentable speech. *Communications of the ACM* 44(2):69–75, 2001.

Fleishman, G., In-box invasion. *Wired* 9(3):87, 2001.

Graven, M., Leave me alone. *PC Magazine* Jan. 16:151–159, 2001.

Grossman, W., To protect and self-serve. *Scientific American* March:31, 2001.

Harris, N., Privacy concerns rise as plans for tracking cell-phone users unfold: location technology offers safety and services, but some fear it may be abused. *The Wall Street Journal,* Nov. 19, 1999:B4.

Hatlestad, L., Privacy matters. *Red Herring* Jan. 16:48–56, 2001.

Marshall, C., Getting to know you. *Business 2.0* March 20:52–55, 2001.

Mayor, T., Someone to watch over you. *CIO* March 1:83–88, 2001.

Medford, C., Know who I am. *PC Magazine* Jan. 16:134–148, 2001.

Plante, R., R. Crutcher, and R. McGrath, The NCSA astronomy digital image library: from data archiving to data publishing. *Future Generation Computing Systems* 16:49–61, 1999.

Poe, R., Courtesy calls. *Business 2.0* May 1:52–56, 2001.

Rosenberg, R., Handhelds to be Harvard medical students' first assist. *The Boston Globe,* May 7, 2001:C2.

Rotenberg, M., *The Privacy Law Sourcebook 1999: United States Law, International Law, and Recent Developments.* 1999, Washington, D.C.: Electronic Privacy Information Center.

Schmit, R., Online privacy: alleged abuses shape new law. *The Wall Street Journal,* Feb. 29, 2000:B1.

Seltzer, L., Monitoring software. *PC Magazine* March 6:26–28, 2001.

Skykes, C., *The End of Privacy.* 1999, New York: St. Martin Press.

Viega, J., T. Kohno, and B. Potter, Trust (and mistrust) in secure applications. *Communications of the ACM* 44(2):31–36, 2001.

Chapter 9

Avrin, D., et al., Simulation of disaster recovery of a picture archiving and communications system using off-site hierarchal storage management. *Journal of Digital Imaging* 13(2):168–170, 2000.

Baker, N., *Double Fold.* 2001, New York: Random House.

Boxer, S., A century's photo history destined for life in a mine. *The New York Times,* April 15, 2001:B1.

Copeland, R., An optical rosetta stone. *Information Week* April 30:73, 2001.

Elkington, N., ed. *Digital Imaging Technology for Preservation.* 1994, Mountain View, CA: The Research Libraries Group, Inc.

Freiberger, P., and M. Swaine, *Fire in the Valley: The Making of the Personal Computer.* 1984, New York: McGraw-Hill.

Gershenfeld, N., *When Things Start to Think.* 1999, New York: Henry Holt and Company.

Gladwell, M., *The Tipping Point.* 2000, New York: Little, Brown and Company.

Glater, J., Telecommuting's big experiment: federal employees are urged to work outside of the office. *The New York Times,* May 9, 2001:C7.

Kurzweil, R., *The Age of Spiritual Machines: When Computers Exceed Human Intelligence.* 1999, New York: Viking.

McKean, J., *Information Masters.* 1999, New York: John Wiley & Sons.

Murray, B., CD-ROM archivability. *NML Bits* 2(2):4, 1992.

Reich, R., *The Future of Success.* 2001, New York: Alfred A. Knopf.

Takahashi, D., The age of erasable hardware. *Red Herring* May 1:144–148, 2001.

Resources

Archival Services

Because archiving is usually performed on very valuable documents and data, it's usually better to work with a local service instead of risking a situation of disks or papers being lost in the mail. However, as a point of reference, National Archiving Services' Web site is worth visiting to get an idea of the range of services available from archival service companies.

National Archiving Services, Ltd.
777 North James Road
Columbus, OH 43219
614.235.7000
www.nationalarchival.com

One of the services worth noting is Norsam Technologies, which isn't yet open for general commercial business. Their technology of micro-etching nickel disks holds promise for very long-term archiving.

Norsam Technologies
5285 N.E. Elam Young Parkway, Suite A100
Hillsboro, OR 97124
877.476.7627
info@norsam.com
www.rosettaproject.org

Archival Supplies

For traditional photographic prints and slides, Exposures offers a wide selection of acid-free mounting hardware and enclosures. They offer an Archival Mist that deacidifies paper documents, acid-free glue sticks, and acid-free mounting papers.

Exposures
1 Memory Lane
Oshkosh, WI 54903
800.222.4947
www.exposuresonline.com

Audio Digitization and Processing Software/Hardware

Digitizing cassette and reel-to-reel tapes so that the audio can be stored on CD or digital tape can be accomplished with the PC's built-in sound capture hardware. However, for the greatest fidelity and the ability to reduce hissing, pops, and other analog noise, special hardware and software filters are useful. Many retail music centers that specialize in digital music and synthesizers have a range of audio capture hardware and software. For readers without access to a local dealer, Sound Chaser offers a wide selection of hardware and software for manipulating audio.

Sound Chaser
1175 G Street, Suite C
Arcata, CA 95521
800.549.4371
www.soundchaser.com

The top-selling software for digital sound editing and translation includes Steinberg's Wavelab, Syntrillium's Cool Edit Pro, Creamw@re's Triple DAT and Osiris plug-in, Tracer Technology's Dart Pro 32 (specifically made for digitizing vinyl records), and plug-ins from Waves, SEK'D Red Roaster 24-bit, Sonic Foundry's line of products, including Sound Forge and Sound Forge XP (an affordable version of Sound Forge).

Creamw@re
CreamWare US Inc.
855-C Conklin Street
Farmingdale, NY 11735
800.899.1939
www.creamware.com

SEK'D America
407 Stony Point Road
Santa Rosa, CA 95401
800.330.7753
www.sekd.com

Sonic Foundry
Sonic Foundry, Inc.
1617 Sherman Avenue
Madison, WI 53704
800.577.6642
www.sonicfoundry.com

Steinberg North America
21354 Nordhoff Street, Suite 110
Chatsworth, CA 91311
818.993.4161
www.steinberg.net

Syntrillium Software
P.O. Box 62255
Phoenix, AZ 85082-2255
480.941.4327
www.Syntrillium.com

Waves Ltd.
306 West Depot Avenue, Suite 100
Knoxville, TN 37917
865.546.6115
www.waves.com

Although the built-in sound card on most PCs is sufficient for digitizing audio, for the best results the standard sound card can be replaced with one that provides cleaner sound, more on-board RAM for faster digitizing, more dynamic range, and usually a digital output that can output directly to a Digital Audio Tape (DAT) or other digital recording device. The top-selling, moderately priced card is Creative Lab's AWE-64 Gold. Higher-end cards are available from Event Electronics, Digital Audio Labs, Creamw@re, Sonorus, SEK'D, and Frontier Design Group.

Creamw@re
CreamWare US Inc.
855-C Conklin Street
Farmingdale, NY 11735
800.899.1939
www.creamware.com

Creative Labs, Inc.
www.soundblaster.com

Digital Audio Labs
3650 Annapolis Lane North
Plymouth, MN 55447
763.559.9098
www.digitalaudiolabs.com

Event Electronics
P.O. Box 4189
Santa Barbara, CA 93140
Fax: 805.566.7771
www.eventelectronics.com

Frontier Design Group, LLC
199 Heater Road
Lebanon, NH 03766
800.928.3236
www.frontierdesign.com

SEK'D America
407 Stony Point Road
Santa Rosa, CA 95401
800.330.7753
www.sekd.com

Sonorus, Inc.
366 Washington Street
Newburgh, NY 12550
845.562.6000
www.sonorus.com

· ·

DATA RECOVERY SERVICES

The following list is a sampling from dozens of national and international data recovery services. In the United States, DriveSavers is probably the best known service, especially for servers and corporate-sized databases. For a crashed hard drive on a laptop or desktop PC, other services may prove to be cheaper, but I've found the differential worth it for the service DriveSavers provides.

Accurate Data Recovery
18 Hurndale Avenue
Toronto, Ontario M4K 1R7
Canada
888.241.3282
www.a-data.com

CBL Data Recovery Technologies, Inc.
590 Alden Road
Markham, Ontario, Canada L3R 8N2
800.551.3917
www.cbltech.com

DriveSavers
400 Bel Marin Keys Boulevard
Novato, CA 94949
800.440.1904
recovery@drivesavers.com
www.drivesavers.com

DIGITAL MEDIA AND PAPER CD SLEEVES

Most media needs, including CD blanks, can be found at virtually any microcomputer center. The best mail order firms include the hardware and software vendors CDW, MicroWarehouse, and PC Connection, listed below under Hardware and Software Dealers. In addition, Polyline offers a wide selection of media and protective sleeves and cases.

Polyline Corporation
1401 Estes Avenue
Elk Grove Village, IL 60007
800.701.7689

FIRE-RESISTANT SAFES

Most office supply stores, such as Staples and OfficeMax, offer a line of fireproof safes. Safes from Sentry are affordable, and most provide half-hour protection at house-fire temperatures. Higher-end safes that provide longer protection and more secure doors (including gaskets that block the water from hoses and sprinkler systems) are available through office supply stores.

Sentry Group
882 Linden Avenue
Rochester, NY 14625
800.828.1438
www.sentry.com

OfficeMax
800.283.7674
www.officemax.com

Staples, Inc.
500 Staples Drive
P.O. Box 9295
Framingham, MA 01701
800.333.3330
www.staples.com

Hardware and Software Dealers

For media, tape, CD-ROM or DVD drives, power conditioners, data conversion software, and other computer supplies, PC Connection is difficult to beat. Its Web site is especially helpful in providing a list of what types of hardware and software are available for particular problems, arranged by price, manufacturer, or other index. Micro-Warehouse and Computer Discount Warehouse seem especially geared to the corporate purchaser.

CDW Computer Centers, Inc.
200 North Milwaukee Avenue
Vernon Hills, IL 60061
800.838.4239
www.CDW.com

MicroWarehouse
1720 Oak Street
Lakewood, NJ 08701
800.990.0742
www.warehouse.com

PC Connection
730 Milford Road
Merrimack, NH 03054
800.800.1111
www.pcconnection.com

Publishing Perfection
21155 Watertown Road
Waukesha, WI 53186
800.810.1617

The Programmers Paradise
1157 Shrewsbury Avenue
Shrewsbury, NJ 07702
800.445.7899

POWER CONDITIONERS

In the world of uninterruptible power supplies for microcomputers, Advanced Power Conversion (APC) is clearly the most popular brand. Belkin Components and Tripp Lite tend to be better known at larger (more expensive) installations. All of the vendors listed below offer models appropriate for laptops to large server arrays.

Advanced Power Conversion, Inc.
132 Fairgrounds Road
West Kingston, RI 02889
800.800.4272
www.apc.com

Belkin Components, Inc.
501 W. Walnut Street
Compton, CA 90220
310.604.2292
www.belkin.com

Best Power
P. O. Box 280
Necedah, WI 54646
800.356.5794
www.bestpower.com

Opti-UPS
1050 W. Central Avenue, Suite E
Brea, CA 92821
714.674.5080
info@opti-ups.com
www.opti-ups.com

Tripp Lite Worldwide
1111 W. 35th Street
Chicago, IL 60609
773.869.1111
www.tripplite.com

PUBLICATIONS

The National Archives and Records Administration offers a number of free print publications on archiving. In addition, its Web site offers a wealth of information on managing data.

National Archives and Records Administration
Life Cycle Management Division
8601 Adelphi Road
College Park, MD 20740
301.713.6677
records.mgt@arch2.nara.gov
www.nara.gov/publications/recsmgmt.html

For the latest word on electronic privacy in the United States, see the Web sites of several groups that are working to define and address the challenges. The Electronic Privacy Information Center is an advocate's site that reports on the privacy policies of popular sites. Junkbusters is a resource to battle invasive advertising, regardless of the media used. The Privacy Page offers a collection of articles relating to privacy.

Electronic Privacy Information Center
www.Epic.org

Federal Trade Commission
www.FTC.gov

Junkbusters
www.junkbusters.com

The Privacy Page
www.privacy.org

The Privacy Foundation
www.privacyfoundation.org

When it comes to preserving documents, it's hard to pass up the experience of those working at the Library of Congress. In addition, the National Media Laboratory is worth monitoring for announcements on longevity of new digital media, although the information tends to be sporadic.

Library of Congress Preservation Directorate
preserve@loc.gov

National Media Laboratory
www.nml.org

Glossary

A/D conversion	Analog-to-digital conversion. The process of converting voice, music, and other continuous, time-varying signals to discrete digital signals.
Acid-free paper	Paper made with a process that leaves it slightly alkaline. Acid-free or buffered paper lasts longer than nonbuffered paper.
Ad hoc query	A question put to a database, the answer to which cannot be determined before the moment the query is issued.
Algorithm	A process expressed in software.
Amplifier	An electronic circuit that increases the strength or amplitude of a signal.
Amplitude	The extent to which the voltage or current of a signal varies in time. Higher swings in voltage or current correspond to greater amplitude.
Analog network	A network in which voice and other data are sent as continuous, time-varying signals without first being transformed to digital signals by A/D conversion.

Analog signal	An electronic signal that is represented by time-varying voltage levels over a continuous range rather than in discrete steps.
Apache	A popular application for serving Web pages on the Internet. The software is free, open source, and compatible with a variety of operating systems.
Application	A software program, such as a database, spreadsheet, graphics, or word processing program.
Application Service Provider (ASP)	A technology that provides users with access to applications and data through a Web browser, without their needing to purchase and run applications locally.
Appraisal	The process of determining whether data are worth preserving.
Architecture	The general technical layout of a computer or network system.
Archival value	The value of data being maintained in preservation.
Archive	A collection of valuable data.
Archiving	The process of selecting and preserving data for future access or for distribution.
ASCII	American Standard Code for Information Interchange. ASCII code provides a hardware- and software-independent means of sharing data between microcomputers. A standard for data exchange used primarily on microcomputers. EBCDIC is the equivalent standard on IBM mainframes.
Atari	The California-based company, founded in 1972, that helped start the video game industry, providing a platform for game titles such as Pong.
Avatar	A graphical representation of a user that serves as the user's identity in a virtual reality environment. Avatars may look like the user, or they may be totally dissociated and take the form of an animal, alien, or person of the opposite sex.

Bandwidth	A measure of the information-carrying capacity of a medium. Bandwidth is commonly measured in bits per second (bps).
Beta testing	The second stage of product testing, carried out by typical users in a variety of settings that mimic those in which the final product will be used. Beta testing is performed just before a product's release and is used to find and fix bugs, never to redesign features.
Binary	A system of expressing numerical values as a string of 0's and 1's.
Biometrics	A method of verifying the identity of a user based on the user's fingerprints, facial features, retinal pattern, voice, or other personal characteristic.
BIOS (Basic Input/ Output System)	The collection of low-level software codes built into a PC that define the hardware environment. The BIOS is commonly stored in some form of PROM.
Bit	The smallest unit of data in a computer system. Any specific data bit can either be high (1) or low (0).
Bitmapped screen	A display screen where every pixel is represented by at least one bit in memory.
Bits per second (bps)	A measure of the speed at which data is transmitted or received. The maximum bps is limited by the bandwidth of the connection. Kbps, Mbps, and Gbps refer to thousand, millions, and billions of bits per second, respectively.
Bluetooth	A short-range wireless communications standard for linking a wide range of computers, electronics, and telecom devices.
Brick-and-mortar business	A traditional business with a physical presence.
Broadcast	One-way communications from a single transmitter to many receivers, as in broadcast TV and radio.
Browser	A software program that interprets documents on the Web. Netscape Navigator and Microsoft Internet Explorer are the two most popular browsers in use today.

Burn-in	The process, usually performed at the factory, of keeping newly fabricated computer hardware running so that weak elements that fail early on can be identified before the system is shipped to the customer.
CD-I	Compact Disc Interactive. A defunct software and optical hardware standard, introduced by Philips Electronics in the mid 1990s, and intended to provide highly interactive multimedia.
CD-R	CD-Recordable. A CD format that supports the writing of CD-ROMs.
Click-and-mortar business	A traditional business with a significant Web presence. A hybrid between the pure dotCom and brick-and-mortar companies.
Client	A PC or wireless device that communicates over a network both with its peers, other clients, and with a larger computer, called a server, which typically stores data that many workers need to use. The client has just one user; the server has many.
Client-server	A computer architecture in which the workload is split between desktop PCs or handheld wireless devices (clients) and more powerful or higher-capacity computers (servers) that are connected by a network such as the Internet.
Codex	A book, most often a manuscript of classics, scripture, or ancient annals.
Complexity	The science of complex systems. It explores the properties of complex systems at the edge of chaos.
Compression	The manipulation of a signal to minimize bandwidth requirements.
Convergence	The merging of all data and all media into a single digital form.
Customer relations management (CRM)	The process of managing the relationship between a business and its customers.

D/A conversion	Digital-to-analog conversion. The conversion of a discrete digital signal into a continuous, time-varying analog signal.
Data	Numerical quantities or other attributes derived from observation, experiment, or calculation.
Data dictionary	A database about data and database structures. A catalog of all data elements, containing their names, structures, and information about their usage.
Data management	The process of controlling, protecting, and facilitating access to data to provide consumers with timely access to the data they need.
Data mart	A small, single-subject data warehouse used by a single group of users.
Data mining	The process of extracting meaningful relationships from, usually, very large quantities of seemingly unrelated data. Used in marketing, for example, to derive consumer preferences.
Data model	A logical map that represents the inherent properties of the data independently of software, hardware, or machine performance considerations. The model shows data elements grouped into records, as well as the association around those records.
Data transformation	The process of converting data from one form to another, more useful, or standard form. For example, converting degrees Fahrenheit to degrees Centigrade involves data transformation.
Data warehouse	A central database, frequently very large, that can provide authorized users with access to all of a company's information.
Data warehouse management tools	Software that extracts and transforms data from operational systems and loads it into the data warehouse.
DBMS	Database Management System. Used to store, process, and manage data in a systematic way.
Dialect	A regional variation in spoken language.

Digital network	A communications network in which speech and data are first converted to digital form (A/D conversion) before being transmitted on the network.
Digital signature	An encrypted digital tag added to an electronic communication to verify the identity of a customer. Also called an electronic signature.
Digitization	The process of converting an analog representation of data into a digital one.
Document	Recorded information comprising a medium and a message.
Drill-down	A method of exploring detailed data that was used in creating a summary of data.
DSS	Decision Support System. Application for analyzing large quantities of data and performing a wide variety of calculations and projections.
DVD	Digital Versatile Disc. A media format developed in the mid 1990s by Philips and Sony. Although it resembles a standard CD, a DVD has about twenty times the capacity of a CD. Also called Digital Video Disc.
DVD-R	DVD-Recordable. A write-once technology that supports capacities up to nearly 5 GB.
DVD-RAM	DVD-Random Access Memory. A rewriteable DVD format that allows for more than 100,000 rewrites. The medium is double-sided, with a capacity of nearly 5 GB per side.
DVD-RW	DVD-Rewritable. A writeable version of DVD-R. Medium is available in double-sided versions with up to about 5 GB per side. The technology supports 1,000 rewrites.
Early adopter	In marketing circles, a customer who must have the latest and greatest gadget, regardless of cost or inconvenience.
Ease of learning	Regarding a user interface, the ease with which a particular interface can be learned. Contrast with ease of use.

Ease of use	Regarding a user interface, the ease or efficiency with which the interface can be used. An easy-to-use interface may be difficult to learn, and vice versa.
EBCDIC	Extended Binary Coded Decimal Interchange Code. A standard for data exchange used primarily on IBM mainframes. ASCII is the equivalent standard on microcomputers.
ECC	Elliptic Curve Cryptography. A method of encryption and digital signatures that is optimized for computationally limited devices, such as wireless PDAs and cell phones. ECC is more efficient than RSA, the standard encryption used on the wired Web.
EDI	Electronic Data Interchange. A standard transmission format for business information sent from one computer to another, using strings of data.
Encryption	The alteration of transmitted information to keep it secret.
Entity relationship diagramming	A process that visually identifies the relationships between data in a database.
Entropy	A measure of disorder (noise) in a system.
Epigraphy	The study of writings engraved in stone or metal.
Ethernet	The most common form of network used in corporations, with a top speed of 10 Mbps. Because it works like a party line, the network slows dramatically if too many users try to send messages at once.
Firewall	A network security device or software program that can limit unauthorized access to parts of a network.
Full backup	A complete backup of all files in a directory or system. In comparison, an incremental backup includes only changes since the last backup.
Gateway	A software product that allows SQL-based applications to access relational and nonrelational data sources.
GIF	Graphics Interchange Format. A popular data format used for image exchange on the Web.

GUI	Graphical User Interface. The point-and-click interfaces first popularized by the Apple Macintosh and now used by Microsoft Windows. Pictures, not just words, represent features.
HTML	HyperText Markup Language. The most popular programming language used to create documents on the Web.
Human-computer interface	The combination of hardware and software elements that provides the communications channel between a computer and the computer user. Also called the user interface.
Incremental backup	A backup that contains only changes since the last backup. In contrast, a full backup contains copies of all files. Incremental backups are much faster than full backups.
Information	A collection of data and associated explanations, interpretations, and other textual material concerning a particular object, event, or process.
Information Theory	The theory, advanced by Claude Shannon in 1949, that describes, in mathematical terms, a way to precisely measure the uncertainty in the transmission and reception of information. Information Theory defines a way to find the minimum number of bits required to communicate a given message.
Informational value	The value of records for the information they contain as opposed to the value of the media. A child's scribbles on an ancient tablet may be invaluable if the tablet is in good condition, but of little or no informational value.
Infrastructure	In the context of the Internet, the system of servers, cables, hardware, and software that ties the system together to support the operation of the network.
Instant messaging	A type of communications service that allows someone to establish a private conversation with another individual in real time.
Internalization	The process of matching the content in a Web site to suit the language and culture of specific customers.

Internet	*An* internet is a collection of local area networks (LANs) connected by a wide area network (WAN). *The* Internet is the World Wide Web, one of many internets.
Internet phone	A wireless phone that can access the Internet. Smart Phones are also Internet phones.
Intrinsic value	The value and characteristics of an original document. For example, the Declaration of Independence has considerable intrinsic value for economic purposes.
ISO	The International Organization for Standardization, which establishes international information exchange standards.
ISO 9096	A standard for storing data on a CD-ROM. The standard specifies how the data are written to the disk for error correction and the format of the table of contents, allowing CD-ROM controlled by a variety of operating systems to access the data on the disk. ISO 9096 CDs can be read on both Macintosh and Windows machines.
ISP	Internet Service Provider. A commercial organization that provides clients with access to the Internet.
Jargon	The specialized vocabulary of a particular trade or profession.
Java	In the context of this book, a programming language, developed by Sun Microsystems, used to create interactive applications on the Web.
JPEG	Joint Photographic Expert Group. A graphics standard that uses compression to achieve small file sizes. Compare to GIF and TIFF.
Knowledge	Information that is organized, synthesized, or summarized to enhance comprehension, awareness, or understanding. That is, knowledge is a combination of data and an awareness of the context in which the data can be successfully applied.
Legacy system	An existing information system in which a company has already invested considerable time and money. Legacy systems usually present major integration problems when new, potentially incompatible systems are introduced.

Life cycle of records	The concept that data pass through a continuum of phases, from creation, active use, to maintenance.
Linguistics	The scientific study of language.
Linux	A Unix-like operating system that is free, open source, and compatible with a variety of operating systems.
Liquid Crystal Display (LCD)	The flat display technology used in handheld games, laptops, cell phones, and PDAs.
Local Area Network (LAN)	A group of computers, interconnected through wired and/or wireless communications so that they can share data, software, and storage devices. LANs are part of a client-server computing architecture.
Localization	The process of adapting a Web site or user interface to a particular country or region.
Loyalty	A positive inner feeling or emotional bond between a customer and a business or a brand. Loyalty can't be assessed directly but can be inferred from a customer's actions.
Loyalty effect	The quantifiable behavior normally associated with loyalty, such as repeatedly transacting business with a particular retailer or Web site.
Metadata	Data about data: how the structures and calculation rules are stored, information on data sources, definitions, quality, transformations, date of last update, and user access privileges.
Moore's Law	The prediction advanced by Gordon Moore, co-founder of Intel, that the number of transistors per square inch on integrated circuits will double every year. Moore predicted that this trend would continue for the foreseeable future. The law has been amended to predict a doubling approximately every 18 months.
Morphology	The study of the structure of words.
MP3	A standard for encoding digital audio, especially popular for distributing music on the Web.

Multimedia	The integration of motion video, animation, graphics, sound, voice, and text on the computer screen to entertain or educate.
Napster	A company that gained fame by making commercial music recordings available for free copying and distribution on the Web, much to the consternation of the recording industry.
National Archives and Records Administration (NARA)	The independent agency of the executive branch of the U.S. federal government, whose purpose is to select, preserve, and make available to the federal government and the public historically valuable government records. NARA is responsible for preserving documents such as the Declaration of Independence and the Constitution of the United States and for administering the presidential libraries and federal records centers.
Noise	An undesirable electrical signal.
Normalization	The process of reducing a complex data structure into its simplest, most stable structure.
Object-oriented	A method of application development that allows the reuse of program components in other contexts. Objects can inherit properties from other objects.
Open source	Software code that is open to users. Java, Linux, and XML are considered open source. Open source programs can be modified to suit the particular needs of a company or suite of applications. Most applications are proprietary to the manufacturer and are licensed but not modifiable.
Paleography	The study and analysis of the ancient writing on papyrus, wax, parchment, vellum, paper, and other destructible materials.
Paper	Thin sheets of compressed vegetable cellulose fibers, used for writing, printing, packaging, and wrapping. Synthetic fiber papers are made from nylon, Dacron, and Orlon fibers, with or without blends with wood pulp.
Papyrus	A writing material made from the central, spongy material of the stem of the papyrus plant.

Parchment	Formerly, a writing material made from animal hide. Contemporary parchment is high-quality, usually off-white, textured paper.
PDA	Personal Digital Assistant. A handheld electronic organizer that can have Internet access and email functions.
Platform	Systems upon which computing environments are built. Platforms include the Linux operating system, the Microsoft Windows operating system, and the TCP/IP Internet standard. Hardware platforms refer to particular lines of microcomputers, for example, the Macintosh platform.
Pragmatics	The study of the interaction between language and the contexts in which it is used.
Preservation	The process of providing a stable environment for data, using safe handling methods, duplicating unstable materials to stable media, copying fragile materials into usable format, storing records in housing made from stable materials, repairing documents to maintain their original format, establishing pest control, and instituting a disaster recovery plan.
Process management	An evaluation and restructuring of system functions to make certain that processes are carried out in the most efficient and economical way.
Proprietary	Software or hardware controlled by a company. Microsoft Windows and the Macintosh iBook are proprietary software and hardware, respectively.
Proteome	The body's collection of proteins. Given that the human genome, which encodes proteins, has been unraveled, medical researchers have turned to the proteome to further unravel the secrets of inherited diseases and other traits. Like the human genome project, exploring the human proteome will require a massive computational effort.
Protocol	A set of standards that defines, for example, communications between devices.

Push technology	The automatic delivery of information without continuous prompting from the user.
Query response times	The time it takes for the warehouse engine to process a complex query across a large volume of data and return the results to the requester.
Query tools	Software that allows a user to create and direct specific questions to a database.
RDBMS	Relational Database Management System. A system that stores, processes, and manages data arranged in relational tables.
Register	Interfaces that are directly assigned to hardware, accessed by the BIOS in response to commands from the operating system. The hard drive and floppy drive in a PC are each associated with unique registers.
ROI	Return on Investment. The profit made on an investment, evaluated in terms of money, timesavings, reduced complexity, or other measure.
RSA	The encryption algorithm that forms the basis for security on the Internet.
Scalability	A system's ability to support larger or smaller volumes of data and more or fewer users.
Semantic change	The change in the meanings of words over time.
Semantic mapping	The mapping of the meaning of a piece of data.
Semantics	The study of the meaning of language.
Semiotics	The analysis of sign systems.
Server	The computer that serves data or applications to one or more client computers.
SQL	Structured Query Language. The standard data structuring and access language used by relational databases.
Syntax	The study of the structure of phrases and sentences, that is, how words combine to make sentences.
Text-to-Speech (TTS)	Voice synthesis, using email or other text source to drive the voice synthesis process.

Thin client	A "stripped down" application designed specifically to run over a low-bandwidth communications channel.
TIFF	Tagged Image File Format. A standard, noncompressed file format that retains image data without loss (see GIF and JPEG).
Touch point	The point of contact between a customer and a company. Touch points include the wired Web, the wireless Web, telephone, fax, email, and person-to-person conversations.
Tribology	The science and technology of interactive surfaces in relative motion, including the study of friction, lubrication, and wear.
Tyvek	A proprietary material made of paper and plastic, commonly used to make high-strength CD-ROM sleeves and envelopes.
Understanding	The possession of a clear and complete idea of the nature, significance, or explanation of something. It is a personal, internal power to render experience intelligible by assimilating knowledge under broad concepts.
UPS	Uninterruptible Power Supply. A battery-powered device that generates 110 VAC the moment the power from the mains is disrupted. Most UPS systems for microcomputers provide 15 to 20 minutes of emergency power— enough time for one to carefully save files and close the system.
Vellum	High-quality parchment made from calfskin, kidskin, or lambskin.
Voice recognition	The automatic conversion of the spoken word into machine-readable text or computer commands. Voice recognition is especially attractive as an alternative to keyboard and stylus input on handheld wireless devices.
Wide Area Network (WAN)	Multiple local networks tied together, typically using telephone company services. WANs may connect users in different buildings or countries.
WORM	A Write Once, Read Many optical disc technology used for secondary storage.

XML	Extensible Markup Language. A markup language used to create Web pages that can be automatically reformatted to suit the needs of a variety of devices, from Internet phones with postage-stamp-sized displays to large desktop monitors. XML, an open Web standard, not only specifies how the data appear but, like a database, defines what the data represent.
Zip disk	A proprietary, removable, magnetic media standard produced by Iomega. The most popular Zip disk format is 100 MB. However, 250-MB drives that use media of the same dimension as the 100-MB disks are used as well. A 250-MB drive can read and write to 100-MB disks, but an older 100-MB drive cannot read or write to the newer 250-MB disks.

Index

Integrated Services Digital Network
(ISDN) 37
Intel 34, 37, 39
Intel microprocessor, compatibility with 39
Intel Pentium microprocessor, bug in first
release of 85
Intellectual property rights 152, 156, 215, 216
Intentional data corruption 167–168
Intentional destruction 169
Internal Revenue Service (IRS), taxpayer
database 204
Internet 36, 37, 169
Internet Explorer 48
Iomega Zip disks 41, 68, 71, 72
Iomega Zip drive 45

J

Japanese libraries, destruction of, in World
War II 8
Java 86
JPEG (Joint Photographic Expert Group)
files 233
Just-in-time multimedia learning 201
Just-in-time online, and context-specific data
136
Just-in-time publishing 19

K

K–12 schools, and computers 203
Key word indexing 100, 101
Knowledge
defined 9
distinction between data and 10

L

Language
and the communication of context 10
and the extension of meaning through
analogy 10
defined 17
shifts in 11
Languages, computer 46, 86
Laptop computers
and corporate espionage 164
theft of 173
Legal issues, in virtual worlds 215
Libraries
and digital collections 206

user demographics, changes in 217
Library patrons, cost and time issues 217
Liquid crystal displays (LCDs) 80
Lister Hill building, National Library of
Medicine 229, 230
Location-based services, and privacy 222
Low Earth Orbit (LEO) 75
Low-friction coatings, for magnetic tape 81
Low-level variability 42

M

Machine intelligence, and developer
responsibility 215
Macintosh-Windows cross-compatibility
issue 251
Macro viruses 174
Magnetic disks 68
and air pollution 81
erasing 69
failure rates of 81
formatting process 68
size 69
Magnetic media 68–69
Magnetic tape cartridges 69, 71
Magneto-optical (MO) discs and cartridges
70–71
Magneto-optical discs, failure rates of 81
Mainframe computers 34, 236
Matrix of potential PC configuration
variables 51–53
Mean Time Between Failure (MTBF)
rating 80
Media 59–71
deterioration of 78–83
expected lifetimes of 81
performance characteristics 60–64
trends 71
types of 65–71
Media performance characteristics 60–64
capacity 61
compatability 60, 61
cost 63
durability 63
speed 61
stability 64
tribology 63
Media selection 248
Media types 65–71
flash memory 67
magnetic media 68–69

optical media 70–71
solid-state memory 65
Media-based entertainment/education 201
Medium Earth Orbit (MEO) 75
Memories, and data retention 83
Memory Stick (Sony) 131
Mesopotamia, and history of writing 5
Metadata 121
  compared to knowledge 9
  defined 9
Microdrives 69
Microfilm 233, 258
  as storage medium for newspaper clip-
    pings/journal articles/ legal documents/
    photographs 255
  of color prints/drawings 255
Microprocessors 37–39
  and in-home systems 202
  hard bugs 85
  new releases 39
Microsoft antitrust case 165
Microwave hops 76
Microwave repeater stations 202
Migration 14–16
Migration of data 12
Military communications satellites, launch
  failures of 76
Minicomputers 35
MiniDisc 84
MiniDisc technology 71
Mir Russian space station 76
MO discs 70, 71
Mobile phones 20
Modem speed 36, 37
Modern library 19
Modern paper book, appearance of 18
Monitors 42
Monks, in Dark Age libraries 7
Moore's Law 39
Morphology 17
Movable type, invention of 18
MP3 players vs. CD players 217
MTBF rating 80
Multimedia 21, 23
Museums, and digital collections 206

N

Napster 154
National Archives and Records Administra-
  tion (NARA) 233, 235
and controlled destruction of data 235
and data and media management 233
and microfilm 233
Center for Electronic Records 233
guidelines of 234
proactive stance against potential
  disasters 234
selective digitizing by 233
National Library of Russia 8
National recovery services 189
Natural disaster 168
Network Attached Storage (NAS) 71
Network data models 120
Network failure 169
Network protocols 49
Network-based data archival service 37
Network-based storage technologies 71
Networks 36, 37, 49
  architecture 36
  complexity of 37
  high-speed versus normal-speed 36
  service disruptions 37
Neuromancer (Gibson) 158
New data modalities 200
New digital technologies, and printed book
  purchases 19
New York Public Library 19
Night shift workers, and operator error 171
Nintendo game consoles 35
Non-tangible documents, authoring for
  ephemeral media 216

O

Object-oriented data models 120, 121
Obsolescence 83–87
Occupational Safety and Health Administra-
  tion (OSHA) 160
Odyssey home game console 32
Onboard GPS-based navigation system 202
Online addictions, psychological implica-
  tions of 216
Online booksellers 19
Online mediation, and dynamics of legal
  system 215
Online merchants, and HTML-based
  tracking devices 221
Open computing systems 49
Operating environments, changes in 16
Operating system 45
  defined 45

threats, determining how best to resolve 181

threats, identifying/ranking 180

Rolling power outages, and network service disruptions 37

ROM (Read-Only Memory) 66

Routers 78

S

Satellite communications, economics of 76

Satellite services 200

Satellite TV signals, unscrambling 173

Satellites 73, 76
- competition with cable and terrestrial services 202
- lifetime of 73
- versatility and functionality provided by 73
- volume of data handled by 73

Schools, and digital computing/communications 203

Science fiction, and exploration 157

Secondary storage 40

Secure ID cards 122, 164

Security, and DBMS 118

Security policy, instituting 165

Security procedures 164

Self-modifying hardware 260

Self-publishing movement 206

Servers 78

SGML 47

Singapore medical system 198

Sledge microprocessor (AMD) 39

Smart cards 173

Smart environments 200, 202

Smart phones 203

SmartMedia 131

Social bookstore chains 19

Socio-technologic future 209–225

Software 44–49
- application software 46
- defined 44
- languages 46
- operating system 45
- trends 48
- utilities 46

Software drivers 45

Software extensions 46

Software failure 172, 173

Software firewalls 237

Software robots 200

Software tool selection 250

Software viruses 174

Solid-state memory 65

Space Station Alpha 159, 160, 169

Speed 61
- and transfer of data 11

Sputnik 76

Stability 64

Standards, shifts in 11, 12

State governments, and the Web 207

Static electricity 172

Static RAM (SRAM) 66

Statistical probabilities 176

Stolen identities 154

Stone engravings 12

Storage Area Networks (SANs) 71

Storage devices 40

Storage media 80
- ephemeral nature of 8
- longevity of 12–13
- shifts in 11

Storage Service Provider (SSP) 168, 181

Streamer tape 41

Supercomputers 34, 65

Super-high resolution display and graphics accelerators 42

Surges 171

Survival, and data 4, 9

Synchronization, and DBMS 118

Syntax 17

SyQuest cartridge system 72

T

Technologic devices and processes, dependence on 56, 59

Technological obsolescence 83–87

Technology, as change agent 200–203

Teledesic network 75

Television, evolution from simple virtual reality device 219

Terrestrial and satellite repeaters 78

Terrestrial microwave hops 76

Text-only archives 108

Text-to-speech (TTS) engines 215

Theft 154, 173, 174

Theft of data 154, 156

3D graphic engines 30

Touch points 128, 129

Transaction monitors, and operator error 171
Transformed data 134
Tribology 63
Trojan horses 174
Trojan worms 174
Twisted pair 77

U

U.S. Library of Congress 8
U.S. Postal Service, and email market 206
Understanding, defined 9
Uninterrupted power supply (UPS) 122, 172
UNIVAC I 30
Universal vocabularies/standards, difficulties of adopting 114
Uploads of digital data 206
USB standard 14
Utilities 48
Utility theory 177

V

Value chain 133–136
Vandalism 174–175
Vendor failure 175–176
Veterans Administration Hospital System computer systems 204
Video standards 15
Videodiscs 42, 73
Virtual reality 200, 219
    and accuracy/precision 219
    changes in definition of 219
    of music industry 219
Virtual reality systems 201
Virtual worlds, legal issues in 215
Viruses 174
    and DNA 259
Visionary, entrepreneur compared to 203
Voice recognition 33

Volume of data generated/archived, value of data compared to 207
Voyager disk 231, 260

W

Warehousing 111–115
Wax tablets 12
Wax-coated wooden tablets 18
Wearable exercise monitors 200
Web browsers, introduction of 20
Web bugs 222
Web radio 201
Web site content, archiving 253
Windows operating system 45, 46, 49
Wired networks, and corporate espionage 163
Wireless LANs, and privacy 163
Wireless personal information managers 203
Word processing programs 46
World Wide Web (WWW)
    accountability issue 218
    and data gathering 19
    and information storage 11
    as a vehicle for self-publishing 206
    HTML 47
    information sources on 19
    introduction of 20
Worms 174
Writeable CD-ROMs 14
Write-Once-Read-Many (WORM) drives 70
Written information, dissemination of 18, 21
Written word, differences between the spoken word and 17

X

XML 47, 86

Z

Zip disks 14, 41, 68, 71, 72